Claudia Jones
A Life in Exile

I hope she will inspire you too!

Marika

Claudia Jones

A Life in Exile

Marika Sherwood
with
Donald Hinds
Colin Prescod
and
the 1996 Claudia Jones Symposium

Lawrence & Wishart
LONDON

Lawrence & Wishart Limited
99a Wallis Road
London E9 5LN

First published 1999

British Library Cataloguing in Publication data.
A catalogue record for this book is available from the
British Library.

ISBN 0 85315 882 7

Typeset in Liverpool by
Derek Doyle & Associates.
Printed and bound in Great Britain by
Redwood Books, Trowbridge

Contents

Notes on contributors   9
The symposium speakers   11
Introduction   15

1 Claudia in the USA   20
2 Claudia settles in London   35
3 Claudia and The British Communist Party   62
4 The political activist   89
5 *The West Indian Gazette*   125
6 Carnival   150
7 Her death, burial and legacy   163

Symposium

Session 1: My friend Claudia   178
Session 2: The political activist   187
Session 3: The West Indian Gazzette   196
Session 4: Carnival   204

Index   217

For Claudia and Pearl Prescod and all the
other women in this book

In memoriam of
Billy Strachan and Gertrude Elias
who did not live to see this book in print

Contributors

Donald Hinds grew up in Jamaica where he began writing stories at the age of 14. He joined his mother in London in 1955 and became the fifth Black bus conductor at London Transport's Brixton garage. Having gained some qualifications at evening classes, ten years later, he joined the Post Office as a minor civil servant. In 1966 he published *Journey to an Illusion - the West Indian in Britain*. He has written six novels (as yet unpublished) and numerous short stories, some of which have been published or broadcast. Continuing to study part-time, he obtained his Bachelor's and then Master's degree. He taught history at Tulse Hill School and then became head of history at Geoffrey Chaucer School. He now lectures part-time at South Bank University, and is working on yet another novel.

Colin Prescod was born in Trinidad. He came to Britain in 1958 to join his mother. He was senior lecturer at the Polytechnic of North London from 1969 to 1989, teaching sociology, political economy and Caribbean studies. Having already been involved in film-making, he moved to the BBC as head of the African/Caribbean Unit until 1993. Currently he is a freelance television producer, and co-project director of the European Multicultural Media Agency. He is also chair of the Institute of Race Relations, and a member of the editorial working committee of its journal *Race and Class*; Board director of the Association for the Cultural Advancement of Visual Arts; and chair of The Drum, an African-Asian-Caribbean arts project in Birmingham. His most recent publications are *On Route - late 20th century carnival arts in the UK*, 1998, of which he is co-editor and a contributor; and, as editor, *Through the Looking Glass*, 1998, on socially engaged art for children and of 'Dealing with difference, beyond ethnicity', in *Intercultural Arts Education and Municipal Policy*, 1997.

Marika Sherwood was born in Hungary, emigrated to Australia and then the UK. She worked as a school teacher in London and briefly in

Sicily. Training as a counsellor and then as a psychotherapist, she worked as a student counsellor at the Polytechnic of North London, where with Colin Prescod she initiated a number of projects for Black students and for teachers. She then moved to teaching in further and adult education in London and the USA. Concentrating on research from the mid-1980s, she has published many articles on various aspects of the history of Black peoples in Britain. A founder member of the Black and Asian Studies Association since 1991, she is still its secretary, conference organiser, and editor of its *Newsletter*. Especially interested in the political organisations of the 1930-1950 period, her most recent books are *The 1945 Manchester Pan-African Congress Revisited* (with Hakim Adi), New Beacon Books, London 1995, and *Kwame Nkrumah: the years abroad 1935-1947*, Freedom Publications, Accra 1996 and *Ernest Bowen and printers' unions in British Guiana and Trinidad 1927-1941*, Savannah Press, London 1999.

The Symposium Speakers

Ranjana Sidhanta Ash is a freelance writer and lecturer. From 1983 to 1996 she was editor of the Heinemann Asian Writers Series, which she also instigated. She has been an Associate Fellow at the Centre for Reseach on Asian Migration at the University of Warwick. Her book, *South Asian Women Writing in Britain*, was published in 1994. Despite many disagreements, she remained a member of the Communist Party until 1993.

William Ash is a writer, novelist and dramatist and was a very active member of the Movement for Colonial Freedom. He worked for many years at BBC Radio's drama department, where he dramatised eleven books, including some by African and Indian writers, and had three of his original plays performed. His five non-fiction works include *The Way to Write Radio Drama*, published in 1985 and since reprinted. The author of eleven novels, his most recent is *But My Fist is Free* (1997).

Trevor Carter came to Britain from Trinidad in 1954 and qualified as a teacher. He headed a department in a Hackney comprehensive school and was a member of the Rampton/Swann Committee of enquiry into the 'education of West Indian children' in British schools. For some years he was the chair of the Caribbean Teachers' Association and of the Black Theatre Co-operative; he also served as a member of the West Indian Standing Conference. Virtually since his arrival in Britain he has been a member of the Communist Party, now the Democratic Left. Trevor's book, *Shattering Illusions*, was published by Lawrence and Wishart in 1986.

Pearl Connor was born in Trinidad, where she was an active member of the Carib Theatre, founded by Beryl McBurnie, and the Trinidad and Tobago Youth Movement, led by Jack Kelshall and Lenox Pierre, which campaigned for independence and a federated West Indies. She came to Britain in 1948 to study law, and also attended the Rose

Burford School of Speech and Drama. She married the actor/producer Edric Connor and with him started the Afro-Asian Caribbean Agency which, apart from helping artists, writers and performers find work, also campaigned for their equal treatment; it was closed in 1976. Involved in the political struggles of the time, the Connor home became a meeting place for Black politicians passing through London. In 1963 they established the Negro Theatre Workshop. Three years after Edric's death in 1968, Pearl married Joe Mogotsi. She continued working both in the theatre and politically, and is currently using all her legal training to attempt to get from the new South Africa the many years of royalty payments due to the Manhattan Brothers.

Gertrude Elias was born in Vienna, where she studied art and worked as a book-jacket designer, illustrator and cartoonist. As her work was highly political, she had to work under many names. She left Vienna for London in 1938 and attempted to continue her career despite the prejudice against women artists and, post-war, against people of the Left. However, her career advanced as did her political involvements: for example, she designed posters for the Movement for Colonial Freedom and became involved in the north African freedom movements and Middle East affairs, writing articles on them for many journals. In 1975 she was appointed exhibition organiser of the Camden Council for International Co-operation and mounted 'The World As We See It' to mark the UN's Decade for Women; another exhibition followed in 1982. Gertrude died in 1998.

Richard Hart, Jamaican trade union leader, political activist, historian and lawyer, was imprisoned by the British during the Second World War; and was among those expelled by the People's National Party in 1952 for being communist/left wing. From its foundation in 1946 until its demise in 1953 he was secretary of the Caribbean Labour Congress. In 1965 he emigrated to Britain, but returned to the Caribbean in 1982 to become the legal consultant to the government and then Attorney General (a civil service, not Cabinet appointment) in revolutionary Grenada. When the USA invaded, he returned to Britain and became co-founder and chair of Caribbean Labour Solidarity. A prolific lecturer and writer, he is continuing his chronicle of Jamaican history in two new books *Towards Decolonisation*, UWI, 1998, and *From Occupation to Independence*, Pluto Press, 1998; there are two more books in the pipeline.

Pansy Jeffrey came to the UK in 1946 from the then British Guiana to study nursing. She was an active member of the newly formed West Indian Students' Union, where she met her husband-to-be, Lionel Jeffrey, who was also politically active. Both belonged to the Caribbean Labour Congress, on whose committee Pansy was the Women's Representative. She also served on the Entertainments Committee of the West Indian Students' Union. After a brief return to Guiana, after the 1958 anti-Black riots in Notting Hill she was appointed as the Black social worker/adviser attached to the local Citizens' Advice Bureau. In this capacity she not only served the Black community directly but sat on many committees relating to issues concerning the Black community. Exhaustion from the demands of her work forced her into early retirement in 1987, but she is still involved in her capacity of president of Pepperpot, an old people's centre which she was instrumental in setting up in the 1980s.

Joe Mogotsi of South Africa is a composer and singer. He founded the Manhattan Brothers which made recordings and toured Southern Africa in the 1930s and 1940s, doing shows in nightclubs (for whites only) and in halls they hired themselves. In 1961 Joe came to Britain in the show 'King Kong', starring Miriam Makeba. When the show folded, those of the Manhattan Brothers that had come with it regrouped in Britain and embarked on a world tour. In the 1970s revival of 'Showboat', he was understudy for 'Joe', the character played by Paul Robeson in the original 1928 production. Still composing, his songs are now performed by 'Joe Mogotsi and the Manhattans', a new group formed when many of the original Brothers retired. With his wife Pearl Connor, for many years Joe Mogotsi has helped South African artists obtain work in the UK and abroad.

Alex Pascall was born in Grenada. He came to Britain in 1959 and found work with London Transport while singing and drumming with a variety of groups. In 1972 he began discussions with the BBC over the need for a special programme for Black people. This resulted in 'Black Londoners', which by 1978 was a daily one hour long radio program. In 1984 the BBC closed down the programme. He was appointed national co-ordinator of Caribbean Focus '86, a showcase for Caribbean culture which moved from the Commonwealth Institute to tour nation-wide. In 1985 he was a founder member of the Foundation for European Carnival Cities which links carnival-holding cities and presents education programmes on carnival. He also continues to work in radio.

David Roussel-Milner was born in England. As an accountant, he joined the Royal Marines, then worked as a trainee bank manager in Madrid. Returning to England he became secretary of his mother's firm, Carmen Commonwealth Hairdressers, sang in pop groups, began to write for the Black media and became politically active, e.g. as a founder member of the Martin Luther King Foundation. In 1980 he became finance officer at the Arts Council, and began a long struggle against institutional racism within that government-sponsored organisation, while continuing to write. He was forced into retirement after a heart attack in 1985, but continues with his work against racism and for the fostering and promulgation of carnival and Black Arts.

Corinne Skinner-Carter trained as a dancer in Trinidad, specialising in Shango. She danced with the leading dance companies there before coming to Britain in 1959. Here she has worked mainly as an actress, appearing in many TV 'soap operas', such as the 15-part *Empire Road* as well as in Black-made feature films such as *Pressure* (1975), *Burning an Illusion* (1981) and *Elphida* (1987).

Billy Strachan (1921-1998) of Jamaica came to Britain to volunteer for the RAF in 1940. Accepted as a wireless operator, after flying thirty missions he was trained as a pilot and flew a further fifteen missions. After the war he returned to Jamaica, but could not find rewarding work, so returned to the UK and trained as a lawyer. Not interested in private practice, he worked as Clerk to the Justices at Magistrates Courts (i.e., as legal adviser to lay magistrates). Having resigned from the Communist Party, he was appointed Senior Chief Clerk of the West Central Division, the first Black man to achieve such a position. Secretary of the London branch of the Caribbean Labour Congress, he was the publisher of its newspaper, *Caribbean News,* and was for many years an informal adviser to Cheddi Jagan, one of Guyana's political leaders. He was the author of three legal books, *Adoption, The Drinking Driver and the Law* and *Matrimonial Proceedings in Magistrates Courts,* as well as of innumerable legal and political articles. Billy died in 1998.

Introduction

Claudia

Claudia Jones – wasn't she the founder of the Caribbean carnival in Britain and of Britain's first major Black post-war newspaper? Yes. That, and much more.

Claudia lived for less than fifty years, but what she accomplished during her brief life is quite amazing. A Trinidadian by birth, she spent the formative years of her life in the United States. Raised mainly by her father during the Depression in Harlem, with only high school education, she rose to become a leader in the Communist Party of the USA. She became a journalist and the editor of one of the Party's papers. She wrote pamphlets and theoretical articles for the Party. She went on US-wide recruitment drives. She was such a fantastic public speaker that she could hold Madison Square Gardens spellbound. She became the friend of Paul and Essie Robeson. Throughout all this, she had to struggle with the vestiges of childhood tuberculosis.

After the Second World War, the US government persecuted her together with the other leading Communists. Years of hounding resulted in heart disease, which was exacerbated by a year's imprisonment. Extradition to Britain followed.

Claudia arrived in London in December 1955. She was very ill. She knew no-one, except a few fellow Communist exiles. Naturally she expected to be embraced by the British Communist Party. This did not happen, probably because she was far too outspoken about racial prejudice within the Party.

In the 1950s the racial situation in Britain deteriorated almost daily as the numbers of immigrants arriving from the colonies and India increased. The newly-arrived were met with anti-immigrant campaigns and fascist organising on the streets. In 1958 anti-Black riots swept many British cities. In 1959 a Black man was killed on a London street by a gang of white youths for no other reason than that he was Black. This was a lynching.

As the Communist Party did nothing to protest about this, Claudia moved outside the Party to organise resistance. She formed groups, she formed coalitions. She persuaded Caribbeans, Africans and Indians to co-operate. She organised meetings, marches, demonstrations, petitions, lobbies, and hunger-strikes. She worked with other anti-imperialist organisations. Recognising that art and culture can be used for political purposes, she organised talent quests and beauty contests. (In those days that a Black woman could be beautiful was an unknown concept.) She introduced African-American artists and writers to a Black British audience. In all this she had the support of Paul Robeson, who had returned to Britain in 1958. And all the while she was in and out of hospital.

With very little financial support, Claudia published and edited the *West Indian Gazette*, a monthly paper that covered British and world political, economic and cultural news. The *Gazette* was also a campaigning tool. Additionally, its office served as an advice bureau for Black peoples as well as a discussion forum with visiting Black political figures such as Norman Manley and W.E.B. Du Bois. And all the while she was in and out of hospital.

In was not until 1962 that Claudia was granted a passport. She then travelled to Moscow where she met Henry Winston, another senior CPUSA offical, just released from a long period of imprisonment. She became so ill that she was hospitalised for a month. In 1964 she travelled to Japan for an anti-hydrogen bomb conference, and then visited China. She was so ill that soon after her return she died.

The 1996 symposium on Claudia

By the beginning of the 1990s some of the elders I knew in the Black communities, who had been politically active in the 1940s, were dying. Thus reconstructing histories, given the paucity of written material, was becoming increasingly difficult. One day it dawned on me that 'something had to be done' about Claudia Jones before it was too late.

But Claudia was of the 1950s and 1960s, a period I had not researched. Who should be interviewed? As I was involved in other projects, how could it be done quickly? I consulted my friend and colleague of many years, Colin Prescod, whose mother had been Claudia's friend. Colin agreed with my sense of urgency. We decided to invite all those we knew who had been involved with Claudia to an all-day symposium. A general invitation to participate was published in the left-wing press. The Norman Melburn and Barry Amiel Trust agreed to fund the enterprise. The Institute of Commonwealth Studies let us use its facilities. The National Sound Archive contributed by tape-recording the day. Our intention was to publish the transcripts as a book.

Some thirty people responded to our call. We divided the day into four discrete sessions: 'My friend Claudia'; 'Claudia the political activist'; 'the *West Indian Gazette*'; and 'Carnival'. We asked particularly knowledgeable colleagues to introduce each session. The sons of two women close to Claudia chaired the sessions. David Roussel-Milner, the son of Carmen England, despite recent hospitalisation, consented to introduce the day and chair the first session. Colin, the son of Pearl Prescod, chaired the remaining sessions.

The day was long; many people contributed and at times the atmosphere was very emotional. The affection and respect for Claudia was palpable. But there were also some notable absentees and some people there who could have spoken but chose not to do so.

When Colin and I read the transcripts (very ably typed by Susan Hutton), we realised that a possible reason, apart from illness, for both the silences and the absences were the long-standing difficulties, for example between non-communists, ex-communists and present members of the Communist Party (renamed Democratic Left), and over many fraught issues related to Carnival. So some people would have to be re-interviewed and we would have to see those who had not attended the symposium.

The research and the book

Our discussions resulted in the decision to undertake not only the new and re-interviews, but also archival research. That is, to produce a book of which the transcripts were only a part – though an integral part. We asked Donald Hinds, who had worked as a reporter on the *Gazette*, to write the chapter on the paper. Colin, who lives on the edge of the Carnival route and who had participated in this now vastly popular event for many years, would write the Carnival chapter. I would write the rest, as well as edit the transcripts – with the approval of the speakers.

To research such a fabulous woman was a daunting task. It became more so as the work progressed and I felt increasingly overawed by Claudia. Battling with heart disease and poverty, a foreigner in Britain, she accomplished more in her brief nine years in England than most of us achieve in a healthy lifetime. Could I ever find out enough, understand enough, to do her justice?

Written material on Claudia is very scarce. The papers deposited in the Communist Party Archive in Manchester's National Labour History Museum have obviously been culled. There is almost no trace of Claudia in the Government's files at the Public Record Office. An appeal to the Foreign and Commonwealth Office drew a negative response. The Home Office Records Management Services' J.M. Lloyd was more helpful: he found a file that contained some police surveillance records on Claudia in relation to the riots in Notting Hill. However, the undoubtedly voluminous correspondence regarding her passport applications, her multi-form political activities, her travels abroad and MI5 (surveillance) records have not been released.

What of Claudia's papers? She died in a room brimming with books, pamphlets and papers. I discuss the possible fate of some of these in the chapter on her death. However, much remained in her room that was taken over by her friend Manchanda (Manu). He kept everything. When he died in 1985, Diane Langford, his ex-partner, sorted out his belongings. She kept what she could but some of the material was too fragile and mildewed. Diane remembers Manu complaining that 'people had taken material and had not returned it'. (There was – and is – no archive in Britain where the papers could have been deposited.) What Diane kept, she has let us borrow. This was a fantastic boon and we are all hugely grateful to Diane, for both the loan and for keeping the papers safe all these years. The preserved papers, the Estate of A. Manchanda, are referred to throughout this book as the Langford Collection.

The paucity of written material has been augmented by interviews. We spoke with too many people, including past and present members of the Communist Party/Democratic Left, to name them individually here. Their names appear in the footnotes. I, as an outsider to Claudia's life and times, feel much honoured by the welcome I received and the trust reposed in me by Claudia's friends, colleagues, and comrades in Britain and in the United States. My feeling towards them is as towards Claudia – can I do justice to their faith in me, and to their high regard for Claudia?

I must also thank the many colleagues who gave me information, written and verbal, for the footnotes. These are copious as so many of the people and events mentioned in the transcripts and text will be unfamiliar to many readers. I also owe thanks to the staff at the Marx Memorial Library and the archivists at the National Labour History Museum and Hull University Library; and to Diana Lachatanere, the curator of manuscripts; and all the staff the Schomburg Center in New York. All went beyond the call of duty in aiding my search for information about Claudia. Dr Walter A. Hill of the National Archives in Washington also falls into this category.

My request for information on Claudia published in the communist, left-wing and local press sadly elicited no response.

The transcripts, as they appear here, have been heavily edited to eliminate tautologies, repetitions, and some digressions; where extracts have been quoted in the main text, they have been omitted from the transcripts at the end; it was necessary to keep the book down to a manageable size. I have not turned the spoken word into carefully constructed sentences as it seemed important to retain the flavour of the exchanges.

Finally, I want to thank Claudia. For being such an inspiration. For lifting my tiredness, whether physical or mental, by her example. For saying (not that she ever would have – or would she?) 'look, if you believe in something, just get on with it'. For being a loving, laughing, warm, generous, encouraging, wholly committed example to us all, who never judged anyone by the colour of their Party card or the colour of their skin.

Marika Sherwood
London, June 1998

Claudia in the USA

Claudia Cumberbatch was born on 21 February 1915 in the Belmont section of Port-of-Spain, capital city of the British colony of Trinidad.[1] According to her own account, her mother's family were land owners; her father, Charles's, in the hotel business. But Claudia was not to spend very long in the country of her birth. The financial upheavals following the end of World War One, which included a drop in the price of cocoa, affected the Cumberbatch family's fortunes. Hoping to improve their prospects Mr and Mrs Cumberbatch emigrated to New York, USA, in 1922; their four daughters followed two years later. Claudia was attending Harriet Beecher Stowe Junior High School when her mother, a garment worker, died in about 1927. In the midst of the Depression Mr Cumberbatch lost his job as the editor of a West Indian newspaper. He took work as a furrier but when this employment ended he was left with little choice and had to accept the only work available: 'superintendent of an apartment in Harlem'. The family was so poor that though she had been elected 'mayor' of the student body, and was due to receive the Theodore Roosevelt Award for Good Citizenship, Claudia could not attend her junior high school graduation ceremony as there was no money for the 'graduation outfit'.[2] Her father's janitor's apartment was so damp that she contracted tuberculosis in 1932 and had to leave Wadleigh High School for a year's convalescence.

On graduating from Wadleigh High, Claudia found work in a laundry. Then, not wanting to 'become like her fellow workers who were young Negro women fainting regularly because of the unbearable conditions of overwork, speed-up, etc in the heat of summer', she moved to a factory, then to a Harlem 'millinery store and then a lingerie shop as a salesgirl'. In 1940 Claudia married Abraham Scholnick, but nothing is known either of her husband or of the marriage, which was dissolved in 1947.[3] Clearly dissatisfied with the limitations on her life, Claudia joined a drama group at the National Urban League, a 'Negro' organisation one of whose aims was to increase opportunities for young people. She also began to write for a Harlem journal, which eventually led to her contributing a weekly column, 'Claudia's Comments'.

Harlem was Claudia's home throughout her life in the USA. In 1935 she had lived at 13 West 113th Street; her last address was 504 West 103rd Street, just seven blocks south of the accepted Harlem border.

Claudia joins the Young Communist League

In February 1936, prompted by the Communist Party's spirited defence of the Scottsboro boys, Claudia joined the youth section of the Party, the Young Communist League (YCL).[4] Though Claudia gave up the opportunities offered by the Federal Theater Project for a job on the CPUSA's *Daily Worker*, she did not altogether abandon her interest in the stage: she continued acting with the National Urban League's troupe 'in many churches in the Harlem community and in Brooklyn'. She was also active in numerous social clubs in the community, in the Junior NAACP and played tennis at a local club.[5]

By 1937 Claudia was a member of the *Worker's* editorial staff.[6] Clearly indefatigable, she became very active in the Young Communist League, serving as its Harlem organiser, then on its National Council, and subsequently as New York State educational director and State chairman.[7] Becoming associate editor of the YCL's *Weekly Review* she also worked with the National Negro Congress (NNC) and the Southern Negro Youth Congress.[8] In 1938 Claudia was made editor of the *Weekly Review*. During the war the YCL was transformed into American Youth for Democracy, and she became editor of its monthly journal, *Spotlight*.

Full member of the CPUSA

In 1945, Claudia 'graduated' from the YCL into the CPUSA. She was appointed editor for Negro Affairs on the *Daily Worker*, and became executive secretary of the National Negro Commission in the same year. In 1947 she was re-assigned to work among women; as executive secretary of the National Women's Commission she toured all 43 states in the following four years.[9] In 1948 she was elected to the National Committee of the CPUSA.[10] Claudia was moved to work on the National Peace Commission in 1952, which again involved touring the country in support of the local peace centres which became especially active during the Korean War, advocating peaceful co-existence.[11] In 1953 she took over the editorship of *Negro Affairs Quarterly*, working 'in special fields among Negro people and participating as a member of the NAC'.[12]

Claudia at Willie McGhee rally 1951, *courtesy of the Schomburg Center, New York Public Library.*

Trials and imprisonment

In January 1948 Claudia was arrested for the first time, incarcerated on Ellis Island and threatened with deportation to Trinidad. She was not a US citizen as her application for citizenship in 1940 had been refused because of her communist affiliation. The American Committee for the Protection of the Foreign Born, a Party-supported organisation, bailed her out of jail. To publicise and gain support for her, an emergency conference was called in Harlem by communist and West Indian leaders, and a demonstration was organised at the Department of Immigration offices on 2 February; readers of the *Worker* were encouraged to send letters of protest to President Truman. Supported by the Committee, Claudia refused to participate in the hearings held later in the year on the basis that they were illegal; the Government was forced to grant an adjournment.[13] When her deportation was eventually ordered in June 1951, the Committee lodged an appeal.[14]

Claudia was again arrested, with sixteen other communists, in June

1951, and then released on bail. A few months later, in October, she was arrested yet again, this time under the McCarran Act. She was once more interned on Ellis Island, in a special McCarran Wing, before again being released on bail.[15] She was tried, convicted, sentenced to a year and a day in prison, and fined $2000. The charges against her were that she had contravened the Smith Act by teaching and advocating the overthrow of the US Government by force and violence; that she helped to organise the Communist Party whose aim was the same; and that she had issued a directive to this effect which was circulated in the Party's theoretical journal *Public Affairs*.[16] That she advocated the overthrow of the Government by *violent* means was in the testimony of Government spy, paid informant and known liar, Harvey Matusow.[17] She appealed to the Supreme Court, but it refused to hear her appeal. The Party paid the fine.

Not surprisingly the pace of work and the trials took their toll. In July 1951 at the end of her trial and that of sixteen other second rank communist leaders arrested in that year, she suffered heart failure. She was in hospital for three weeks and was diagnosed as suffering from hypertensive cardio-vascular disease. At the end of the year she was back in hospital with coronary heart disease.

In January 1955 after the Supreme Court refused to hear her appeal, Claudia began sentence at the Federal Reformatory for Women at Alderson, West Virginia. There she joined her comrades Betty Gannett and Elizabeth Gurley Flynn, both of whom had had longer prison terms imposed on them. In prison Claudia learned to weave, winning a state prize at the local county fair for her placemats![18] She also did a lot of clay modelling and taught other women how to model, as well as teaching one how to play the piano. Her father visited Claudia regularly, though according to Gurley Flynn, he was 'elderly and not too well'.[19]

During her imprisonment Claudia's health deteriorated further. She was diagnosed as suffering from coronary arteriosclerosis and arrested tuberculosis. Despite this diagnosis she was not allowed her course of prescribed drugs until her comrades asked the British consul in New York to intervene on her behalf.

The Communist Party arranged Claudia's defence during the numerous hearings and trials and worked to prevent her deportation under the McCarran Act. A delegation, including Paul Robeson and Claudia's father, pleaded with the Parole Board in May 1955 for her early release.[20] National and international support (including the West Indian Independence Party of Trinidad & Tobago) was organised to press for her release. The Civil Rights Congress, a communist organisation for which Claudia had gone on recruiting drives in 1951, also

FAREWELL TO CLAUDIA
(October 24, 1955)

Nearer and nearer drew this day, dear comrade,
When I from you must sadly part,
Day after day, a dark foreboding sorrow,
Crept through my anxious heart.

No more to see you striding down the pathway,
No more to see your smiling eyes and radiant face.
No more to hear your gay and pealing laughter,
No more encircled by your love, in this sad place.

How I will miss you, words will fail to utter,
I am alone, my thoughts unshared, these weary days,
I feel bereft and empty, on this gray and dreary morning,
Facing my lonely future, hemmed in by prison ways.

Sometimes I feel you've never been in Alderson,
So full of life, so detached from here you seem.
So proud of walk, of talk, or work, of being,
Your presence here is like a fading fevered dream.

Yet as the sun shines now, through fog and darkness.
I feel a sudden joy that you are gone,
That once again you walk the streets of Harlem,
That today for you at least, is Freedom's dawn.

I will be strong in our common faith, dear comrade,
I will be self-sufficient, to our ideals firm and true,
I will be strong to keep my mind and soul outside a prison,
Encouraged and inspired by ever loving memories of you.

Elizabeth Gurley Flynn's farewell poem to Claudia. From Elizabeth
Gurley Flynn, *My Life as a Political Prisoner*, New World Paperbacks,
International Publishers (1963), New York 1976

tried to have her sentence reduced on health grounds.[21] The National
Committee to Defend Negro Leadership was also involved in the fight
for Claudia; it solicited the help of the British National Council for

Civil Liberties, both to persuade the British consul in New York to take an interest in her case and then to ensure that she would be extradited to Britain, not to Trinidad.[22] The Party also attempted to alert the liberal left-wing in Britain to the situation faced by Claudia. Writing to the weekly *New Statesman and Nation* on 8 March 1955, William L. Patterson, of the Civil Rights Congress, detailed the lack of medical care for Claudia's during her imprisonment. He urged readers to write to the US Attorney General asking for the suspension of Claudia's sentence. Patterson's letter was not published.[23]

Although the Party and the Congress lost on both counts, Claudia was released early, but only because of the time she had earned for 'good behaviour'. On 25 October 1955 she left Alderson accompanied by her father. Claudia arrived in New York to find over one hundred and fifty of her supporters awaiting her at the railway station. That evening a 'homecoming reception' was held for her at the Bottle & Cork Club in Harlem. Though she managed to attend this, she was immediately hospitalised again, but only pending deportation.

Claudia threatened to sue the US Government, claiming wrongful imprisonment and fighting her deportation order. Her actions resulted in the Government eventually proposing that she could leave for Britain voluntarily if she discontinued litigation.[24] In the meanwhile, the Party had approached the British consul in New York to ascertain whether she would be prosecuted in Trinidad, and if the much needed medical facilities were available there.[25] How and which officialdom made the decision that Claudia should be deported to Britain is not known. The governor of Trinidad, expecting her arrival, was worried that she 'may prove troublesome' (an anonymous civil servant in London noted in the margin: 'So are we!')[26] The governor was much relieved when he was informed that Claudia was going to the UK. He warned the Colonial Office that 'she might become a source of infection amongst all Colonials in Britain'.

A sad farewell

Three hundred and fifty people attended Claudia's Farewell Reception, organised by the Party, on 7 December 1955 at Harlem's Hotel Teresa.[27] Among those to pay tribute to Claudia were William Patterson and Paul Robeson. Patterson's lengthy address, partly devoted to the Black struggle, said of Claudia:

> ... our dear friend and comrade embodies all that is best in our vast heritage of struggle. Claudia is one of the magnificent daughters adopted

of a new nation conceived in slavery, dedicated to the proposition that freedom and equality of opportunity is the goal that nature and society have set for all mankind. Claudia reflects ... all that was best in the character and activities of Harriet Tubman (and) Sojourner Truth ... Claudia had amazing talents on which to build ... Claudia, we say au-revoir, but not goodbye ... Go, beloved friend. Get well, heroic fighter ...[28]

Paul Robeson and his wife Essie – a journalist and also politcally active – were both close to Claudia. Robeson, who had visited Claudia that afternoon, but who could not be present at the reception, sent a message:

Claudia belongs to us, belongs to America ... Claudia has enriched our land ... In her dedicated work and leadership Claudia has given new life to the finest traditions of our country ... the struggle for Negro liberation, for women's rights, for human dignity and fulfillment ... We know that the great contributions she has made here will be continued in her work abroad ... She will contribute greatly ... to the colonial liberation struggles ... Let us be mindful of the friends and dear ones she leaves among us – her father who has stood so staunchly by her side – and cherish them for her ... Dear Claudia, our hearts go with you ... Be assured that we will work hard to bring you back to a better America – and an America that will welcome you as one of her finest daughters.[29]

If these speeches alone were not enough to bring tears to Claudia's eyes, the many messages, cards and gifts she received must have caused the sick woman's tears to flow. There were financial donations, and gifts of warm clothes from trade unions, neighbours, and friends in Detroit and Seattle; from the Manhattan Labor Youth League; from Brooklyn comrades; the Estonian Workers Club in Manhattan; from her fellow prison inmate, Elizabeth Gurley Flynn; and many others whose names are illegible. Bernard Weller (about whom nothing is known) pressed $200 into her hand. Telegrams arrived from Chicago comrades, the editors and staff of the *Daily* and *Sunday Worker*, and from W.E.B. Du Bois and his wife Shirley Graham.[30]

In her farewell statement Claudia claimed that the Smith Act and the McCarran Act under which she was deported were 'racist immigration laws, directed especially against West Indians from whose proud heritage I spring ... The laws are the shame of America'. In an earlier speech she had pointed out that it was 'ironic that the time and money and energy spent in the prosecution of me is not applied to the white supremacists in the South who are daily calling for force and violent opposition against Supreme Court decisions ordering the integration of American schools.'[31]

Two hundred people were at the quayside the next day to wave her farewell on the *SS Queen Elizabeth*. Among the telegrams waiting for her in her cabin was one from Harriet Magil which read: 'What is an ocean between us. We know how to build bridges. Love.'[32]

Presumably the CPUSA warned the Communist Party of Great Britain (CPGB) of Claudia's imminent arrival, but without access to CPUSA files and with the complete absence of such correspondence in the CPGB archives, we do not know what precisely was said. The Party certainly did not forget Claudia after she left the USA. Not only did she maintain a personal correspondence with leading Party members such as Bill Foster and Ben Davis (detailed in the next chapter), but Claudia also received financial help. In 1957 Ben Davis wrote:

> I will take up the question of finance as soon as I return to work tomorrow. Certainly you should have gotten aid by now. Elizabeth [presumably Gurley Flynn] will help.

A few months later Davis wrote apologetically that,

> a major financial crisis faces the Party ... This, no doubt, is why nothing has been forthcoming from the Party to you. It has been raised often enough and sharply enough by many of us.[33]

Only one letter written on CPUSA letterhead remains in the Langford Collection of Claudia's papers. Headquarters staff member Phil Bard wrote on 8 September 1959 that he had 'asked about you from everyone who has returned from London. We have been informed that you could use some help now and all of us here feel that we should do our best ... Everybody sends their love to you and we hope to hear from you soon.' The letter enclosed $50.

The Party also maintained its links with Claudia by asking her to write for its publications. She wrote an article which appeared in *The Worker* of 2 November 1958, about the riots in Britain.[34] In 1964 *Freedomways* asked her to write an extensive article on 'the Caribbean Community in London', which was duly printed in its Third Quarter 1964 issue.[35]

The Communist Party of the USA

In order to understand Claudia's relations with the Communist Party of Great Britain which is described in Chapter 3, it is necessary to understand some facets of its sister party in the USA, which was formed in 1919.

At its 1928 Congress the Communist International (Comintern) was critical of the CPUSA's failure to attract Blacks to the Party. Perhaps taking a lead from the success of the Garvey movement's 'Back to Africa' slogan, it initiated the 'national self-determination' policy and pressed for its application to the southern states of the USA. This idea, of some kind of separate state for Blacks, was never clearly formulated and was at first resisted. However, on the basis that 'a campaign for a Negro republic was tied up with a campaign in the party ranks against white chauvinism' (i.e., racism), eventually most African-American members apparently fell in line.[36] Another, more successful, attempt to foster interest in communism in the southern states was the formation of the Sharecroppers Union, which soon had a membership numbered in the thousands.

From the 1930s the Party's legal arm, International Labor Defense (ILD), took up work for Negroes, assisting those on trial and taking up cases it made famous, such as the trial of the Scottsboro boys. The ILD also gave financial aid to those it designated political prisoners and by 1936 thirty per cent of this aid was going to the families of Black inmates.[37] In the northern cities communists organised grass-roots action in the ghettoes. This included returning evicted tenants to their homes, pushing for more financial and other aid from city administrations during the Depression, and boycotting stores that refused to employ Blacks.

Contrary to its British counterpart, the CPUSA paid some attention to the Comintern's injunction to recruit Black members and not to neglect the special injustices suffered by Black and colonial peoples. How successfully the Party fulfilled its mandate is yet to be fully assessed. It is estimated that in 1930 there were, at most, 238 Black members out of a total membership of 7,500. (This is less than half of the proportion of Blacks in the total population, which was 9.7 per cent in 1930.)

According to some accounts, of the 2300 registered members of the Harlem section in 1936, 30 per cent were 'Negroes'; the numbers of Black women members increased from 187 in 1937 to 307 in 1938.[38] Gerald Horne gives the membership in the soon-to-be Black ghetto as 2800, and points out that there were seven Blacks on the Party's Central Committee.[39] Whichever is the correct figure, George Blake, the organiser of the Harlem Division, noted that 'these figures conceal the tragedy of several thousand members lost in the course of five years'. The fluctuation and instability was particularly serious in the Negro sections of Harlem.[40] By 1939 there were approximately 7000 Black Party members.[41]

Race and gender

In the mid-1930s the Comintern changed its policy to the Popular Front, that is, co-operation with liberal, middle-class organisations such as the NAACP and the National Urban League. A new body, the National Negro Congress, was formed in 1936. With many prominent, non-communist 'Negroes' among its leadership, the NNC attracted wide membership. Its purpose was to work on civil rights issues, demanding full equality and the abolition of all forms of segregation. It campaigned, for example, against Mussolini's invasion of Abyssinia, against prejudiced school texts and even organised classes on African-American history.[42]

It was also during this era that one of the two national labour organisations, the Congress of Industrial Organisations (CIO), and the Party drew quite close, and thus some headway was made in opening up employment opportunities for 'Negroes' in industries from which they had previously been excluded. However, the Party's policy that it 'would fight for the right of Negroes for jobs, but would guarantee that white workers would not be fired', led to disagreements with some influential Black members. It was probably his opposition to this development that led to the expulsion of Barbados-born Richard B. Moore, who had been a senior official in both the ILD and the NNC.[43]

The CPUSA made some attempt to deal with racism within its own ranks. Though the Party enforced the abolition of Jim Crow (segregation) at its meetings, that did not necessarily break down barriers. Louise Thompson, writing of 'Negro women in our Party', noted that,

> when they [Negro women] come to our meetings or affairs, they do not feel that they fit in, they do not feel as much a part of it as even our Negro men comrades ... When we have dances ... Negro girls ... would be glad to attend ... if they were danced with – not made wallflowers.

Nor was all well on the race and gender issue. In 1933 16 per cent of the CPUSA's around 20,000 members were women; of these, approximately three hundred were Black.[44] Thompson believed that attracting Negro women to the Party would root it in the Black community. But 'as there were far too few Negro women in positions of leadership', this would be impossible to achieve.[45] A conference on women's work held in Detroit in 1937 pointed out that the Party was not doing enough for women workers who all experienced special problems.[46] A Party Conference on Negro Women in June that year advocated that 'special attention [should be paid] to Negro women on the basis of their special problems'.[47] These proposals filtered through to the YCL Convention of 1939 where one of the eleven panels was devoted to the question of how to recruit more young women.[48]

Margaret Cowl, director of work among women, pointed out in 1936 that while the Party advocated that both men and women had to 'stand shoulder to shoulder' to fight capitalism, it paid no attention to issues such as equal pay, maternity leave and equality between Black and white women. In 1940 Cowl suggested that the most important question for women was not the right to work, but equal pay. Some communist women were also proposing the theoretical thesis that all women – even communist women – were oppressed by their men.[49]

The papers of the CPUSA have not been opened to researchers, and hence nothing is known of its National Women's Commission, which, according to Robert Shaffer, was disbanded in 1940.[50]

The effects of the war

With the signing of the Hitler-Stalin Non-Aggression Pact in 1939, together with the Comintern's insistence that all Parties should drop their anti-fascist policies, many, including African-Americans, left the Party. The NNC was denuded of its non-communist leadership, which led to the departure of many members when they realised that the remaining leaders were exclusively communist. Claudia, along with some Harlem and other national Black leaders,

> remained loyal to the organisations and struggled to salvage its reputa-
> tion as an exponent of racial equality ... They kept alive the cultural
> struggle of the Popular Front and in doing so maintained much of their
> influence among Harlem's creative artists and college-educated youths.[51]

In 1940 the attempt to resuscitate the NNC, with the help of the CIO and a communist leadership which included Claudia, failed, largely because of Party's open support of the USSR's Hitler policy.[52]

At the end of the war the policy of national self-determination for African-Americans in the southern states of the USA, which had been somewhat sidelined in the 1930s, was brought to the fore again. While some argued against it, Claudia stated the case for self-determination in two articles in the Party's theoretical journal, *Public Affairs*. The essence of Claudia's argument was that Black peoples' attitudes to the question could not be allowed to determine policy. This should be based on objective conditions, 'and upon this basis express the fundamental demands (land, equality, freedom) of the oppressed Negro people'.[53] Her articles generated a great response, by both Blacks and whites, supporting both sides. In 1947 the Party's new secretary, William Z. Foster, pronounced on the conundrum: there would be no immediate 'propaganda for a Negro Republic; the precise meaning [of the phrase, Negro Republic] would become clearer in time'.[54]

Elizabeth Gurley Flynn had been the principal Communist spokesperson on women's issues during World War Two. Assuming leadership of the National Women's Commission, she re-established it as the Congress of American Women in 1945.[55] Flynn emphasised that the right of women to work should be extended post-war, and succeeded in having this included in the 1945 Party 'platform'. She also pressed for female representation in the trade unions and in 1947 advocated not only the equality of Black and white women, but the equality of women with men in the political, economic, legal, professional and cultural spheres of life.[56] With the approach of the Cold War, America began its witch-hunt against communists. The first arrests were in July 1948, when twelve members of the national executive, including two African-Americans, were arrested under the Smith Act. One of the five defence lawyers, himself later imprisoned, was Ben Davis, Claudia's friend and comrade for many years. With the persecution, membership of the Party diminished and activities were naturally curtailed, though, as we have seen, valiant efforts were made by Claudia and others to continue the struggle.

Notes

1. Unless otherwise stated this outline of Claudia's life is compiled from encyclopaedias, biographical dictionaries, e.g. D. Clark Hine et al, *Black Women in America*, Indiana University Press, Bloomington 1993.
2. Claudia Jones to Comrade Foster, 6 December 1955, Tamiment Library, New York University, Howard 'Stretch' Johnson Papers, box 1.
3. *Ibid*. According to her divorce certificate issued at Ciudad Juàrez, Mexico on 27 February 1947, Claudia had sued Scholnick on the basis of incompatibility. The couple had married in September 1940 and had no children (Divorce Certificate in Langford Collection.)
4. The Scottsboro Boys were nine 'Negro' youths accused, without any evidence, of raping two white girls. Two of the accused were juveniles aged 13 and 14. The girls recanted their original accusation but the boys were still charged. The CPUSA orchestrated a national and then an international defence committee which toured Britain and Europe in 1932. The trials and appeals (1931-35) resulted in five men being freed and four being sentenced to life imprisonment.

5. See note 2. The National Association for the Advancement of Coloured People, a protest organisation was formed in 1909 by Black and white liberals.

6. Henry Winston, *Life Begins with Freedom*, New York 1977, p23. Ellie Jaffe wrote to me from Hyde Park, New York, on 26 June 1998 that Claudia had been editor of the *Weekly Review* from c.1941. 'We all accepted Claudia's editorship without reservations. Her being black was warmly welcomed.' Claudia attended Mr Jaffe's wedding in 1942 'as a warm friend': "Cross-race friendships" were, of course, more prevalent in radical circles than in the general population.' (I want to thank Gertrude Falk for putting me in touch with her cousin.)

7. According Henry Winston, its Black executive secretary, 'the conception of the YCL is that it is first and foremost an educational organisation. Its education will be based upon the teachings of Marxism-Leninism ... Such an education must be combined with practical activity, which gives the League its other side: that of a service organisation, first to the labor movement and second, to all mankind'. (Henry Winston, 'An understanding of the YCL Convention', *Party Organiser*, July 1937, pp17-19)

8. The Southern Negro Youth Congress was set up in 1937 as an affiliate of the National Negro Congress. The National Negro Congress was a communist-led organisation, initially supported by the Urban League and other Black organisations. It campaigned, for example, against lynching, and for improved schools, recreational space and wider job opportunities for Harlem's Black youth. See W. Burghardt Turner & Joyce Moore Turner, *Richard B. Moore, Caribbean Militant in Harlem*, Pluto Press, London 1992, p65.

9. See note 2.

10. *Daily Worker*, 23 January 1948.

11. See note 2.

12. *Ibid*. Did Claudia mean the NNC?

13. *Daily Worker*, 23 January 1948, 19 September 1948.

14. *Daily Compass*, 27 June 1951.

15. Ellis Island was a reception centre for immigrants and a detention centre for deportees.

16. Schomburg Center: Civil Rights Congress Papers, Pt. II, reel 37, #0259.

17. See Harvey Matusow, *False Witness*, Cameron & Kahn, New York 1955.

18. See note 2.

19. Elizabeth Gurley Flynn, *My Life as a Political Prisoner*, International Publishers, New York 1976, p64. There are many mentions of Claudia here; Flynn's poem, 'Farewell to Claudia' is on p211. Flynn died shortly before Claudia, in September 1964.

20. African-American singer, actor and political activist Paul Robeson was involved in the anti-imperialist movement in the USA; he was chairperson of the Council on African Affairs (1937-1955), which campaigned on such issues. See for example, Martin Dubermann, *Paul Robeson*, Alfred A.

Knopf, New York 1988; Lloyd L. Brown, *The Young Paul Robeson*, Westview, Boulder 1997.

21. *Daily Worker*, 18 March 1955, 26 April 1955, 11 May 1955, 17 May 1955, 9 June 1955, 1 September 1955, 3 November 1955; Gerald Horne, *Communist Front?* New Jersey 1988, pp169, 229, 311; Schomburg Center: Civil Rights Congress Papers, Pt.I, reel 11, #0672; Pt.II, reel 37, #0259.

22. The NCCL's correspondence with the British Government and with Claudia's US colleagues is at the Hull University Library: NCCL Papers, DCL/53/9.

23. William Patterson to the editor, *New Statesman & Nation*, Moorland-Spingarn Research Centre, Patterson Papers, box 9, file 48. I searched the *New Statesman & Nation* from March to 7 May. African-American William Patterson was the National Executive Secretary of the CPUSA's Civil Rights Congress. He had initiated the petition, 'We Charge Genocide' to the United Nations in 1951. See William L. Patterson, *The Man Who Cried Genocide*, International Publishers New York 1971, pp179-181.

24. *New York Times*, 18 November 1955. Unfortunately neither the correspondence with the British consul in New York nor the papers on her deportation have been preserved by the Foreign Office.

25. Unsourced newspaper cutting dated 28 October 1955, Tamiment Library, New York University, Cedric Belfrage Papers, box 3.

26. Trinidad Monthly political reports 11 October 1955, p5; 14 December 1955, p4; PRO: CO1031/1804.

27. *Daily Worker*, 30 October 1955.

28. Patterson's speech in the Langford Collection. Harriet Tubman escaped from slavery in the southern United States and then led many others to freedom in the North. Sojourner Truth, a slave in the North, once freedom was declared, spent her life campaigning against slavery and for women's equality.

29. Paul Robeson's speech in Langford Collection.

30. The pan-Africanist scholar, writer and civil rights activist W.E.B. Du Bois was one of the founders of the NAACP. He moved to Ghana in 1961 after repudiating the USA and joining the Communist Party.

31. *Daily Worker*, 10 November 1955, 12 December 1955.

32. It has not been possible to discover anything about Harriet Magil.

33. In Langford Collection: Ben Davis to Claudia, 2 September 1957; 25 January 1958.

34. There might well have been other articles; I did not search the US Communist press for the whole of the period of Claudia's sojourn in Britain.

35. Correspondence with *Freedomways* in Langford Collection. *Freedomways* was a quarterly 'review of the freedom movement'. Its editor, Esther Jackson, who had asked Claudia to write the article, is the wife of James Jackson - who was for many years a member of the CPUSA's Central Committee. The article was reprinted in the radical (and short-lived) London journal *Black Liberator* 1 December 1978, pp28-37.

36. M. Fitzgerald, M. Furmanovsky & R. Hill, 'The Comintern and American Blacks 1919-1943', in Robert A. Hill (ed), *The Marcus Garvey and UNIA Papers*, vol.5, University of California Press, Berkeley 1986, p849.

37. *Ibid.*, p849.

38. Mark Naison, *Communists in Harlem During the Depression*, Grove Press, New York 1983; Turner & Turner, 1992 (note 8); Susan Campbell, '"Black Bolsheviks!" and the recognition of African-America's right to self-determination by the CPUSA', *Science & Society*, 58/4, pp440-470.

39. Gerald Horne, 'The Red and the Black', in Michael E. Brown et al (eds), *New Studies in the Politics and Culture of US Communism*, Monthly Review Press, New York 1993, p214.

40. George Blake, 'The Party in Harlem, New York', *Party Organiser*, June 1938, pp14-19. In order to increase and stabilise Party membership Blake advocated the 'incorporation of the best traditions of Negro life ... and cultural forms of the struggle of the Negro people into the very center of our units and branches' (p17).

41. See Fitzgerald (note 36), pp841-854.

42. Turner & Turner (note 8), p65.

43. *Ibid.*, p68.

44. *Party Organiser*, August 1937, pp25-7.

45. Robert Shaffer, 'Women and the CPUSA 1930-1940', *Socialist Review* no.45, 9/3 1979, pp73-118.

46. *Ibid.*

47. *Party Organiser*, June 1937, pp22-24.

48. *Ibid.*, p25.

49. Shaffer 1979 (note 45), p96.

50. Rebecca Hill, 'Nothing Personal? Women in the Communist Movement 1940-1956', BA Thesis, Wesleyan University 1991; Shaffer, 1979 (note 45), pp80, 87.

51. Shaffer (note 45), p97.

52. Naison 1983 (note 38), p288.

53. Claudia Jones, 'Pre-Convention Discussion Articles; Discussion by Claudia Jones', *Public Affairs*, 24/8, August 1945, pp717-720; and 'On the right of self-determination in the Black Belt', *Public Affairs*, 25 January 1946.

54. William A. Nolan, *Communism Versus the Negro*, Henry Regnery, Chicago 1951, p60.

55. Despite the official change in name, it was still usually referred to as the National Women's Commission.

56. According to researcher Rebecca Hill, 1991, (note 50), the National Women's Commission was little more than a paper organisation, and Elizabeth Gurley Flynn had no fundamental concern with women's issues and almost never attended the Commission's meetings.

Claudia Settles
in London

Claudia was obviously loved, respected and valued by her friends and comrades in the USA, who continued their links with her after her enforced departure from America. In his letter to Claudia, soon after the birth of his daughter Emily, Ben Davis wrote:

> Emily ... is a bit swarthy in complexion, with black hair and black eyebrows – and a fat round delicate face. If she grows up that way, she'll rival the best of them in attractiveness. I should only hope that she develops your spirit, intellectual capacity and staunchness of convictions. Nina, I believe, would hope the same thing ... I would hope too that she should develop your personality and her own type of beauty, of which you have your own.[1]

Davis, 'Negro' communist New York City Councilman, had been a comrade of Claudia's in Harlem since the 1930s.[2] He maintained a correspondence with her probably until his death, although the last preserved letter is from 1962. Much of the correspondence deals with CPUSA matters or sends news of friends such as Essie and Paul Robeson. The letters also discuss political and theoretical issues and comment on Claudia's activities in Britain. Davis and Claudia were clearly involved in ongoing discussions on many issues affecting the CPUSA during its period of rapid change, but perhaps especially on the 'Negro question' and the fading fortunes of the Women's Commission. Davis missed Claudia's companianship:

> Sure do miss you, gal. If I hadn't been so damned disoriented myself, I think I would have put up a one-man successful fight to keep you over here ... It seems to me that you are an American, not a 'British citizen'. This is where you spent your life and made your contributions to American democracy – and they were very important contributions. Only in the technical sense – frankly not even that – are you a 'British citizen'. Then if you're an American, you should be here, not there...[3]

One of Davis's constant concerns was Claudia's ill-health. He advocated that Claudia should remain in England only as long as it took her to get a passport, and then leave for 'where your health will get the very best expert care by those who have more than a professional interest. This is primary and indispensable for your future, personal and political'.[4] But Claudia did not get a passport for some time and her health continued to worry Davis: for example, on 29 May 1959 he asked: 'How are you getting on – your health? Are you taking care of yourself? What do the doctors say?'

Davis, in his warm and informative letters, continued to boost Claudia's morale and lessen her sense of isolation from the world she had known so well, and from communist comrades of her own stature. His letters are signed: 'With admiration and warmth' and 'Love to you, a very fine and great woman'. His final preserved letter begins: 'You are indeed the same Claudia – brilliant, charming, warm and articulate' and concludes with: 'I lost track of your paper and that should be re-established. Most of all, I lost contact with you and that is calamitous.'[5]

The honorary chairperson of the CPUSA, Bill Foster, kept in touch with Claudia, at least during her first year of exile.[6] His two letters also express concern for her health, and also mix the personal and the political. In his letter of 30 April 1956, Foster notes that 'we read all your discussions of various questions with interest, particularly what you had to say on the Negro question'. He and his wife both sent their love and good wishes to Claudia.

From these and the other odd letters that have survived (there is one, for example, from Betty Gannett and her family), it is obvious that Claudia had many close friends.[7] At least for a while she maintained her interest in, and contributions to, Party discussions, which, to judge by the few remaining letters, were received with the respect her status within the Party merited.

The most comprehensive set of preserved letters is from Helois Robinson.[8] These span the years 1956 to 1962, when Helois either died or became too incapacitated to continue the correspondence. Helois's letters, as Davis's, were partly political, partly personal. She sent news of her own and other communist women's activities, as well as news of her family. She and others maintained some contact with Claudia's sisters Lynne, Lindsay and Yvonne as well as with her father, who, it would appear, died in early 1956.

Helois not only sent news but also responded to what must have been Claudia's pleas for financial support. In many of her letters she either mentions sums sent (for example, $55 in June 1956) or that she is going to, or has spoken to, comrades about Claudia's plight in Britain.

As the Party was short of funds in 1956, Helois formed a 'group of twelve of your friends to take some responsibility toward your needs'.[9] (An unknown sum was sent, probably by this group, in December 1957.) Four years later Helois fell seriously ill with multiple sclerosis. On her way to Moscow for treatment she stopped briefly in London to see Claudia. Concerned about her friend's still precarious financial situation, Helois again promised help: 'I do think I will be able to raise the question of your needs to a greater extent and have taken some responsibility', she wrote on 19 May 1960. Two months later she sent Claudia $50 as 'down payment', and a further unknown sum in October of the same year.[10]

Helois also assisted by soliciting subscriptions to the *Gazette*, and by helping Claudia keep abreast of events in Afro-America: on 23 July 1957 she wrote that 'a few of us will send you subscriptions to four of the Negro press'. (The CPUSA sent her the *Daily Worker*.)

Claudia's political situation in Britain concerned Helois as much as it had Ben Davis (see chapter 3). 'Please let me know if the organisation has made any commitment to you', she wrote to Claudia on 15 June 1956.

In 1960 after Mae Williamson, also exiled to Britain in 1955, had visited the USA, Helois informed Claudia that she (Helois) had 'run into a few people who have seen Mae Williamson during her stay here and I have the feeling that she herself has not done real justice to you and to the situation which confronts you generally'.[11]

Another friend with whom Claudia maintained contact, though only one letter has been preserved, was Howard 'Stretch' Johnson.[12] In a telephone conversation with me Mr Johnson candidly revealed that many years ago he and Claudia had been lovers.[13] A close friendship succeeded this, as borne out by Claudia's letter to Mr Johnson, in which she relates her two month-long hospitalisation and continuing medical supervision. 'The doctor has assured me that with proper care, rest etc. I should in several months be enabled to resume normal living and work ... it is impossible to be both uprooted and ill.' After detailing her housing problems – it had been a request for financial assistance that had led her to telephone him a few days previously – Claudia goes on to discuss CPUSA politics, especially the policies to be taken regarding 'national self-determination for the Negro people'. Having reiterated her belief in this policy in 1945, Claudia now argued against the Party declaring the policy obsolete.[14] She concludes by chiding 'Stretch' for sending 'tid-bits about mutual friends', but not about his wife, Martha, and daughters.[15]

It is possible that Claudia also left behind in the USA the current man in her life, about whom all we know is a name: Pasquale. In one of her letters, dated 2 February 1956, Helois had written that it 'would be nice if Pasquale could join you on holiday in the South of England'. In the 'autobiography history' that Claudia sent Bill Foster in December 1955, she ended with a scrawled note: 'My plans are to remarry in England within the next few months'.[16] Was she planning to marry Pasquale? (It is possible that this is a pseudonym. Claudia and her comrades must have been aware of the possibility of their correspondence being opened by either – or both – the US and British secret services.) However, this relationship did not last, as on 23 July 1957 Helois wrote to Claudia that she 'could well understand your reaction to Pasquale. I certainly hope that it will [be] very soon when you will have consolidated your life in this direction [sic]. You have so much to offer the right guy.'

We know nothing of Claudia's relationship with her sisters; evidently she maintained ties with her sister Yvonne, who sent her $50 in October 1960.[17] Claudia was close to her father, addressing him as 'My dear Daddy' in the letter she wrote to him on 19 December 1955, enclosing her 'Ship's Log so that you may see how we spent our Crossing'. Unfortunately only a remnant has been preserved of her own carbon copy – the log of the first and a little of her second day on board the *Queen Elizabeth* bound for England. She recalls 'fifty of my closest colleagues and friends, neighbors, Negro and white, and their children, my father and my sister' who had come to see her off.

> Tonight my mind, heart and thoughts are still in the land I belong to and know and its people with whom I have worked and struggled for social progress – tonight my mind and heart and deepest thoughts are with my comrades – the finest representations of the people of the United States of America. They are with my magnificent family whom I love and miss
> ...

Friends sent Claudia news of her father: 'Jim' wrote on 30 December 1955 that 'your father was over to dinner ... We drank toasts to you and your health.' Two weeks later Betty Gannett in a long letter, which included letters from her husband and children, included a note about Mr Cumberbatch: 'What strength your father has! I love to visit with him. Though he misses you terribly, he's holding up well. He promised to spend an evening with us ... when he finishes the series of tests etc in connection with his kidney condition.'[18]

With her close comrades, friends and family left behind in the USA, it is not surprising that Claudia should admit in public that 'it is hard to make up for a lifetime among comrades and friends who have fought the good fight against all odds'.[19] Her good friend Ben Davis tried to alert her to the situation in which she would find herself in Britain: 'You have been – understandably and inevitably – in a state of ab- normal tension, complex readjustment and anxiety ever since you were released from prison. You need time for calm judgement under condi- tions of your environment and not on the basis of the intense desires which you cultivated under prison conditions [sic].'[20]

Making a life in Britain

Claudia certainly did not find herself in an environment conducive to the 'calm judgement' or to the recovery of her health, as advocated by Ben Davis. She arrived in Britain to face a complex situation vis-à-vis the British Communist Party, racial discrimination, divisions between resident Blacks, and her own continuing ill health. Moreover she was bereft of her friends and comrades, with little money, and was then virtually disowned by the Communist 'family' here. She knew no-one here except fellow-exiles and was unfamiliar with both British and Caribbean culture and use of language.

Immediately on her arrival Claudia stayed with Mae and John Williamson, and on her discharge from hospital with another exiled couple, Charlie and Mikki Doyle, in south-west London.[21] However, in April 1956, probably not many weeks after her discharge, she wrote to 'Stretch' Johnson that she believed that not only did the Doyles themselves have to 'find new accommodations', but that she thought 'they have had enough with being hosts, so have I, as a guest'. So Claudia, despite her illness, set about finding a flat in a city which was suffering a grave housing shortage.

Illness

Claudia's first bout of illness had been when she was hospitalised for a year at the age of 17 for tuberculosis. In July 1953 she collapsed with heart failure which was diagnosed as hypertensive cardio-vascular disease. Released from hospital after three weeks, she was ordered to rest and continued to receive treatment for hypertension. She collapsed again in December with 'coronary heart disease', resulting in further hospitalisation and enforced rest. On admission to prison in January 1955 she was diagnosed as having 'arrested tuberculosis, cardiac disease, coronary arteriosclerosis and essential hypertension'.[22] On her release from prison she was hospitalised in New York, and then again soon after her arrival in the UK. St. Stephen's Hospital, London, reported in December 1955 that Claudia suffered from 'combined hypertensive and arteriosclerotic heart disease'; her TB had healed, but she had 'calcifying pleuritis and more recent infection', as well as 'non-specific bronchitis with emphysema'. Moreover, she was found to be in a 'moderate drug-induced confusional state'.[23]

After being released from hospital in April 1956 she attended a 'bi-weekly clinic for chemical tests to my reaction to anti-coagulants'.[24] By April she must have given up all hope of obtaining a passport and thus of travelling to Prague and then the USSR for medical treatment.

In her letter to Claudia of 6 February 1957, Helois Robinson noted Claudia's 'recent sojourn in hospital'. At the end of the year, when she was able to travel to southern France for a holiday, she must again have been ill as a French prescription for medication has been preserved in the Langford Collection. In June 1958 she was back in St Stephen's Hospital. During her visit to Moscow in 1962 she was so unwell that she had to be hospitalised for some weeks.

It is hardly surprising that Claudia's ill-health continued. Some claim that she chain-smoked, at least in the *Gazette* office, but as comrades in America do not recall her smoking, this must have been due to the new stresses she was experiencing. Trying to keep a monthly newspaper going in an office that also served as an informal Citizens' Advice Bureau, a political discussion centre and a necessary port-of-call for visiting dignitaries from the Black world, as well as participate in (if not organise) the many events and demonstrations of those years must have taken a heavy toll on Claudia's health. What is surprising is that she managed to do it all, despite her poor health.

Finding somewhere to live

The immediate task she faced in early 1956 was finding somewhere to live. According to her 12 April letter to 'Stretch', she had been looking for a month and a half. As an undated note in the British Communist Party archives states that 'Nora must get cracking and find her a flat', it may have been through the Party that in May 1956 Claudia succeeded in renting a flat in south London from Reverend Hewlett Johnson, the 'Red' Dean of Canterbury.[25] The Dean did not charge her the usual fee for 'fixtures and fittings', which Claudia had at the beginning of the search asked the CPUSA, *not* the CPGB, to cover.[26] By 1959 the Dean had to threaten Claudia with eviction because of unpaid rent. He offered to accept her 'latest proposal' in April 1959 regarding outstanding payments, but as another cheque of Claudia's was returned as 'void' by the bank in July, one has to presume that this arrangement broke down. Nevertheless, Claudia continued to live at 6 Meadow Road until about April 1960, when she moved to north London.[27]

Trying to earn a living

It is not known when the CPGB placed Claudia at the New China News Agency, nor when she was removed from there (see chapter 3). What is perfectly clear from the undated statement she sent to Party headquarters is that she was under great stress: the layout and quality of the typing is not up to the standard of her other writings. She had been made to feel a 'burden', she wrote, 'and not a useful member of the agency'. She admitted that it might be 'problematic ... to get jobs as befits their knowledge, experience and contribution' for all the exiles, but surely the Party would not have placed her there if it had not been believed that she could be other than a 'burden'.[28] That a woman of Claudia's vast experience, recent imprisonment and serious illness should be reduced to writing such a memorandum is a grave indictment of the CPGB. Certainly this situation would not have been conducive to the 'calm' advocated by Ben Davis.

A number of questions remain unresolved: was Claudia unemployed after she was dismissed from the News Agency? If so, when? Is that the reason why she had fallen behind with the rent? In April 1956 she was still unemployed, as she told 'Stretch' that if she received assistance for housing from the US Party, that 'would enable me to live for another several months on what I have left'. In a letter to Ben Davis in mid-1957 Claudia wrote, 'my health is holding its own, although I have a constant struggle to do what I want to do, work an 8 hour day to earn a living and then make a political contribution. It's an adjustment that hasn't been easy, or I should say, hasn't been fully made ... I chafe against it.'

Two months later she was 'looking for a different job – not so taxing on my energies. If the balance of what I was promised last summer could be forthcoming, it would help no end.' She also hoped to take a holiday soon.[29]

Without any further information, and as the Inland Revenue (i.e., income tax) department only keep records for six years, it has not possible to discover where Claudia worked between her time at the News Agency, and before she started at *West Indian Gazette*.[30] What is clear is that she had waged a determined struggle against ill health and impoverishment.

Financial worries were constant. In March 1958 she was compelled to borrow £30 from the CPGB. She must have been truly penniless to have been forced into this position. The Party reluctantly lent her the money, repayable in three months; 'I do hope you will be able to make a better go of things in the coming period', warned Party chairman Harry Pollitt.[31] Three months later Claudia wrote to the Party from her sickbed at St Stephen's Hospital: she was 'in the process of arranging for money owed me on my job to be forwarded', in order to meet the 20 June deadline for repaying the loan.[32] (Pollitt had earlier taken a somewhat different line with Claudia – before he was confronted by her boldness. In March 1956 he sent her a copy of his Political Report to the CPGB's 24th National Congress; the note enclosing it reads: 'I apologise for not having been in to see you ... You might like to read the Political Report ... My love, if you will have it, Harry')

Among the smattering of Claudia's preserved papers there is much evidence of her impecunious position. Her motor insurance was terminated in 1961 because of non-payment of the premium.[33] The *Gazette*'s accountant was preparing to sue her over unpaid fees in February 1961. In April 1962 she added up the personal loans she had received – the sum came to £232 of which, she noted, she had only repaid £65. In October 1963 she was sentenced to 7 days' imprisonment for not attending a hearing regarding outstanding amounts owed to a travel company for over a year; she paid £5 to avoid going to jail. In 1964 she was sued for non-payment of council rates, and less than a month before her death she was sent a stern letter by the bank about not having met the *Gazette*'s overdraft repayments. That her situation was so dire is hardly surprising: as she noted in a scrap of an undated letter, 'the revenues from the paper have never given me a proper full-time salary. I live on what monies my family still send me from the U.S. – & £4 a week editorial expenses ...'

Things were so bad that Claudia resorted to betting on horse-races – with what luck is unknown![34]

One person who did his best to help Claudia was Pablo Picasso. It is believed that she had met him during her visit to France (see below). Picasso was much taken by her and gave her two drawings to sell in order to raise money. However, her then colleague Jan Carew believes that she did not sell them; if that is the case, then they disappeared when she died.[35] There were also two benefactors in Britain to whom she could turn when in the direst of straits.[36]

Passport problems

As Claudia's temporary travel document was confiscated on her arrival in Britain, the Communist Party tried, but failed, to persuade the Home Office to grant her a passport. Claudia decided to take matters into her own hands. In June 1957 she asked for a passport to enable her to travel to Nice in southern France. She told the Passport Office that she had received an invitation to holiday there from her friend Mrs Paola Tomasini. She also wrote to Dr Eric Williams, the Prime Minister of Trinidad, as she had been given to understand that the Trinidad authorities would be consulted about her application. Finally, on 22 August 1957 she was granted a passport limited to travel in France and she duly left for a much needed holiday on 5 November. Who paid for this? Probably French comrades, as Helois wrote to her that she was 'happy you were afforded the vacation by our French Friends'.[37]

In March 1958, on receiving an invitation from the Bulgarian Peace Committee to speak in Sofia on the occasion of Paul Robeson's 60th birthday celebrations, Claudia requested an extension of her passport. Having learned from a Passport Office official that the restrictions on her travel had been imposed by the Government of Trinidad via the Colonial Office, Claudia wrote again to Prime Minister Williams. Williams referred her letter to the Colonial Secretariat, where the Acting Colonial Secretary (i.e., the British Government's representative) promised to 'look into the matter'.[38] Claudia, clearly not trusting officialdom, asked left-wing barrister D.N. Pritt for help. Pritt suggested that Labour MP Sir Dingle Foot should be asked to make enquiries. Foot tried to intervene, but must have received a negative response from the Colonial Office as he was soon forced into expressing his regrets to Claudia.[39]

The British Foreign and Commonwealth Office, which has custody of the Colonial Office files, claims to be 'unable to trace any reference to Claudia Jones in the FO [Foreign Office] and CO [Colonial Office] Files'.[40] Therefore it is not possible to determine whether there is any substance to Ben Davis's 'firm opinion that the State Dept. is directly and primarily responsible for the limitations which the British Government is putting upon your travel'.[41]

It was not until mid-1962 that Claudia's passport was extended to cover 'the British Commonwealth and all Foreign Countries'. Why the restrictions were removed is not known. Could the Soviets have requested that she be issued with a passport, as she had been invited to go to Moscow? Would the British Government have acquiesced to such a request? Not very likely. It has been suggested that Eric Williams, as Prime Minister of newly independent Trinidad and Tobago granted her a passport. But this was not so: not only did Claudia travel on a British passport, but the extension of her passport is dated 28 May 1962, which predates independence. As Claudia is remembered as expressing her gratitude to Williams, it is possible that he did exert some pressure on the British Government.[42] Without access to official papers, we shall never know the reasons why the Government decided to grant Claudia an unrestricted passport.

Friends and lovers

As in the USA, Claudia's closest friends were also her political associates – and most were women. Though she shared exile with the Williamsons and the Doyles, there is no trace of her having retained – or established – a friendship with them. Was this perhaps due to the white ex-CPUSA members being offered roles and positions within the CPGB, while Claudia was offered nothing? Did they not put up a fight on her behalf? To judge by Helois Robinson's comment on Mae Williamson (p37), it seems they did not.

It cannot have been easy to build a new circle of friends and colleagues as there were no Black communists in senior positions within the Party and very few Black people with any political experience, except perhaps in the Caribbean. White/Black friendships were generally uncommon in Britain in the 1950s and 1960s. Thus both her colour and her experience at the centre of the CPUSA would have isolated Claudia.

It seems that Claudia's earliest friendships in Britain were with people from abroad, those with international experience: Amy Ashwood Garvey; Eslanda Goode Robeson and her husband, Paul.

We do not know if Amy (Marcus Garvey's first wife) and Claudia knew each other in the USA, but it is quite possible that they had met. Having parted from Garvey after helping him set up the Universal Negro Improvement Association in both Jamaica and New York, Amy never succeeded in establishing a political niche for herself. Amy's search for a satisfactory life resulted in almost constant movement between the USA, the Caribbean, Britain and West Africa. In New York in the 1940s she had campaigned for Adam Clayton Powell's bid for a seat in Congress. When she decided to return to Britain in August 1945, Ben Davis and the West Indian activists, Ethelred Brown and Charles Petioni (both of whom Claudia must have known), were among the guests at the farewell party organised by the Council on African Affairs – whose chairperson was Paul Robeson.[43]

Amy took the chair at the first session of the Pan-African Congress of 1945, organised by George Padmore, one of her colleagues from her previous sojourn in London.[44] She then left for Liberia and Ghana, returning to England in 1949. In 1953 she was in the Caribbean and in

1957 in Ghana for the independence celebrations. What she did in Britain between these trips is unclear; it is believed that she worked as a social worker in Birmingham and in London.[45] In 1958 she emerged as the founder of the Association for the Advancement of Coloured People (see chapter 4) and from this time onwards was associated with Claudia and for a while with the *Gazette*.

Though Amy was often abroad during Claudia's years in Britain, the two women retained a friendship, as evidenced by the two letters and telegrams from 1964 which have survived. Both letters were written from the Liberian Consulate at Las Palmas, where Amy was recuperating from illness. The first letter asks Claudia to move Amy's possessions out of Amy's London home, which she was about to lose due to non-payment of the mortgage. The second letter asks for Claudia's immediate intervention in the matter of the repatriation of the remains of Marcus Garvey from London to Jamaica. Apparently Garvey's second wife had resuscitated her efforts of 1940 in this regard. Amy had thwarted the earlier move and was determined to do so again, or to be the one to bene-fit from it. 'You are my dearest friend', Amy wrote. 'I am putting the matter in your hands ... My dear if we can put this over ... the great publicity should send my books sky high ... We could make a great thing of this and my dear I thought of Pearl going there and singing Garvey's favourite hymn.'[46] How Claudia dealt with this matter is not known. However, after proving that she and Marcus had never been divorced and thus she had the rights to his remains, Amy signed release papers once her expenses to return to London and her outstanding bills in Las Palmas had been paid by the Jamaican Government.[47]

Eslanda and Paul Robeson were old colleagues: Essie had written the introduction to Claudia's pamphlet, *Ben Davis Fighter for Freedom* (New York, 1954), which demanded amnesty for the imprisoned Davis. Claudia, while she was editor of *Weekly Review*, had inter-viewed Paul for the 22 June 1943 issue. To judge by Paul's farewell message to Claudia in December 1955 (see chapter 1), he knew her well and held her in high regard. Having regained his passport in 1958 after a world-wide effort for its restoration, the Robesons left New York for Britain almost immediately and lived there for the next five years.[48] Unfortunately, without access to the Robesons' papers, it is not possi-ble to give an account of this undoubtedly close relationship.[49] However, photographs and brief mentions in the *Gazette* give us some indications. On 27 June 1959 the *Gazette* gave a 'Meet Paul Robeson' reception at Lambeth Town Hall, which was followed by a similar reception at St Pancras Town Hall on 18 July. Essie accompanied her husband on both occasions.[50]

Nadia Cattouse, Paul Robeson and Claudia. *Estate of A. Manchanda.*
Photographer unknown.

The next year, on 28 September, Paul was featured at a *Gazette* Anniversary Concert, where he is reported to have advocated the use of 'art as a weapon for freedom, be it in Africa, the Caribbean, Cuba or British Guiana'. In her welcoming speech, Claudia asked those present to drink a 'toast to [the Robesons'] continued contributions, their health and future successes in their respective fields ... The Robesons stand [for] the idea of equality [of] security, peace, human dignity and the brotherhood of all peoples'.[51]

We know of no further official association between Paul and Claudia. Essie, apart from appearing on platforms with – or organised by – Claudia, also wrote for the *Gazette*. In 1959 she wrote on the Accra All African People's Conference; in May 1961 on 'The Commonwealth: the Largest Political Family'; and her interview with Jomo Kenyatta was printed in the December 1961 issue.[52]

Only two pieces of correspondence between Claudia and Essie remain in the Langford Collection. The first is a carbon copy of a letter from Claudia on *West Indian Gazette* letterhead, dated 6 June 1960. Claudia was, 'at a point where both exhaustion and the weight of the problems are weighting me down a bit. WE CANNOT FAIL. Too much has gone into the establishment of this paper – too much in terms of work, concepts and sacrifice, personal and otherwise for this to happen.' She was considering calling a meeting in the middle of the month of people who might be willing to invest in the *Gazette*; or should a public company be launched to raise enough money to buy a printing press and employ a full time secretary and to pay the editor?[53]

> I need to discuss some of these urgent matters with compatriots in whom I have the deepest confidence of judgement and support ... Darling Essie, I hate to burden you both. Please let me hear from you.

Claudia was also thinking of a Midsummer Folk Festival, Concert and Talent Quest; she wondered whether Paul would be free to participate.

The second fragment in existence is a letter from Essie to Claudia, whose tone confirms their long friendship. The first page is missing so there is no date or sender's address, but it was written from abroad. The two closely-typed pages show concern for Paul's health: his illness in Moscow in 1958-59 and even during his performance in *Othello* from April to November 1959, and his current illness and hospitalisation. She also speaks of the immense strains of being 'PAUL ROBESON' and wanting to live up to people's expectations, but how he simply cannot any longer. The doctors told her that Paul would only be 'out of the jungle' if he could acknowledge and tell 'everybody that he is through with that phase of his life'. But how was Paul to be made to see this? 'Put on your thinking caps', she asked Claudia.[54]

What of friends in Britain? This is how Claudia's friends and colleagues described her at the Symposium held in London in 1996:

> **Pearl Connor** We came across each other in 1956 ... Claudia was one of the most charismatic Caribbean women I ever knew ... She linked her political stance with the artistic and cultural achievements of our people ... Claudia was like a meteor flying swiftly across our sky, a brilliant light which brightened our landscape, pointing the way forward ... The glow of her personality remains an inspiration to us all ... Claudia was somebody really very important, a great stimulus to us all ... Such leadership is rare and when we get it we treasure it ... She made you fearless. There was some quality in Claudia that gave you an impetus and a feeling that you could win, that you could succeed...

Bill Ash It is almost incredible to think that anyone who did not even enjoy the best of health could have achieved as much on the world stage as Claudia did in under ten years, and yet she never gave the impression of being a dour committed character driven to the edge of endurance by all the calls she was prepared to accept on her time and energy. She was a beautiful woman full of life and gaiety and delightful to be with.

I love to remember the times we were together for other than purely political purposes, as when Ranjana and I went with her and Manchanda to Stratford-on-Avon to see Paul Robeson performing Othello and to visit with him afterwards.

Ranjana Ash I'm proud to call myself a friend of Claudia Jones ... That woman was not well but she did it all ... Something that we must remember, that she made us think about uniting struggles ... Because she was a dynamic personality; anyone who thinks that these isms make people all very serious should remember this marvellous woman as she came in laughing, brilliant, full of energy ... Claudia as a person was constantly bedevilled by very poor health. I have seen people using that as an excuse for not doing all that they could. This was a woman who never once mentioned her physical disabilities, her health.

She educated many of us. We knew Langston Hughes, we knew Paul Robeson, but you know, she was keeping up with all the newer writers.[55] When Baldwin's first novel came out, I think she gave a long review in the *Gazette*... How many of you remember a brilliant play by a Black American playwright, Lorraine Hansberry, called 'A Raisin in the Sun' which opened here I think in '59? Do you remember Ruby Dee and Ossie Davis?[56] Well she and Ossie did lots of things. It was through Claudia that we heard of their recitations ... [and] of African American writers. I am so grateful to Claudia for having found the time to remain a truly cultivated woman besides being a political dynamo.

When she was living in a place in Brixton, she was very hospitable and was forever throwing parties, and they were lots of fun and things happening. [Once] Claudia scalded her arm ... It must have been excruciatingly painful, but she had planned a programme with some local women and other people ... In spite of that scalded arm she carried through that programme ... She was always inviting people and people visited her from the struggle in the States, and for those of us who hadn't met her 'names' it was wonderful ... That was going to be the way I would know Claudia over and over again.

David Rousell-Milner Claudia taught me how to write, it was the first attempt I had ever made and she taught me a great deal. This was often at a Chinese restaurant up near the Oval, a restaurant we often used to go to, and usually it was some Chinese soup because we didn't eat a great deal but we enjoyed the Chinese soup. She had a very gentle way about her, a very gentle way of convincing me and directing me as a young man, showing me where my ideas really were going astray, and bit by bit I moved to the Left. But as a friend she just wasn't there to sort of say, 'No, you're wrong about that'; she was someone who led. With me, gently. With other people she could be tough when she needed to be, but certainly with me she was very gentle and it succeeded.

Alex Pascall That was a lady! She was beautiful in every sense, not just the physique that you saw outside. When Claudia spoke, oh Lord! everybody just ... your body tingled, there was something about this lady. And I think that's the way we have to remember Claudia.

These are friends and acquaintances who loved and admired Claudia. But was it a relationship of equals? There were certainly no Black colleagues here of her own wide experience and status, and seemingly friendship with British whites was not a possibility. According to Dorothy Kuya, then a young communist about to enrol at college to complete her teacher-training, who lived not far from her in the two years before her death, Claudia was a 'very private and serious person ... She did not have much time for gossip ... Claudia never talked a great deal, and did not talk about herself.'[57] Trevor Carter, Party member then, as now: 'Claudia did not have to disguise her emotions with me, but she did not treat me as an equal – she saw me as a young comrade'.[58] Roy Sawh, one of many comrades who used to sell the *Gazette* on street corners, told me that 'Claudia helped shape my political mental process', but 'we were not close, no'.[59]

Did Claudia need affection and support? Some of this could have been provided by the women in her life, such as Ranjana Ash, Nadia Cattouse, Pearl Connor, Amy Ashwood Garvey, Pearl Prescod, Lyn Jones and the Baden-Semper sisters; and after 1958, Essie Robeson.[60] But most of these women were considerably younger, involved in their own affairs and careers, and some were not as 'political' as Claudia. 'We all ran when she wanted us for some project or other. But we were all too busy – I never so much as had a cup of coffee with her', Pearl Connor told me. Nadia Cattouse in many conversations echoes Pearl's memories.[61] Lyn Jones, who sometimes helped out in the *Gazette* office, and who exchanged home visits with Claudia, believes that no-one was close to her.[62] Whom did she find to share her concerns, her perspective on communism, her political commitment?

Among her new friends of Caribbean origins were the writers Jan

Carew, George Lamming and Andrew Salkey, all of them 'political', but again much younger and more inexperienced than she was. Jan Carew's memories confirm Claudia's particular solitariness: he thought Claudia 'unique – there was no woman like her in England, of any colour. She had no peer ... She was a grand person, very generous as a human being. Never gave any clues as to the personal hardships she was enduring, of her hand-to-mouth existence. She was very proud and kept her personal feelings to herself'.[63] Ricky Cambridge, a newly-arrived young Trinidadian in 1961, was attracted to Claudia through the politics of the *Gazette*. His face pensive with memories, he remembers Claudia as 'charismatic, a great speaker ... In complete command of the situation and herself ... Unperturbed by anything outside the cause'. He, too, was unaware of both her illness and her penury.[64] Andrew Salkey told writer Anne Walmsley that Claudia had been 'a marvellous teacher of people like myself ...[I learned from her] 'that Marxism and racism were not exclusive'.[65] Pat Salkey described to me Claudia attending the Sunday get-togethers at the Salkey household in Holland Park, and that she often came with a group, which sometimes included the musician Rudolph Dunbar, but not with a close personal friend.[66]

However, some Caribbeans, though much impressed by her, stayed away from Claudia. Some because they were members of the CPGB and were aware that the Party and Claudia 'had reservations about each other'; others because they were anti-communist; a few because of her close association with Manchanda, who was seen as 'difficult and dogmatic'.[67]

There was, at least for a while, an African-American in her life: a 'tall, handsome seaman', Trevor Carter recalled. Josephine Florent, who worked for the British-Polish Friendship Society in Portland Place in the 1950s, remembers Claudia, who was friendly with some-one there, coming to eat at the Warsaw Club accompanied by a 'charming, pleasant light-skinned Black man, who always wore a trilby hat'. Josephine and her partner and Claudia and her friend were occasionally taken out to dinner in Marylebone by wealthier colleagues from the Society and its journal *New Poland*.[68] It is possible that one of these men was George Bowrin, as John La Rose believes that he and Claudia were close to each other during the final days of the *Caribbean News* and the birth of the *West Indian Gazette*.[69] (See chapter 3.)

Manu

A more permanent role in Claudia's life was played by Abhimanyu Manchanda, known as Manu. To eke out what must have been meagre wages offered by the job found her by the CPGB at the New China News Agency (see chapter 3), Claudia sub-let a room in her flat to Manu, a fellow communist. However, as the rent was frequently unpaid, one has to surmise that neither Claudia nor Manu had a steady, or a sufficient, income. It is not known why Manu came to Britain, some say that he was expelled by the Communist Party in India.[70] From a middle-class family, he had been a leader of the Student Federation of India. He was well educated and worked in London intermittently as a supply teacher. Manu was a man of 'intellectual self-confidence, well versed in Marxism-Leninism', but 'he had to have his own way. He became extremely annoyed if he didn't win the vote and threatened to leave whatever organisation he was with', recalls his Indian Workers' Association (IWA) colleague Avtar Jouhl.[71] Ranjana Ash remembers him as 'very dogmatic and critical', while Nadia Cattouse confirms that he 'walked out if people didn't agree with him'. Others are even less flattering, remembering him as a 'confidence trickster who used her contacts to get money out of them'. Jan Carew recalls 'constant arguing over some issue or other; but this quarrelling wasn't serious'. Pearl Connor thought him a 'total curse ... he was a block – kept people away'. Lyn Jones, who confirms that many thought Manu used Claudia, adds that Claudia never indicated that and always spoke of him fondly. 'She wasn't as important to him and he was to her', Jones believes. Ricky Cambridge, who does not remember Manu being around Claudia much in the 1962-64 period, when he was frequently in the *Gazette* office, remembers him as being very 'accusatory' and a 'die-hard, argumentative communist', who (mistakenly) thought much of himself as a theoretician.[72] Why is there such an almost universal dislike of Manchanda? Was it perhaps because he was so dogmatic, and would never compromise, and had little patience with those who did not share his vehemently expressed political views?

It is believed that Claudia might have met Manchanda through the International Committee of the CPGB. Taja Sahota, who was then the chairman of this Committee, had obtained a list of Indian Party members from the Committee and used this to set up branches of the Indian Workers' Association; Claudia and Manu were the key workers in setting up the London branch. Manu divided his efforts and energies between working for the *Gazette* and for the IWA, which could only pay him expenses but not a salary. At that time the IWA only had a Punjabi paper and could not afford also to produce an English-language one; the Association hoped to be able to use the *Gazette* to propagate its views and inform and educate non-Punjabi Indians in Britain.[73] Manu became general secretary of the London branch of the IWA in 1956.[74]

Claudia and Manu shared the two-bedroom flat at 6 Meadows Road. At least in the beginning, the relationship was intimate; but it was never easy. Avtar Jouhl recalls that 'there used to be arguments between Claudia and Manu ... She sometimes treated him like a school-child.' As evidenced by the little remaining correspondence, the initial love affair may have moved to more of a comradeship as the years passed. Thus Manu's two letters to Claudia while she was in France in 1957, addressed to 'My sweet darling', show much concern for her health, and send news of common acquaintances. The bulk of the letters is an account of how Manu has fulfilled the many requests and instructions that Claudia had sent regarding the redirecting of mail, the payment of bills and other matters, and he assured her that he had cleaned 'the sitting room, your bedroom, my room and the kitchen'. Manu reiterates how much he misses her 'not the least [because] I had started depending upon you to spur me on to do things ... This was done by my mother ... you have taken over this admirably!' He had been to dinner with Charlie and Mikki Doyle, who had been 'rather indulgent towards [me], of course because of you'. He had, he admitted, caused 'some excitement because of my increasingly rude interruptions'.[75]

In 1959 Manu, in a letter addressed to Claudia as 'Miss Jones', announced that he was getting in touch with solicitors in order to 'dissociate with both the *Gazette* and the Coloured Peoples' Publishing House'. This was occasioned by her 'very chaotic, most inefficient, uneconomic and unsystematic working'. This might have been true, as Claudia had editorial but not publishing experience, and there were no funds to employ a manager or a book-keeper. However, in light of Taja Sahota's recollection of Manu's room at Meadow Road being as untidy as Claudia's was neat, the rationale of the resignation has to be read with caution and scepticism.[76] Manu certainly did not leave the paper, though his role had become 'casual', as Claudia admitted in a letter to him dated 31 August 1961. There had been 'recriminations', which Claudia wanted to bring to an end by clarifying Manu's role on the paper: he was to be circulation and business manager. Claudia outlined conditions for a working relationship, which banned the discussion of personal matters in the office and name calling; she wanted 'demarcation of roles, a schedule of meetings and fund-raising to permit the employment of more staff and the clearing of debts', which amounted to £490.

Two letters from Manu to Claudia while she was in the USSR in 1962 have been preserved. These are addressed to 'Dear Claudia' and are almost completely devoid of anything personal, concentrating on the *Gazette*'s unpaid bills and material for future issues of the paper. This seems to indicate that the arrangements outlined by Claudia the previous year had not been put into practice. Manu's letter of 29 August lists outstanding bills, which, excluding the printing of the *Gazette*, came to £233. A number of creditors were threatening legal action and the electricity at 138 Cranforth Gardens, where Claudia then lived, had been cut off. But there is still a note of care and concern in the letter: though Manu castigates Claudia for the 'mess' she had left behind, he also hopes that she will be able to have a holiday once she is discharged from hospital. Manu promised not only to 'keep the paper going but to expand both the circulation and advertisements'. The next epistle, a post card, informed Claudia that the landlords were trying to repossess the *Gazette* offices and that as the printing of the September issue had not been fully paid, the November issue was in jeopardy.

It would seem that at this time, between 1960-1963, Claudia and Manu did not share living quarters. In 1962 Manu's address was 110 Fitzjohns Avenue, Hampstead, while Claudia lived at 58 Lisburne Road, also in Hampstead, but some distance from Manu's flat.

Despite this physical separation, Claudia and Manu remained close. On her second day in Moscow in 1962 she wrote him a three and a half page letter, replete with her excitement at being in the city and at her reception by the staff of *Soviet Woman*. She hoped that her health would permit her to go to a 'Central Asian Republic – to the sun and especially to see one of the places where the national question was solved'. She then discusses 'things I left somewhat in a mess' (the *Gazette* bills, etc.) and concludes with her appreciation 'for all you're doing to help out'.

Claudia's second letter from the USSR was written from hospital, where after nine days she was allowed to sit up and walk a little. Despite her obvious illness she worries about how Manu is coping with the 'plethora of problems' she had left in his 'lap'. She was using her 'enforced rest' to write an 'article for my hosts', planned to write a short story on her hospitalisation, and was learning Russian. She also wrote some poems.

Claudia's final letter from the USSR tells of her considerable anxiety about finding alternative accommodation in London. But she quickly moves on to discuss recent political events and their coverage in the *Gazette*. She queries the lack of book reviews, the missing beauty column, and criticises the lack of news as opposed to 'declarations'. She is pleased with the sports page but reprimands Manu for his editorial: 'oh my dear please watch the length of sentences and length of words ... Not a treatise or a legal argument, an editorial to be understood by average people.' She is also highly critical of Manu's changes to the

Gazette's masthead, which he had clearly not discussed with her. 'I know this is an old pet fancy of yours', she wrote. A masthead should not be 'tampered with lightly'. His alterations destroyed the visual link between 'Afro-Asians, West Indians and other Caribbean people'. She planned to be back by mid-November, after the 'great Soviet holiday for which celebrations I've been invited to stay...'[77]

Having been advised by Soviet physicians not to travel by air, Claudia did not arrive in London until 21 November.[78] It is possible that it was on her return that she moved into rooms in Lisburne Road, North London.

In July 1963 Claudia wrote to Manu from St Stephens Hospital admitting that she 'must learn to curb my temper. Underlying it all is the frustration of our mutual positions and the material difficulties.' She had been told he was not well, and gives instructions regarding financial matters at the *Gazette*. (This letter is addressed to Manu at 58 Lisburne Road, but begins 'I tried reaching you at your house only to find you out. Thinking you might be at Lisburne Rd – no luck either when I phoned.' Presumably Manu had keys to Claudia's flat.)

Little remains of Claudia's correspondence from Japan or China. A card from Japan dated 9 August 1964 reads: 'Yesterday I laid a rose for you and me at Hiroshima renewing our pledge for "No more Hiroshimas"'. A month later Claudia wrote to Manu to say that she had intended to send him a card for his birthday – on 4 September – but had not been able to as she was again in hospital. She tells Manu, with evident excitement, of all that she had been seeing and learning, including the 'complex inter-relations of agriculture to industry' and the various methods being introduced, as 'to feed a nation one had to find ways to eke more out of the land, individual labour was not enough'. Claudia worries about not having heard from Manu – is his 'health holding up?' ... 'I needn't emphasise how thankful I am that as a colleague and compatriot (you are a 'West Indian' – and I 'Indian') our links lie in our common thinking, common outlook and shared struggles – to say nothing here of friendship. You again have made it possible for this trip to be extended. Please write – and do take care ... PS I'm sure you saw the item in *Hsinhua* when the Latin American Delegation including C. Jones met Chr. Mao. *That* was quite a day![79]

The final piece of correspondence is a card from Shanghai, dated 21 September, in which Claudia complains of a lack of letters from Manu. 'Please write', she concludes the brief note. 'Hope you're OK. Love, Claudia.

Claudia's passport is stamped by the Hong Kong Immigration

Department on 5 October 1964. Had she paid a brief visit to Viet Nam, as suggested by Mr Sahota? Fairly shortly after her return to London Manu must have left on his trip to China as he was not in Britain when Claudia died, so soon after her return – on Christmas Eve 1964.

Self analysis

Claudia's autobiography has vanished, but a few pages of self-analysis, of introspection have been preserved. These pages reveal Claudia as few, or perhaps none, knew her.

> Tonight I tried to imagine what life would be like in the future – personal, that is, for on the broad highway of Tomorrow, despite craggy hills and unforeseen gullies, I am certain that mankind will take the high road to a socialist future.
>
> My certitude for this broad future has never matched my certitude for my personal fortunes. I have not been endowed either with the ability to apply that certitude – or indeed to experience its harbingers. Perhaps dialectically, this is why: my very certitude and commitment has over-shadowed in the eyes of some my personal interest in people. To those with whom I share this broad vision this seeming weakness has been resented more kindly, if not resented – rejected. Whereas this character-istic has impinged on personal relationships, it has nevertheless served as a liberating force making and shaping the being that I have become. I, in turn, have rejected any tendency to reduce this result even perhaps to stifle its evocation.
>
> Evocation is a mutual emotion. To evoke a response of togetherness – in all things (maturity tells me this is probably impossible in a single relationship) and remembering human limitations there must be togeth-erness. Togetherness also is not an abstraction; its inner laws and contradictions must be studied.
>
> Yet another characteristic may be strength of character and a tendency to fight weakness – not to openly sympathize with it. Is it because a lurking fear exists that capitulation to manifested weakness in others (even when not self-imposed) may in turn impinge on what I regard as essentially impermissible?
>
> In the strongest I have witnessed impermissible weakness. I do not exclude myself, but I have never been able to condone personal weak-nesses and, therein, perhaps is another antagonistic contradiction: regarding the impermissibility of personal weakness as fundamental, not entirely lacking in my own share of these, I seek to counter my own (and

others) with a harshness that is also impermissible in close human relationships.

For most of my adult years this has been the essence of my approach; the raison d'etre of my function. I find I have been praised for a single mindedness of purpose – and this is true enough; only my sincerest friends have observed the one-sidedness of my existence – something (again the characteristic rears its head!) I have hardly allowed myself to admit – far less to fully examine!

Perhaps as third reason (happily I do not publicly avow or practice this characteristic) at root has been a 'protective' one – against personal injury. Those who truly know me know this – and I have often known even as I strike back, the verbal blows from which I flee are nourished in identical soil.

Fearing the perpetuation of this one-sidedness in personal relations, I persist in it; fearing the disappointment of non-togetherness. Knowing that evocation of a different approach means change on my part, I have no certitude that change will strengthen togetherness. But this certitude is related not only to faith in the future – which is not blind but scientific; one needs must apply some scientific enquiry to all phenomena. And if one resists that inquiry can it be because one knows that the application of that very science will reveal an uneven development; or that one fears to admit failure, or even that one's own limitations will stand naked and bare? Is it that in so examining the very characteristic will be proven a nugatory patterning the [illegible] violation of it? Or even that it will be found that one is so languid [illegible]?

Penchant that I have for introspective discussion, I seem to have wound up where I began, I bore no-one but myself. I have admitted nothing; but sought to analyze all this for self-understanding; I find I have deluded myself – conscious though I ever am that delusion is unrealistic, can never replace togetherness or evoke happiness – nor sympathetic friendship or understanding.

And as I become too aware of this state, to even try to change – I realise I not only have become lethargic in these matters (a state not to be emulated!) but positively without sense. All weavers know of tangled skeins. The Bard thought they became 'threads to deceive'. Sometimes they can be untangled and sometimes they serve as webs. How I believe in the Loom of Language! and in the Family of Man![80]

Notes

1. Davis to Claudia, 25 January 1958. Unless stated otherwise, material in

this chapter is from what remains of Claudia's papers in the Langford Collection. Ben Davis had married his secretary at about the time or shortly after Claudia's expulsion.

2. Davis was first imprisoned during the McCarthy era in 1948. He was re-arrested in the 1950s and died in 1964. Claudia duly noted his burial in the *Gazette*.
3. Davis to Claudia, 16 August 1959. Davis was a lawyer.
4. Davis to Claudia, 9 September 1956.
5. Davis to Claudia, 25 January 1958; 29 May 1959; 15 September 1962.
6. He was living in semi-retirement due to a heart condition.
7. Betty Gannett was imprisoned with Claudia in Alderson; at the time of her imprisonment she was National Education Director of the CPUSA; after her release she continued in senior posts in education and in public relations and was on the editorial board of *Political Affairs*.
8. A Black woman, Helois Robinson was an 'outstanding leader in the labour and civil rights movement', according to James and Esther Jackson, who remember her being at the reception given to Paul and Essie Robeson on their return from the UK in December 1963. From a telephone conversation, 16 May 1998
9. Robinson to Claudia, 15 June 1956.
10. Robinson to Claudia, 7 July 1960; October 1960.
11. Mae was the wife of John Williamson, who had been Labour Secretary of the CPUSA before his imprisonment and exile. He wrote a fairly regular column for the British *Daily Worker*, was given the leadership of the campaign to have Paul Robeson's passport restored, and became librarian of the Marx Memorial Library. It is interesting to note that Mae could travel whereas Claudia was not given a passport until 1962.
12. In the late 1930s Johnson had been leader of the Harlem YCL at a time when many Harlem intellectuals and artists were associated with communism – or at least with its internationalist vision. Johnson had once been a dancer at the Cotton Club and an actor at the Negro People's Theater. Later in life, after a period spent 'underground' because of the McCarthyite persecutions, he taught sociology at the State University of New York.
13. Telephone conversation with Mr Johnson in Galveston, Texas, April 1997.
14. 'Discussion article by Claudia Jones, *Political Affairs*, August 1945, pp717-720.
15. Claudia to Howard 'Stretch' Johnson, 21 April 1956, Tamiment Library, New York University, Collection 161, H.S. Johnson Papers, Box 1.
16. Claudia to Comrade Foster, in H.S. Johnson Papers, *ibid*. It has not been possible to discover the identity of Pasquale.
17. My attempts to locate Claudia's sisters have been unsuccessful.
18. Betty Gannett to Claudia, 18 January 1956. (The letter is dated incorrectly as '1955'.)
19. *The Worker*, 2 November 1958, p2.

20. Davis to Claudia, 9 February 1956.
21. Initially letters from the USA were addressed c/o the Williamsons, then c/o the Doyles. Deported to Britain, Charlie Doyle became a shop steward for the Electricians' Union and Mikki Doyle eventually became the women's editor of the *Morning Star*.
22. Claudia to Comrade Foster, 6 December 1955, H.S. Johnson Papers, note 15.
23. Report from Phillip Harvey, heart specialist, St Stephen's Hospital, 30 December 1955, NMLH: CP/CENT/DISC/03/06. One cannot but wonder about the cause of the 'drug-induced confusional state': was this deliberately induced?
24. Claudia to Howard 'Stretch' Johnson, 21 April 1956, H.S. Johnson Papers, note 15.
25. Undated note in NMLH: CP/CENT/DISC/03/06. There is nothing in the Hewlett Johnson Papers at the University of Kent regarding Claudia, but there is some correspondence with Paul Robeson and William Patterson of the CPUSA.
26. Helois Robinson to Claudia, 17 May 1956; Claudia to Howard 'Stretch' Johnson, 21 April 1956, H.S. Johnson Papers, note 15.
27. Dean Hewlett Johnson to Claudia, 6 April 1959. Claudia's new address was 10 Felix Avenue, London N.8.
28. Undated memorandum in NMLH: CP/CENT/DISC/03/06.
29. Claudia to Ben Davis, 15 &16 May 1957 and 8 July 1957, Schomburg Center: Davis Papers, Sc Micro R 6129, Reel 1. In the USA, as a full time worker for the Party, Claudia did not have to separate earning a living from political activity.
30. Letters to author from Inland Revenue 13 August 1997 and from the Dept. of Social Security 24 September 1997, which stated that no information can be disclosed for research purposes.
31. Harry Pollitt to Claudia, 25 March 1958, NMLH: CP/CENT/DISC/03/06.
32. Claudia to Bill Wainwright, 20 June 1958, NMLH: CP/CENT/SEC/20.
33. The *Gazette* had bought a battered old car; Claudia had to learn to drive and in the process ran the car into a wall.
34. There is a scrap of paper with the names of horses at Kempton Park racecourse in the Langford Collection. Diane Langford told me that Manu had preserved her betting slips.
35. Telephone interview with Jan Carew in Pennsylvania, 6 May 1998. Ricky Cambridge recalls only a drawing of Harriet Tubman in the Lisburne Road flat. Interview, London, 16 & 28 May 1998.
36. Interview with Nadia Cattouse, London, 14 May 1998. Apparently only one of these benefactors is still alive; this person does not want his name revealed out of respect for Claudia.
37. Helois Robinson to Claudia, 21 December 1957.
38. Claudia to Colonial Office, 25 March 1958; Claudia to Dr Eric Williams,

25 March 1958; Acting Colonial Secretary, Trinidad to Claudia, 14 June 1958. There is no trace of this correspondence in the Colonial Office papers at the Public Record Office.

39. D.N. Pritt to Claudia, 30 March 1958; Sir Dingle Foot to Claudia, 28 March 1958. Both men were lawyers and both had been much involved in colonial issues, for example defending Kwame Nkrumah and Jomo Kenyatta against charges brought by the British Government.

40. Letter to author 31 July 1997. I could find nothing on this period of Claudia's life in the National Archives in Washington.

41. Davis to Claudia 2 September 1957. Mr Walter B. Hill of the US National Archives has 'searched the indexes of the Departments of State and Justice [but] failed to identify any file or correspondence that dealt with Davis'. Letter from Mr Hill 7 April 1998, to whom I wish express my gratitude for his help with this research.

42. Telephone interview with Lyn Jones, London, 27 May 1998, who had worked in the Trinidad and Tobago High Commission in London for many years. The UK Passport Agency informed me, in a letter dated 3 September 1998, that no no correspondence relating to passports is preserved.

43. Lionel M. Yard, *Amy Ashwood Garvey*, Associated Publishers, nd, 120.

44. Amy had lived in Britain in the early 1920s and again from 1925 to 1938. See Hakim Adi & Marika Sherwood, *The Manchester 1945 Pan-African Congress Revisited*, New Beacon Books, London 1995.

45. Tony Martin, 'Amy Ashwood Garvey, Wife No.1', *Jamaica Journal*, 20 March 1987, pp32-36. (I must thank my colleague John Cowley for giving me a copy of this article.)

46. Amy Ashwood Garvey to Claudia, 23 June 1964; 2 July 1964. Amy's manuscripts on Garvey were never published and appear to have been lost. Presumably Amy was refering to Pearl Prescod, the Trinidad-born actress and singer.

47. Yard, note 43, pp204-208.

48. *Daily Worker*, 12 July 1958, p1. The Robesons arrived on 11 July 1958; among those welcoming them at the airport were Cheddi Jagan and Viscount Stansgate, better known as Anthony Wedgwood Benn, MP.

49. Despite pre-arrangements with the Moorland-Spingarn Research Center and Paul Robeson Jr to see his parents' papers, and a confirmation of this the day after I arrived in the US in November 1997, the following day Mr Robeson closed the papers to all researchers. The papers were still closed in early 1999.

50. Essie, as a reporter for Associated Negro Press of Chicago, had recently attended the West Indies Federation Inaugural Conference and the All-African People's Conference in Accra, organised by George Padmore.

51. *West Indian Gazette*, November 1960, p3. Such ideas must have been very close to Claudia's own views on the role of art and culture.

52. The US Embassy found one of the articles on the Accra conference so

alarming that it warned the State Dept. in Washington that Essie was stirring 'Africans and Asians alike against Westerners', see Martin Duberman, *Paul Robeson*, Alfred Knopf, New York 1988, p732, n.18.

53. The Coloured People's Publishing Co., which published the *Gazette*, was a private company. Claudia was, of course, the editor.

54. The letter might have been written from Berlin, where Robeson was hospitalised from August to December 1963. Paul and Essie, who was to die of cancer two years later, returned to the US on 22 December 1963.

55. African-American poet and writer Langston Hughes (1902-1967) came to prominence during the Harlem Renaissance, the flowering, and recognition, of 'Negro' artistic talent in the USA.

56. African-American acting couple, often involved in political activities in the USA.

57. Telephone interview with Ms Kuya in Liverpool, 9 February 1998. Dorothy Kuya was born in Liverpool of African descent. She saw 'quite a bit' of Claudia during that time, but does not recall her speaking at or attending a CP meeting. She was one of the few British Black women to join the Party.

58. Interview with Trevor Carter, London 2 September 1997. Some might believe the two halves of this statement to be somewhat contradictory.

59. Interview, London, 21 May 1998. Roy Sawh came to the UK from British Guiana in 1958; he studied in Moscow from 1960 to 1962. On his return he was associated with the founding of the Racial Adjustment Action Society and then the Universal Coloured People's Assocation. He is the author of *Where I Stand*, Hansib, London 1987.

60. On Nadia Cattouse, Pearl Connor and Pearl Prescod, see Stephen Bourne, *Black in the British Frame*, Cassell, London 1998, and Jim Pines (ed), *Black and White in Colour*, BFI Publishing, London 1992.

61. Interviews with Pearl Connor, London, 15 May 1998 and Nadia Cattouse e.g. 14 May 1998.

62. Telephone interview with Lyn Jones, London, 27 May 1998.

63. Telephone interview with Jan Carew in Pennsylvania 6 May 1998.

64. Interview with Ricky Cambridge, London 28 May 1998.

65. Anne Walmsley, *The Caribbean Artists Movement 1966-1972*, New Beacon Books, London 1992, p45.

66. Telephone interview with Pat Salkey, London, 8 May 1998.

67. Interview with John La Rose, London, 7 May 1998 and with Sonny Black, London, 28 May 1998. A long-standing trade union and political activist in his native Trinidad and also in Venezuela, John La Rose settled in London in 1961. He was educated about conditions in Britain, he recalls, by Claudia and Pansy Jeffrey, then an advice worker and activist in Notting Hill. Also Trinidadian, Sonny Black came to Britain in 1961 as manager of the Dixiland Steel Band. He is now a promoter of Caribbean and African music and artistic director of the Commonwealth Arts and Culture Foundation.

68. Interviews with Trevor Carter, London, 4 May 1997 and with Josephine Florent, London, 14 April 1998 and 5 April 1998. Josephine, partly of St.Lucian descent, was a member of the CPGB for much of her life.
69. Interview with John La Rose, London, 7 May 1998.
70. Some informants claim that Manu had not been expelled by the Party in India and that this was a groundless charge levelled against him by the CPGB. Interview with Taja Sahota, Leamington Spa, 10 March 1998.
71. Interview with Avtar Jouhl, Birmingham 21 January 1998.
72. Interviews with Ranjana Ash, London, 14 January 1998; Nadia Cattouse, London, 5 February 1998; Pearl Connor, London, 15 May 1998; Ricky Cambridge, London, 28 May 1998; telephone interviews with ex-CPGB member Jenny Williams, 14 January 1998 and Lyn Jones, London, 27 May 1998; telephone interview with Jan Carew in Pennsylvania, 6 May 1998.
73. Interview with Taja Sahota, Leamington Spa, 10 March 1998.
74. The IWA had been formed in Coventry in 1938. The post-war years and the attainment of independence led to a period of quiescence, but under mainly communist leadership the organisation was flourishing again by the 1950s. There is no definitive history of the IWA; see John De Witt, *Indian Workers Association in Britain*, OUP, London 1969.
75. Manu to Claudia, 11 November 1957 & 29 November 1957.
76. Interview with Taja Sahota, Leamington Spa 10 March 1998.
77. Claudia in Moscow to Manu, at 110 Fitzjohns Ave, 21 August 1962, 31 August 1962, 25 October 1962.
78. Telegram from Claudia to Manu, 19 November 1962.
79. Claudia from China to Manu, 7 September 1964.
80. Claudia's handwritten pages are not always easy to decipher. Nothing has been altered in the transcript.

Claudia and the British Communist Party

In order to understand Claudia's relations with the British Communist Party (CPGB) it is necessary to explore the Party's attitudes and policies towrads colonialism and racism. It is also important to examine the Party's relationship with Black peoples in Britain. Though the US Communist Party's (CPUSA) relationship with Black members was not wholly successful, perhaps a major difference between the two parties was that the CPUSA acknowledged the issue of race while the CPGB did not. Moreover, the US Party's leadership included many Black members, while the British had none. The CPGB's attitude to racial matters, and its incomprehension of its own racism, were to have radical effects on Claudia's life in Britain.

Party policy on colonies

In the pre-war years relations between Black peoples in Britain and the Communist Party were almost non-existent, despite Comintern instructions to foster relationships with both the colonies and colonials in Britain. Though a number of Black peoples of African, Asian and Caribbean descent were members of the Party, their particular situation and concerns were rarely addressed by the Party.[1] Historian Hakim Adi relates that Palme Dutt, the Communist Party of Great Britain's theoretician, at a conference of the British Empire Communist Parties in 1947, only advocated independence for colonies/dependencies with 'national movements', by which Dutt apparently meant communist parties.[2] It is hardly likely that Dutt did not know that communist parties were banned in all the colonies, so why did he follow the standard British line that colonies were 'not ready' for independence? In the following year Jamaican Richard Hart in a scathing criticism accused the Party of political naivety and ignorance of West Indian and West African political demands. Richard Hart was then the leading Marxist in the

Caribbean and the secretary of the Caribbean Labour Congress. He decided not to send his detailed criticism to London; this accused Dutt of ignorance of the existing situation in the different colonies and their national movements, of homogenising the colonies and of not elucidating the difference between 'dominion status' and 'independence'. In the more moderate but still forceful letter he did send, Hart wrote, '... it appears that you are not aware of the progress made by our national movement and do not appreciate the fact that we demand *Dominion status now* ... I am sure that now that this has been made clear to you, you will do what lies in your power to make this generally known ...' [3]

By the Party's second 'Conference of the Communist and Workers Parties of Countries within the Sphere of British Imperialism' in April 1954, some lessons had apparently been learned, perhaps as a result of pressure from more vociferous Black members in London. Ade Thomas spoke on Nigeria, and there were three representatives of the Caribbean: Billy Strachan spoke on 'Terror in the West Indies', George Bowrin on 'The Struggles in Trinidad' and Ranji Chandrisingh on 'Terror in British Guiana'.[4] The somewhat verbose manifesto issued by the Conference contained some 'immediate objectives': the end of the 'shameful wars in Malaya and Kenya; mutual support in the daily battle for higher living standards and democratic rights; to unite for the aim of national independence and self-determination of all our peoples and to secure the withdrawal of troops from all the territories dominated by British imperialism and to unite in the fight for peace against the menace of a new world war'. The manifesto also noted that 'in Britain the Communist Party has a special responsibility ... to draw the widest sections of the labour movement and the peoples into common action with the struggle of the colonial and semi-colonial peoples'.[5]

Methods for achieving their aims

One has to presume the Conference left matters in the Party's hands. But how safe were these? A few months later, Harry Pollitt[6] published his statement on 'The national independence of the colonies', which was a section of the CPGB's general manifesto, *The British Road to Socialism*.[7] Pollitt spent considerable space outlining the 'American war policy' and the 'key task' of the CPGB as 'the fight for peace'. He advocated, without defining, a 'fraternal association of the British people and the liberated peoples of the present Empire', but then, most confusingly, went on to say that this could only be attained once 'the peoples of the present Empire [have] achieved their complete independence as a result of the joint fight by the British and colonial peoples'. A much more important and revealing inconsistency is his later advocacy of how Britain would 'supply the vast market opened up by the liberation of the subject peoples with the capital goods, the steel, coal, locomotives and machine tools they need to carry through the most rapid industrialisation of their countries, as well as manufactured consumer goods to raise the standard of living of their peoples. In return we would receive the foodstuffs, timber and raw materials needed for our own economic development.' That this would be a somewhat unequal exchange, that newly-independent countries might choose to purchase their capital and consumer goods elsewhere and develop their own industries, and the crucial issue of who controlled the international markets in which these raw materials were sold, as well as banking and insurance, neither the CPGB nor Pollitt considered.

According to Party historian Noreen Branson, it was through pressure from 'some West Indian members' that the precise 'formulation' of the statement on colonies was debated.[8] Cris Le Maitre remembers more precisely: it was the Aggregate Meeting of the West Indies Committee that sent in the much debated 'formulation'.[9] Some suggestions had also been sent to the Party by the branches regarding policy towards the future relationship of Britain to her ex-colonies. There was further discussion at the pre-Congress meetings, where a 'minority position' was proposed, that is, for 'fraternal relations' with Britain, as defined by the Aggregate Meeting. Seemingly for the first time, the Executive Committee's formulation was defeated by 298 votes to 210. Claudia Jones supported the minority statement.[10]

Party policy on racial discrimination in Britain

> When I raised the question with him, George Padmore said, 'Look my brother, no communist party can rise above the general culture of the people to any extent, and if there is racism in the United States, you are going to find it within that party. You must always remember that.
>
> (Trevor Carter at the 1996 Symposium)

According to Billy Strachan, it was pressure from the International Committee of the CPGB that led to the Party issuing in February 1955 a 'Charter of Rights for Coloured Workers in Britain'. The Charter stated that the motto 'United We Stand, Divided We Fall' was applicable to both 'British and coloured workers'. (The Party's confusion here is

obvious: the 'coloured' workers were as 'British' as their 'white' peers.)
There were four points in the Charter: racial discrimination should be
made into a 'penal offence'; 'government restrictions and discrimination
against coloured workers entering Britain' should be opposed; there
should be equality in employment, wages and employment conditions;
coloured workers should be encouraged to join 'their appropriate trade
unions on equal conditions of entry with British workers'.

In the 19 March 1955 issue of *World News* (p238), 'Talking Points
on ... Colonial Workers in Britain' explained that most of these workers had left their colonies of origin because of dire unemployment. The
recently passed McCarran Act closed the doors of the USA to
Caribbeans seeking work, which forced them to turn instead to Britain
where they found racial discrimination to be ubiquitous. The labour
movement, the paper urged, should declare itself 'opposed to any form
of discrimination and ... win the coloured workers for the trade
unions...' The Party emphasised that the 'real solution to the problem
[was to] free the colonies and end imperialist exploitation'. Thus the
Party avoided analysing why 'colonial workers' were seen as a 'problem', and in doing so confounded the issues of racial discrimination and
the effects of imperialism.

A few months later *No Colour Bar for Britain*, a CPGB pamphlet
by Phil Bolsover, was issued. The pamphlet begins:

> There is a great opportunity before British working people. We are being
> offered a partnership. Acceptance will immensely increase our strength.
> Rejection can only cause disastrous division. It is the partnership of
> British working people with colonial people ... It has been open ever
> since the British Empire became an empire. But now suddenly it comes
> with new and personal force. For it is being offered to us on our
> doorsteps ... The need for this unity now confronts us on the street, now
> confronts us in the factory, nor is it a ... matter of local town hall poli-
> tics. Having passed our resolutions we Socialists, we trade unionists ...we
> progressively minded people are now called on to back them by action –
> action here (p3).

Bolsover points out that workers should be making demands of the
Government, for jobs, housing and other social improvements, not
attacking each other. 'Tories and employers ... see dangers in an alliance
between coloured workers and white workers; the more far-seeing
recognise that such an alliance can have important effects both at home
and throughout the Empire' (p10).

This outspoken statement was followed by a pamphlet issued by the

London District Committee of the CPGB which followed the same line of argument. *Brothers in the Fight for a Better Life* named 'grasping landlords and profit-grabbing bosses' as the common enemies of workers, 'whether born here in London or in Trinidad or Dublin or Lagos. These workers (should be drawn into) trade unions, tenants' organisations and political organisation to prevent employers using them as cheap labour and landlords using them to force rents up'. Despite considerable evidence to the contrary, the pamphleteers believed that 'in almost every case they will find a welcome among trade unionists'. It was perhaps mixed feelings about immigration that led them to advocate the 'need to find a solution to the desperate poverty which drives these families to leave their homes and travel thousands of miles to a strange land' (p14).

Both these pamphlets are a great advance on the sterile debates on policy towards colonies at Party congresses and in another pamphlet of that era, *London Labour and Colonial Freedom*, published in 1954. This recounts purely labour struggles since the eighteenth century on nearly all of its 16 pages. The remainder outlines the Party's work in India and that of the League Against Imperialism in the 1930s, together with the more recent support for British Guiana's struggles with the British Government. It ends with a quotation from the *British Road to Socialism* which clearly reveals the Party's instrumental and imperialist approach to colonial independence. Independence should be granted as,

> only by this means can Britain be assured of the normal supplies of the vital food and raw materials necessary for her economic life, obtaining these in equal exchange for the products of British industry ... This would provide the basis for a new, close, voluntary and fraternal association ... to defend in common their freedom against American imperialist aggression.

However, even the more positive pamphlets, while advocating action, sadly do not indicate what form that action might take. There is no mention at all, for example, of the necessity of convincing trade unions of the error of the racist policies a number of them espoused at this time.[11] An admittedly cursory look through the *Daily Worker* did not reveal reports of street-level action against racist landlords, employers or councils.

The question must be asked: how did it happen that though the Party had previously ignored this issue, by the mid-1950s it had become a subject for pamphleteers? According to Billy Strachan, who became a member in 1949, the new vision of the world emanated from the International Committee. Who pressed for it? After all, two 'coloured' men, Rajani Palme Dutt and Desmond Buckle had been members of the Committee for some time, yet the issue had not been raised previously. It could only have been the Committee's new, clearly more vociferous members, H.B. Lim and Strachan himself.[12] However, the role of other Caribbean communists must not be discounted. For example, there was a West Indian circle at the London School of Economics and Political Science, chaired by Yusuf Hussein, which discussed, *inter alia*, the proposed ban on immigration from the Caribbean. The group's concern was taken up by the Aggregate Meeting, which in turn informed the International Committee. The parent committee asked the West Indians to prepare a paper on the issue. This was done and presented to Rajani Palme Dutt, the chair of the International Committee, by Billy Strachan, Cris Le Maitre and Ranji Chandrisingh. One of the West Indians' concerns was the effect that such a ban would have on the Caribbean. However, Dutt dismissed their worries with an assurance that 'it won't happen'.[13]

Though the issue of racism was not raised at the two Empire conferences, there was clearly some interest in it, and it was incorporated in the revised 1958 version of *The British Road to Socialism*. In this a sentence appears in an extended section on Socialist Democracy: 'All forms of discrimination on grounds of race or colour need to be made illegal'(p24). This one sentence appeared in a slightly different form in the previous text, under the section on Colonial Freedom, where it was stated that the 'British labour movement needs to fight the colour bar'.[14] However, George Matthews in introducing the 'Alliance of British People with the Peoples of the Empire' section of the *British Road* to the 25th Party Congress in 1957, did not mention racial prejudice.[15] What Matthews stressed in his speech was that 'the British people must put an end to colonial oppression *for their own sakes*, and not only for the sake of the colonial peoples themselves' (his emphasis). Was this a pragmatic or an instrumental approach, given that Matthews argued that 'the problems [of empire] account in a large measure for the burdens on the British working people'?[16]

The Party's relationship to Black members

Noreen Branson's fourth volume of the *History of the CPGB* details public pronouncements, resolutions and the occasional pamphlet, but

tells us nothing at all about any activities on behalf of colonial independence or racial discrimination in the UK. She mentions no Black
members.[17] Is this because, as Barbados-born Peter Blackman, CPGB
member and volunteer worker at the Party's headquarters in King
Street, once stated: '...The CP didn't *see us* [Blacks]. In all the years I
worked with Bradley, I never even had a drink with him.'[18] (Bradley
was the secretary of the CPGB's Colonial Bureau; Blackman worked
with him daily on the production of bulletins, pamphlets, and other
materials.) Cris Le Maitre in a recent discussion told me that 'colonials
found it easier to talk to European communists than with Brits'.[19]

Emile Burns organised classes in Marxism exclusively for West
African students in London. The students who attended these, mainly
Nigerians, were also enabled to attend international communist conferences. (The Party's approach to such segregation, whether for special
classes or branches/committees, underwent a succession of changes.)
The Nigerians were critical of the Party's attitude towards them. Some
of them complained that the Party's *For a Lasting Peace and People's
Democracy*, a pamphlet on the Nigerian political situation, had been
produced without sufficient consultation with them. (It should be
noted that many students in this period were not 19 year-olds, but were
often mature men and women with years of work, and in some cases,
political activity behind them.) The students claimed that the Party was
'not prepared to consider our views in preparing materials for the
formulation of a policy concerning our country' and that the behaviour
of 'Dutt, (Idris) Cox and co. is so arrogant as to smell of imperialist
methods'.[20] That no Nigerians – or other Africans – were appointed to
the CPGB's Nigerian Commission demonstrated the Party's attitude
towards Africans and must have fuelled the students' anger.

In about 1949 the Party set up a West Indies Committee in London
in response to demands by Caribbeans who found that their concerns
were irrelevant to most 'white' Party members.[21] They were also
dismayed by the 'racist and colonialist attitudes that ran through the
veins of most white people, Communists included'.[22] According to
Cris Le Maitre, there were divergent views about the need for such a
committee. While there was general agreement that 'if you scrape the
skin off a British communist you'll find an imperialist', some were
against special branches on the basis that colonial issues should be
raised at branch meetings under 'International Affairs', which was
always on the agenda.[23] From 1949 to 1952 the Committee published a
monthly *West Indian Newsletter*.[24] It seems that eventually there were
a number of West Indian committees which met together in King Street
as the 'aggregate committee'; Cris Le Maitre was convenor and Idris

Cox the rapporteur.[25] Of the fifty or so members in the 1950s, very few remained after the Committee was dissolved in 1956. The West Indies Committee was replaced by the West Indies Advisory Committee which included many whites.

> Claudia's arrival in this country co-incided with rifts within the international communist movement. Kruschev's speech denouncing Stalin at the 60th Congress of the Communist Party of the Soviet Union had a serious impact on Black comrades, particularly those people who were involved in political movements at home and in the international communist movement ... [It] impacted particularly on those of us who were in the Caribbean Labour Congress, those of us who were in the League of Coloured Peoples, and those of us who were members of the West Indies Committee of the Communist Party.
>
> The West Indian Committee was a sub-committee of the international committee of the Communist Party and the boss of that was Palme Dutt ... The Black comrades were split, there were those of us who said 'long live the Marshall' [Stalin], and those of us who said, 'Kruschev is right'. So there was a problem. And out of that not only grew a problem of how to deal with Kruschev's speech but how to deal with our work, not only on the streets and in the trade unions et cetera, but also the media. There was a conflict on our paper the *Caribbean News*. Billy [Strachan] was the editor and publisher of *Caribbean News*, and he'd been the leading light in the West Indian Committee. Claudia came just then.
>
> (Trevor Carter at the 1996 Symposium)

The Caribbean Labour Congress (CLC), founded in Barbados in 1945, advocated radical social change and the formation of an independent West Indian federation. A branch of the CLC was formed in Britain in May 1948, under the aegis of the CPGB, though the exact relationship is not clear. Billy Strachan was the London CLC's secretary.[26] The London CLC received little support but much 'good advice' from the Party, as founding member Nichols wrote to Richard Hart, the CLC's secretary in Jamaica. 'Quite candidly it's difficult to get help from the Party ... although the Colonial Department wholeheartedly supports our proposals ...'[27] The CLC kept in touch with its parent body in Jamaica and with US organisations such as the Council on African Affairs and the Civil Rights Congress, both supported by the CPUSA.[28] By the early 1950s it had spawned three 'branches', the Birmingham and Leeds CLCs and the Merseyside West Indian Association.[29]

The Party was said to be equally unsupporting when the CLC launched its monthly newspaper, *Caribbean News*, in September 1952, even though all the paper's workers, including the editors and publishers (at various times, Strachan, Chandrisingh and Le Maitre) were communists. According to Strachan, 'nobody was paid, we had no salaries, no money'.[30] Perhaps the Party's aid came indirectly, as the paper was printed free by 'a good comrade who was a printer'.[31]

Though the focus of the CLC and thus of the *Caribbean News* was Caribbean independence, it also campaigned against racial discrimination in the workplace and exhorted Black workers to join trade unions, despite the racial antagonism of many of them.[32] The Party itself, according to Billy Strachan, 'didn't know what racism was ... The race issue was low down on the CP's agenda'.[33] *Caribbean News* was last produced in June 1956, after it had been taken over by the newly elected secretary of the CLC, George Bowrin.[34] In an undated 'Review of Mass Work and our Tasks' with West Indians, possibly written by Claudia in about 1959, the author noted that:

> after the winding up of the CLC many of the CLC cadre had serious complaints of the Party ... G. Bowrin [was] only a formal Party member last year ... [He] asserted 'that Marxism-Leninism is not synonymous with the Communist Party and that the British CP even in 100 years can't have real sympathy and understand[ing] of colonial peoples.[35]

Perhaps the Party's attitude is best exemplified in a letter from Idris Cox, head of the International Department, to Richard Hart in Jamaica: 'I am in close touch with our friend Billie and his colleagues and every now and again we manage to have a discussion on West Indian problems, particularly those of West Indians in Britain.'[36] That such discussions should have been so unusual in the months leading up to the passing of the Immigration Act of 1962, which severely restricted migration from the Caribbean, is most revealing.

How had this situation developed? In the 1930s the Comintern had instructed the Party not only to work with colonies and colonials, but also to rid itself of 'white chauvinism' – that is, racial prejudice. While the response to the former was minimal, to the latter it was non-existent. In the 1950s there was no Comintern to chide the non-responsive Party, which would have been as concerned with its survival in the 1950s as it had been in the 1930s, and thus might have felt it could not espouse unpopular issues.[37] That, of course, might be a reason, but not an excuse. It also seems that loyalty to the Party prevented its Black members from becoming more vociferous in their criticisms – or were these simply ignored?

Though self-criticism was supposedly a keystone of the Party at least in the 1930s, it apparently never occurred to the Party leadership that it should question its own attitudes and behaviour towards 'colonials'. As Billy Strachan explained 'How *could* the CP understand racism? Harry Pollitt [the general secretary] was a self-educated man, but of the working class ... He had no knowledge of the world ... He would not have known where Africa was.'[38] This ignorance probably extends to the Caribbean: Richard Hart, then the foremost Marxist activist in the West Indies, has stated that the CPGB 'had shown no interest in us' (the Marxist group in Jamaica). During his visit to Jamaica during a health cruise Pollitt did not meet with Hart and his colleagues.[39]

The CPGB was a centralist party, obeying diktats emanating from headquarters. Thus the lack of understanding of racial, colonial and independence issues, the bewilderment at the complexities of the situations in the colonies and within the nationalist/independence movements, and confusions over whether to have separate sections for various ethnic groups must have influenced Party branches and members throughout the country. Nevertheless, some managed to think for themselves. For example, the Cardiff Party supported the Colonial Defence Association in the 1930s and 1940s and in the years following; and despite pressure from some white members for a separate branch for Blacks, the Party heeded Black members' resistance to such segregation.[40] In Manchester the multi-racial New International Society (NIS), set up under the aegis of the Party by two white and one Black communist, probably foundered, according to its historian, because of Party interference.[41] The NIS, which also had a branch in Liverpool, campaigned vigorously on issues of racial discrimination at home and abroad, against apartheid, the imprisonment of nationalist leaders in Africa, and fundraised to aid 'colonial children' in the two cities.

What do some Black people who were, or are, Party members think of the Party's attitudes in the 1950s and 1960s? Henry Gunter believed that 'Communist Party members [were] as ignorant as other working men – they believed in the Empire and the colonies'. Trevor Carter: 'from the race point of view, we were confused'. Dorothy Kuya: 'the Party was not willing to debate the race issue – they just didn't understand race issues'. Avtar Jouhl: 'the communists were no different from the population in general regarding racial issues'.[42]

Claudia and the CPGB

The important point is that Claudia brought to us her experience in the struggle in the United States, which had a history of Black people, and her work with a Party (although now we can make all sorts of criticisms about the American Party) which was steeped in a Black struggle, that we did not experience in this country ... Claudia was a leader, a leader of the only Western communist party that was steeped in the Black experience ... Once when I went to her with a problem she said 'One of the things you have got to understand, that must be fully a part of you, is that in your life your slogan should be "Struggle begets struggle"'.

(Trevor Carter at 1996 Symposium)

Claudia arrives

On 16 December 1955 the *Daily Worker* noted Claudia's arrival on the *Queen Elizabeth* in Southampton. 'You Are Welcome Here, Claudia', headlined its report, which gave some details of her imprisonment and expulsion by the US Government.[43] What were her plans, the *Worker* asked. 'Well, I'm a champion weaver and I'm a journalist ... But first of all I mean to have a good holiday and a rest', Claudia replied.[44]

Probably with the help of communist comrades, Claudia was almost immediately hospitalised in St Stephen's Hospital in south London. She remained in hospital for almost two months. On her release, the Party arranged for her to stay at the country home of Tamara and Wogan Phillips (Lord Milford) for a month or so, but it is unlikely that she went there.[45] The Party also arranged a reception for Claudia, which might have been where Betty Reid remembers her reciting a poem by Langston Hughes.[46]

During this period, as she had arrived in Britain with merely a travel permit, the Party hoped to get her a passport and then a visa to Prague. There she could get further treatment, and easily travel on to the USSR.[47] It is unclear from the papers remaining at the Communist Party archives whether Claudia hoped to settle in the Soviet Union or merely intended to seek medical treatment. However, despite strenuous efforts by the Party, the passport application was denied on 12 January 1956.[48]

Settling in

The Party also decided to help Claudia find a flat and resolved that if she needed 'financial help at any time we must give it to her'. The Party might have helped with finding accommodation (see chapter 2); whether financial assistance was provided by the Party is unlikely as in April 1956 Claudia asked the CPUSA to help her pay for the 'fixtures and fittings' necessary to obtain a flat.[49]

However, it seems the Party did help Claudia with employment. She was placed in the New China News Agency as a typist and perhaps sub-editor. But Claudia was clearly not very happy with this position. In an undated memorandum sent to the Party's King Street headquarters, she requested a meeting with 'comrades'. Claudia protested her situation, and her removal from the agency, where she had apparently been accused of inefficiency and stirring up problems between 'Comrade Sam' and the other workers. Claudia's memo alleges that relationships among the staff of the agency had been bad when she arrived and that Comrade Sam felt that she had been 'dumped as an invalid on the agency ... as was done in the past. Sam is very bitter about this policy'.[50]

That Claudia was already very uneasy about her relationship to the Party is made clear in her memo:

> Another aspect I want to raise is the Party's evaluation towards me as an individual regarding getting settled down in this country, both politically and financially ... I want clarification as to what basis and what estimate they (the Party) have of my assets to the Party. There have been times when I have resisted concluding that either I'm to be retired from political life or so invalided that I must lead a sedentary life – or if the opposite is true, then not only clarification but some implementation would appear required.

There is no response whatever to her statement in the file in the Communist Party archive.

Her position in England clearly worried her US comrades and would continue to do so for many years. For example, in May 1959 Ben Davis asked Claudia: 'Are you carrying any special assignment in the Party in addition to other work on the paper?'[51] Avis Hutt, who had met Claudia in the Peace Movement, has 'vague memories of the Party not being able to deal with her ... Claudia must have fallen into a no-man's land with the Party here – she was part of no group, no faction'. Jenny Williams, a party member who had heard Claudia speak at meetings organised by 'broader groupings than the CP' in her Kensington neighbourhood, thought her an extremely good speaker. She asked a party official why Claudia was not used more. 'There are difficulties', was the response. Ricky Cambridge, who joined the party in about 1962, remembers relations between Claudia and the CPGB as being 'acrimonious, uneasy, conflictual'.[52]

Claudia challenges the Party

There is a March 1957 report entitled 'West Indians in Britain' in the

Party's archives. Though unsigned, judging by its outspokenness we can assume that Claudia was the author. The paper details the range of discrimination, including in the workplace and from trade unions, faced by West Indians. None of the existing Caribbean associations were 'mass organisations'; the Caribbean Labour Congress' membership was in decline and was isolated from West Indians in London. Except in London, the report states, 'political activity in this field [the problems faced by immigrants] is seriously neglected ... Many Party members also have ideas about "quota schemes" for coloured workers. Certainly no clear stand is being made for equal rights.' The writer advocates relating 'our propaganda for equal rights in Britain with solidarity action with the struggle in the colonies', a re-examination of the Party's Charter of Rights, public support for Fenner Brockway's anti-discrimination bill, contact with West Indian leaders, articles in the *Daily Worker*, and the development of an 'approach to specific problems in particular industries'.

Claudia represented Vauxhall and Tulse Hill at the 25th Congress of the CPGB in 1957. (She is listed as a 'clerical worker at the Stockwell bus garage': is this a job she had taken after being sacked from the China News Agency?) Claudia had asked to speak at the session on the Political Resolution, but had not been allowed to do so. She had wanted to contribute to that session,

> because of my firm belief that on the crucial question of colour discrimination the coloured people resident in this country are waiting for a lead by the British Communist Party ... I hope that on the new draft there will be a rectification of this serious omission in the draft Political Resolution. Such an immediate programme of united struggle and solidarity now is a prime pre-condition for future relations.[53]

The Sunday morning session at which she did speak was devoted to a discussion on *The British Road to Socialism*, the Party's manifesto. After thanking the Party for its efforts 'to secure my entry into Britain', she seized the opportunity offered to make a very forthright statement:

> If, therefore, in my first Party Congress, I turn to address you on the theme of greater solidarity with the struggles of colonial peoples, and with the coloured workers and peoples in Britain, you will understand that it stems from the first-hand experience and confidence that this Party of ours has it within its capacity to make this turn – a needed turn which is in the interest not only of the colonial people but also in the

present and future self-interest of the British working class and people ...

... Colonial, and particularly coloured peoples in Britain will also want to know what policy the Party Congress advances to meet the special problems facing them in the present economic situation – problems which stem from a common origin – the same monopoly capitalists in Britain who exploit the British working class, but who super-exploit the colonies – thereby requiring a joint struggle against the common evil of imperialism...

... It is not a very wise tactic to seek to allay disquiet, uneasiness and dissatisfaction by telling those whose experience has taught them otherwise, that they are foolish, or to dub them as backward. For in terms of their experience, a well-known African proverb might well apply. That proverb runs: 'respect the old, for they have seen the eyes of the morning!'...

... Comrade Emile Burns in his *World News* article raises the question of our helping the so-called 'backward peoples' of the world. The backward peoples of China and the backward people of Czarist Russia were the first to throw off the old regimes, and are now going forward with the most advanced ideology – the ideology of Socialism – while the technically advanced peoples of the Western bourgeois democratic tradition are still steeped in the mire of backward imperialist ideology. And now India is following suit. The anti-imperialist struggles of the backward Afro-Asian nations, from Egypt to Ghana, are today leading the progressive anti-imperialist ideological struggle.

That Claudia had to make such a speech is clearly a reflection of the disparagement of such issues by the Party's hierarchy. The *Daily Worker*, which did not note that she was Trinidadian (or Black), reported that Claudia received 'very enthusiastic support' and reported some of her speech. She was supported by Solly Kaye, who called on the delegates to 'reaffirm the Party's demand that racial and religious discrimination should be made illegal'.[54] The revised version of the *British Road to Socialism* called on 'the British labour movement to fight against the colour bar and racial discrimination, and for full social, economic and political equality of colonial people in Britain' (p16). It also called for racial or colour discrimination to be made illegal (p24). But there was no special section in the thirty pages of the manifesto devoted to this issue. And such vague calls embedded in discussions of other issues were not the strong statement for which Claudia was obviously pushing.

In a letter to her colleague Ben Davis in New York, Claudia reported on the Congress:

At Easter attended my first CPGB Congress – elected as delegate by two branches ... both Right and Left tendencies but nothing like the kind of thing that existed there ... Spoke in debate on the *British Road to Socialism* particularly in relation to socialist Britain and the colonies and ex-colonies ... Thanked comrades for their excellent aid in facilitating my freedom and coming here ... as well as adopting the lessons learned in the US about the fight against racist ideas and practices ... Fundamentally the policy has everything to do with how the present day fight is pursued here ... The pre-Congress discussion revealed the penetration of imperialist ideas in the ranks of the CP on this question ...[55]

Communist activities

It is hardly surprising, in light of the above, that Claudia was sidelined by the CPGB and was never given a position in its leadership (or elsewhere in the Party) commensurate with her abilities, experience and status in the USA. Nevertheless in 1957 she was clearly continuing to participate in communist activities as she wrote to Davis of her 'constant struggle (because of my health) to work an 8-hour day to earn a living and then make a political contribution'.[56]

The Party did not even invite her to write for its publications; Claudia's name appears only once in the *Daily Worker*, in a review of a book by W.E.B. Du Bois. Not even during the anti-Black riots of 1958 was she asked to add her analysis to the many white commentators in the *Worker*. George Matthews, editor of the paper at that time, when questioned about this, said that he was surprised to hear that there were no articles by Claudia in the *Worker*. 'She was pre-occupied with her own journal, but I presume that had she been asked to write for the *Worker*, she would have.'[57]

When she was asked to write, her writing was sabotaged. In a letter to Ben Davis she told him that she 'did an article for *World News* but half of the heart was cut out – indicating many problems'.[58] The article was commissioned for a special issue of *World News*, 'Together Against Imperialism', which appeared on 29 June 1957. In this truncated version, her piece, 'West Indians in Britain', is a very mild article indeed. It outlines the reasons for immigration from the Caribbean, blames the Tories for 'imposing new hardships on the British people' who then scapegoat immigrants for their problems. She argued that 'the common enemy of both British and colonial workers [is] the Tory ruling class and the imperialist system'. While advocating that West Indians should be encouraged to join trade unions, she points out that though some trade unions 'have declared their opposition to racial discriminatory practices, the main weakness has been the failure to carry out any measures to apply this policy in practice'. The article concludes with the warning that 'Our Party is judged among colonial workers by its policy, but much more so by its deeds ... [Our] influence among West Indians in particular will depend on how we step up the fight to help solve their problems, and how we extend help to strengthen their organisations' (pp412, 416).

How little Claudia was valued by the CPGB is illustrated by the *Labour Monthly* conference of 26 October 1958 on 'Britain's Colonies and the Colour Bar'.[59] She is not mentioned in the papers on the conference which are kept in the Communist Party archives. In the account of the conference which appeared in the December issue of *Labour Monthly*, while the contribution of S.O. Bello, 'a West African delegate', is reported, as is that of R. Bennett of the Afro-Asian West Indian Union, Claudia, representing the *West Indian Gazette*, is only listed as one of the 'other speakers'.[60]

Claudia and the CPGB committees

Despite her longstanding friendship with both Essie and Paul Robeson, Claudia was not a member of the National Paul Robeson Committee, set up by the Party to campaign for the return of Robeson's passport by the US Government. Not only was she not a member, but when the Party in Rhondda, Wales, organised a 'Let Robeson Sing' meeting and asked for Claudia as a speaker, John Williamson replied that 'because of her health and certain other matters, I am not too sure about Claudia'.[61] Nor was Claudia an officer of the CP's US Committee, probably set up in 1954, though she might have had some later association with it as in June 1961 the committee decided to approach her to 'come next Thursday and generally help with the work'.[62]

At least in her first few years in Britain, Claudia attended some Party functions. 'We were at a party school at Hastings doing Stalin's book, *The Colonial Question* in 1956. Claudia was there', recalled Trevor Carter at the 1996 Symposium.

Claudia was an active member of the West Indies Committee from the time of her arrival. According to the Committee's secretary, Billy Strachan, he had been informed by the International Committee 'of this great woman coming over from the USA', and had immediately invited her to join the Committee. She was probably also a member of the body that replaced the West Indies Committee, the West Indies

Advisory Committee as circulars regarding meetings in 1963 are in the Langford Collection. However, she must have been less than enthusiastic about the Committee's work: Paul Sealy, the Committee's convenor, reminded Claudia of Standing Orders regarding absenteeism 'in view of your frequent absence from monthly meetings'. Claudia also participated in the Caribbean Labour Congress until its demise around 1956 and subsequently joined the West Indian Students and Workers Association.[63]

In about 1961 Claudia was named one of the sponsors of the Committee for Democratic Rights in the USA and was a member of its Campaign Committee. The Committee issued a leaflet, *Shall Liberty Die in Chains*, which protested against forthcoming legal measures that would require communists to register as 'agents of a foreign power'. It also published the occasional *US Freedom News* and sent deputations to the US Embassy regarding human rights and the forthcoming trials of communists Gus Hall and Ben Davis.

The only other remaining document in the Communist Party archives regarding Claudia is a letter from her to John Gollan, the general secretary, regarding one Frank Bailey, who was applying for re-admission to the Party. Claudia opposed this on the grounds that Bailey had engaged in anti-Party propaganda. Simultaneously she accused the Party of not checking whether those attending meetings were actually members. 'Such looseness of Party functioning cannot help the development of the Party, but can only bring harm. While we are keen to win new Party members and keep old ones, that should not mean that we admit hostile elements and opportunists in the Party.'[64]

Claudia was also a member of the International Affairs Committee. However, as with the West Indies Advisory Group, her commitment had diminished by 1963-1964. Why was this? Taja Sahota recalls that 'all the Indian communists left the CPGB in 1964 ... The CPGB did not like Claudia ... She brought out the *West Indian Gazette* because of their attitude. Idris Cox, who replaced Rajani Palme Dutt as head of the International Department, did not get on with Claudia'.[65] In 1963 Idris Cox informed Claudia that as her attendance at meetings had been 'few and far between', her place would be offered to 'newer comrades with fresh ideas'. However, 'the Committee will welcome consultations with you from time to time on the extremely useful activity you are carrying out' and planned to invite her 'to Committee meetings when matters affecting the West Indies are under discussion'. Both the tone and the content of the letter bespeak the estrangement between Claudia and at least one leading Party cadre.[66] Surely, had Claudia had any hope of the International Affairs Committee, she would have attended meetings as regularly as her health permitted; after all, of all the committees it should have been the one of greatest relevance to her interests, which were much broader than Cox implied.

Though dismissed from this committee, there is among Claudia's papers a circular inviting all the Committee members to attend a discussion on 2 June 1964 on The Struggle Against Racial Discrimination. Claudia had been asked to participate in the 'special commission to combat racialism' set up by the Party in January 1964. John Gollan, the General Secretary, had written to Claudia that the Party 'would very much like to have your participation in this work' and even indicated that if Claudia could not attend the meeting but was willing to participate, she could name her own date and time. Claudia agreed to attend the meeting.[67]

The result of the commission's work was published in May 1964 as a four page flyer, *End Racialism in Britain*, which pointed out that the 1962 Immigration Act was the equivalent of a 'Colour Bar Act' and that 'racial discrimination is an enemy of working class unity, social progress and socialism'. The leaflet pledged the Communist Party to support 'every progressive measure to combat racialism' and stated that the Party opposed quotas for 'coloured immigration'; the CP stood for equality and the repeal of the Act.

The Party had obviously learned to use Claudia when it needed some of her specialist knowledge. She had also contributed to the work of the Political Committee on drafting the Communist Party Policy Statement on the Commonwealth Immigrants Act, as Gollan wrote to her in March 1964 to thank her for 'the extremely useful work put in by you ...'[68]

According to Billy Strachan, Claudia had been briefly a member of the London District Committee.[69] In 1957 the District Committee decided to issue a leaflet 'addressed to West Indians in London' in order to achieve the aims outlined at the Party Congress by 'Solly Kaye, Claudia Jones and others [who] made a powerful case for a stronger fight against any form of racial discrimination and for a greater effort to develop friendship with coloured workers in Britain'.[70]

It has not been possible to discover whether and how Claudia participated in any other CPGB activities, or in branch meetings. Appeals for information in the 'communist' press have not drawn any responses.[71] Dorothy Kuya, who lived near her in north London does not recall Claudia speaking at any CP meetings; Winston Pinder believes she was not a member of a north London Party branch.[72]

A deteriorating relationship?

Did Claudia not actively participate in the Communist Party except when asked to make a specific contribution? Given her general outspokenness and probably her continuing advocacy of making racial discrimination a central Party concern, she could not have been very popular within Party circles. It is as if the CPGB simply did not know how to respond to this fiery, highly experienced Black woman, who was capable of absolutely mesmerising her audience. Gertrude Elias remembers her as 'something new – something we'd not heard before'.[73]

Sam Russell, Moscow correspondent for the *Worker* until 1959, told me that 'after Claudia arrived her relations with the CP became difficult. Her viewpoint was more that of the CPUSA and as the years went past difficulties increased. A lot of people might have been pretty unkind to her.' Betty Reid remembers that there were 'lots of problems Party-wise ... The chap she lived with [Manchanda] was very difficult. We were not on easy terms. I admired her personality and all that she did ... We were cautious – there were problems, including financial ones. In her public persona and in her approach to major aspects of policy she was unusual.'[74]

Trinidadian Trevor Carter, in 1997 a member of the Executive Committee of the Democratic Left (the new name for the CPGB), believes that cultural differences partly accounted for the possible schism between Claudia and Party members. 'There were culture clashes, especially over her spending habits. She ate meals in restaurants and drank spirits while the CPGB drank half-pints of bitter and meals were often tea and biscuits.'[75]

James and Esther Jackson, friends and comrades of Claudia's New York days, whom I interviewed in New York, remember Claudia as a 'very talented organiser and a great orator'.[76] Esther Jackson recalls that she had received many reports of Claudia in London. 'There was racism in the British Party ... For example at a Christmas dinner at a Party VIP's home, they all sang that song "we shall never never be slaves". Claudia walked out. She wasn't about to accept racism in England when she wouldn't accept it here'.[77]

Mr Jackson, who once visited London, felt that the CPGB's attitude was a 'left-over from the Empire. We talked about her problems with racism in Britain.' The US Party was worried about Claudia's 'transfer to the UK – would her experience be used? ... [Henry] Winston intervened regarding Claudia in Britain; for example, he was concerned that she should have a proper rest after her arrival. He might have helped arrange her trip to the USSR.'[78]

Both Mr and Mrs Jackson ridiculed any inference that Claudia was extravagant. She was not particularly interested in clothes: 'Claudia was one of those women who could tie a bright scarf around her neck over an old suit and look a million dollars', they told me. 'Claudia didn't particularly drink here. We heard she drank in Britain and it must have been the stress.'[79] Claudia was the house-guest of both Avtar Jouhl in Birmingham and Taja Sahota in Leamington Spa; neither recall her drinking or smoking.[80]

The gap between how the Party saw the world and how Claudia saw it is illustrated by a letter from Claudia to George Matthews, the editor of the *Daily Worker*, regarding an article in the paper. As she stated in her letter, Claudia had previously telephoned Matthews and they had agreed that she 'read this in a different context than you say did the *Daily Worker* staff ... I quite naturally expect that the *Daily Worker* as a Communist journal will be foremost in fighting the colour bar and I would hope that it will increasingly recognise the subtleties in the struggle against it ...'[81]

Claudia addressed the editor as 'Dear George Matthews', which not only indicates a somewhat distant relationship but perhaps also what little hope she had that Matthews would understand her perspective. Claudia enclosed a letter for publication, referring to the article 'Economic Ban – Not Colour – Sir Learie'. The *Worker* had claimed that Sir Learie Constantine, then High Commissioner for Trinidad, on a visit to Bristol had stated that the 'non-employment of West Indian bus crews on the Bristol buses is not a colour-bar issue at all'. Claudia questioned the accuracy of the *Worker's* report and pointed out that

> The economic fears of *all* workers is what is always played on when the issue of colour-bar comes to the fore. The white worker is encouraged in his fears to fight not the bosses, but the coloured man who 'threatens' his job. The coloured worker is told to 'understand' that the economic recession means he can't take away other men's jobs, etc. Hence to counterpose the economic issue to the fight against the colour bar, or to deny its existence as a factor, only accelerates the disunity of the workers which only benefits the employers and the racialists... To stress the one without the other, in an instance where there is clear evidence of the existence of *both* factors is to renege on our responsibility of exposing colour-bar practices and manifestations.[82]

That Claudia had to offer such basic analysis to the editor and the journalists on the *Daily Worker*, as well as to its readers, bespeaks the distance between them as late as 1963. Her letter was not published.

Conclusion

Clearly Claudia had not given up her enthusiasm for the principles of communism. What she saw – or was allowed to see – of communism in practice in the Soviet Union and in China demonstrated the strides that previously oppressed peoples could take under communist regimes. That there was an obverse side to such progress she did not see, and might well have ignored as a necessity, had she been allowed to see it. She did not raise issues of democracy, or whether all or a majority of the people had consented to the policies of the communist regimes. Nor did she apparently question whether all the policies and practices were in essence 'communist'.

However, from the very fact that from 1958 onwards her activities were apparently focused on the Black community, we can infer that she grew increasingly distant from the British Communist Party. By contrast, in the USA, every activity she participated in, whether in community work in Harlem, or as national organiser of the YCL, as journalist, editor, and in the women's movement, was under the aegis of the US Communist Party. That under the rubric of the CPGB she could not undertake the work with and for Black peoples which she saw as absolutely necessary indicates the gulf that eventually must have separated her from the mainstream and the leadership of the Party. In the words of Betty Reid, of the CPGB's Central Organisation Department, 'she probably had little to do with the Party or I would remember her'.[83]

From the evidence available it seems that Claudia continued to contribute to the Party when asked to on specific issues, but that she had no role in the Party such as she had had in the USA. Having virtually given up on the Party, she was free to use her creative political energies in the Black community.

How little the Party hierachy thought of Claudia is demonstrated by the fact that on her death no obituary appeared in the *Daily Worker*, *Labour Monthly* or *Comment* - nor in *Communist Weekly Review* or *Marxism Today*.

Notes

1. Marika Sherwood, 'The Comintern, the CPGB, Colonies and Black Britons 1920-1938', *Science & Society*, 60/2, Summer 1996.
2. Hakim Adi, 'West Africans and the CP in the 1950s', in Andrews, Fishman and Morgan (eds), *Opening the Books*, Pluto, London 1996, pp176-194.

Any avowed Communist in the colonies would, of course, have been immediately jailed, as many left-wing activists (such as Hart) were during World War Two.

3. 'A criticism of certain weak points in the Conference of British Empire Communist Parties', undated and marked 'not published'; Hart to Rajani Palme Dutt, 21 October 1947, Institute of Commonwealth Studies, Richard Hart Papers, reel 4; see also Stephen Howe, *Anticolonialism in British Politics*, Oxford 1993, p165. The Hart papers are very informative on the CLC in London.

4. Ade Thomas was from Nigeria, Billy Strachan from Jamaica, George Bowrin from Trinidad and Ranji Chandrisingh was from the then British Guiana. Bowrin, a member of the Trinidad Independence Party, had come to Britain to study law; on his return he worked for a while for the Oilfield Workers Trade Union before going into private practice. (I am grateful to John La Rose for this information.)

5. *Allies For Freedom*, Report of the Second Conference of the Communist and Workers Parties of Countries within the Sphere of British Imperialism, Caxton Hall, London 1954.

6. Harry Pollitt (1890-1969) was a founder member of the CPGB in 1920. From 1929 until 1956 he was the Party's secretary; from then until his death he was chairman.

7. *World News*, 10 July 1954, pp543-544. *The British Road to Socialism* was the Party's programme, drafted in 1951 and adopted at the 22nd Congress of 1952. The original statement on 'National Independence of the British People and of all Peoples of the British Empire', though much amended by the 1952 Congress, focused on the danger of US imperialism to people in Britain. A revised draft was prepared for the 1957 Congress which contained the 'over 1,500 amendments from Party organisations'. After the Congress suggestions were again solicited from Party organisations. The quoted text is from the 1958 revised text. It has not been possible to locate the suggestions sent in after the 1957 Congress.

8. Noreen Branson, *History of the Communist Party of Great Britain 1941-1951*, Lawrence and Wishart, London 1997, p238.

9. The CPGB constitution allowed for members with a particular issue in common to come together in 'aggregate' meetings. The issue was whether the wording should be 'fraternal alliance' or 'fraternal relationship'; Keith Carter and others maintained that an independent socialist Caribbean would only wish for *alliances* with other socialist countries. What if Britain was not socialist? Interview with Cris Le Maitre, London, 19 September 1997.

10. *Daily Worker*, 22 April 1957, pp1&4. The Executive Committee was the leadership committee of the CPGB. The structure of the CPGB congresses meant that it was very difficult to overturn proposals from the Executive.

11. See, for example, Bob Hepple, *Race, Jobs, and the Law in Britain*, Allen Lane, The Penguin Press, London 1968.

12. H.B. Lim in his article 'The Labour Party and the Colonies' in *Labour Monthly*, 40/1, January 1958, pp28-31, castigated Labourites for only generalised statements regarding colonial independence and for 'unwillingness to expose and remove the economic machinery of exploitation in the colonies ... Not a word is said about the demands of the colonial peoples for the return of their sterling balances ... '

13. Interview with Cris Le Maitre, London, see note 9. Dutt was wrong; see Chapter 4.

14. *British Road to Socialism*, no date, 'text circulated for comment – to be returned to the Executive Committee by 14 December 1957'.

15. George Matthews was Assistant General Secretary at this time.

16. CPGB, *25th Congress Report*, London 1957, p40.

17. Branson, 1997, see note 8.

18. Sherwood, 1996, see note 1, p148. For unknown reasons, Peter Blackman was not active in CPGB committees.

19. Yusuf Hussein, Trevor Carter and Le Maitre were the leaders of the West Indian delegates to the Fifth Festival of Students, Youth and Workers held in Poland. On their return, they were criticised, on the basis of information furnished by Idris Cox, for 'being underdeveloped for criticising the CPGB in public'. They had been discussing the CPGB's attitudes to the colonies with some Polish communists. Interview with Le Maitre, London, see note 9.

20. Adi, 1996, see note 2, p186.

21. The function of this Committee was to develop policy towards the independence movements and to involve West Indians in the Party. The Committee met every fortnight; once a month it met with the other colonial committees; every three months representatives met with the Political Committee (the top policy-making committee of the CPGB), which then formulated Party policy on the basis on their advice. On the Indian branches, see J. DeWitt Jr., *Indian Workers' Associations in Britain*, Institute of Race Relations, London 1969.

22. Trevor Carter, *Shattering Illusions*, Lawrence & Wishart, London 1986, p56.

23. Interview with Le Maitre, see note 9. The West London West Indian branch met at Le Maitre's home; the first office bearers were Yusuf Hussein (chair) and Randolph Rawlings (secretary); when Rawlings returned to Trinidad, he was replaced by Le Maitre. Le Maitre was also a member of the West London Committee of the CPGB.

24. There are no copies of this in the CPGB archives. The best source is the Hart Papers (see note 3), reel 6, which contains issues from July 1949 (no.1) to December 1950.

25. Interview with Le Maitre, see note 9. There are no documents in the CPGB archives to verify or elucidate informants' memories.

26. In 1951 the CLC's chair was Dr David Pitt. Le Maitre, who had been co-opted to the executive, contested the election for president in 1952; he was

beaten by Ranji Chandrisingh. Sherwood, 1996, see note 1.

27. Nichols to Hart, 30 November 1947, ICSI Hart Papers, note 3, reel 4; see also Howe (note 3), p212.

28. On the Council on African Affairs, see Penny von Eschen, *Race against Empire*, Cornell University Press, Ithaca 1997.

29. Hart Papers, note 3, reel 6; interview with Billy Strachan, London 24 July 1997.

30. *Caribbean News* was sold on the same basis as the *Morning Star*: volunteer sellers had to prepay for non-returnable copies. Interview with Le Maitre, see note 9.

31. The *News* was banned in the Caribbean. D.N. Pritt, the paper's (free) legal advisor suggested a change of name with every printing, e.g. to *Caribbean Torch*, *Times*, etc. The name of the publisher was also to be changed as Strachan et al were also banned. Interview with Le Maitre (see note 9). The change of name did not fool the colonial government: in his monthly political report the governor stated that 49 copies 'under various titles and different editors' had been seized. Report for 15 January 1954, PRO: CO1031/1804.

32. Strachan at Claudia Jones symposium London 1996; Carter 1986, see note 22, pp47-55.

33. Interview with Billy Strachan, London, 21 May 1997.

34. According to Billy Strachan, who was replaced by Bowrin as both secretary and editor, Bowrin and Claudia joined forces in arguing that the paper should not 'expose its communist involvement' and should take a broader perspective. Bowrin won the election resulting from this argument. Interview, London 24 July 1997. Cris Le Maitre recalls that the CLC was replaced – or that some of the non-communist members deserted it to form the West Indian Students and Workers Association under the leadership of Clive Crevelle. Interview with Le Maitre (see note 9).

35. Undated memorandum in Langford Collection.

36. Cox to Hart 16 May 1961, ICSI Hart Papers, note 3, reel 4. A few weeks previously, in a letter dated 21 April 1961, Hart had complained to Cox that he was not receiving Party publications.

37. The CPGB's membership in 1935 was 7,700; in 1939, 17,756; in 1942, 56,000; in 1955, 32,681; and in 1957, 26,472.

38. Interview with Strachan (see note 33).

39. Richard Hart, *Rise and Organise*, London 1989, p148. Hart did meet Pollitt accidentally in the office of the right-wing labour leader Alexander Bustamente, whom Pollitt was visiting.

40. Marika Sherwood, 'Racism and Resistance: Cardiff in the 1930s and 1940s', *Llafur*, 54, 1991, pp51-70; telephone interview with Charlie Swain, Cardiff, 2 October 1993.

41. Michael Herbert, *Never Counted Out*, Dropped Aitches Press, Manchester 1992, pp80-96; see also Marika Sherwood, *Manchester and the Pan-African Congress*, Savannah Press, London 1995, pp71-2. There is not

even an outline of the history of the New International Society in Liverpool.

42. Interviews with Henry Gunter, Birmingham, 11 February 1998; with Trevor Carter, London 2 September 1997; telephone interview with Dorothy Kuya in Liverpool 9 February 1998; with Avtar Jouhl, Birmingham 21 January 1998.

43. Claudia's imprisonment was known outside London. For example, the CPGB-sponsored Conference on Democratic Rights in the USA held in Glasgow in October 1955 sent her greetings on her release. 'Miss Jones', the Conference noted, 'by her courage and adherence to principle in the struggle for democratic rights and racial equality, has set an inspiring example to be followed by others'. Report on Conference, National Museum of Labour History: CP/CENT/ORG/1/10.

44. Claudia learned to weave while imprisoned and won a prize for her work. See Chapter 1.

45. Unfortunately Lady Tamara Milford does not recall whether Claudia did in fact spend any time at her country home. 'There were so many people there, it is impossible to remember', she told me when pressed. Telephone interview 6 August 1997. As Tamara Rust, she had been the publisher of *Woman Today*, which in its January 1956 issue welcomed Claudia to England and wished her a 'recovery to full health', p7.

46. Interview with Betty Reid, London, 29 July 1997.

47. Papers, mainly undated, in NMLH: CP/CENT/DISC/03/06, Jones file.

48. The Passport Office was prepared to issue Claudia with a travel certificate to Trinidad. Passport Office to Claudia Jones, 12 January 1956; Colonial Office to Claudia Jones, 10 April 1956, Langford Collection. (Unless indicated otherwise, all Claudia's correspondence cited henceforth is from this collection.)

49. Papers, mainly undated, in NMLH: CP/CENT/DISC/03/06, Jones file; Jones to Howard 'Stretch' Johnson, 21 April 1956, Tamiment Library, New York University: H.S. Johnson Papers, Collection 161, box 1.

50. Statement by Jones, no date, in NMLH: CP/CENT/DISC/03/06, Jones file. When questioned about this statement, Betty Reid, of the Party's Central Organisation Department, which would have dealt with Claudia's grievance, could recall nothing about it. According to Ms Reid, 'Comrade Sam' was Sam Chen from Liverpool, who was the CPGB's link with the Chinese Party. As an ex-seaman, he had 'no idea how to handle staff'. Chen's interest in women was a constant source of complaint by his English wife. Interview with Ms Reid, London, 29 July 1997.

51. Ben Davis to Claudia Jones, 29 May 1959.

52. Interviews with Avis Hutt, London, 17 March 1998; and Ricky Cambridge, London, 28 May 1998; telephone interview with Jenny Williams, London, 14 January 1998.

53. 25th Congress papers, 'Sunday Morning, No.14, Claudia Jones', NMLH: CP/CENT/CONG/10/08.

54. *Daily Worker*, 22 April 1957, p4.

55. Jones to Ben Davis, 15/16 May 1957, Schomburg Center: Ben Davis Papers, New York, reel 1.

56. Jones to Davis, 8 July 1957, *ibid.* Sadly only two letters from Claudia have survived in this collection.

57. Telephone interview with George Matthews, London, 17 December 1996. I looked at alternate weeks' issues for January to September 1956 and every issue between 2 August – end September 1958, the main period of the riots.

58. Jones to Davis, 8 July 1957, see note 55.

59. *Labour Monthly* had been founded at the instigation (and probably funding) of the Comintern in 1921. It was under the firm control of the Party through its editor, Rajani Palme Dutt. With no official connections with the CPGB it was able to attract a fairly broad readership and list of contributors. See J. Callaghan, *Rajani Palme Dutt*, London 1993, pp42-3. Nothing is known of Ralph Bennett except that he was a communist.

60. NMLH: CP/IND/DUTT/10/06. It is believed that Bello worked on the railways and was a member of the West African Students' Union. (Information from Hakim Adi.) The information officer at Labour Research, Noreen Branson, could find no further details. Telephone conversations 28 April 1998; 19 May 1998.

61. Dave to John Williamson 23 July 1956 and Williamson's reply 30 July 1956, NLHM: CP/CENT/ORG/1/11. An unknown person had written that 'Claudia Jones would be very popular indeed'. Siân Williams, the librarian of the South Wales Miners Federation, for whose help I am most grateful, has not been able to discover the i ntity of this comrade.

62. Minutes of the US Committee, 15 June ´ ɔ1, NMLH: CP/IND/DUTT, possibly file 14/09 (unnumbered when I saw the file). According to Ranjana Ash, Mikki Doyle had 'pushed Bill [Ash] out of heading up the US Committee'. Interview, London, 14 January 1998.

63. Interviews with Billy Strachan, London, 24 July 1997; and with Le Maitre, London, 19 September 1997.

64. Jones to John Gollan, 13 September 1958, NMLH: CP/CENT/DISC/03/06, Frank Bailey file.

65. Interview with Taja Sahota, Leamington Spa, 10 March 1998. Whether the Indians left or were expelled is a disputed issue. Ricky Cambridge remembers Claudia attending only public discussions organised by the Committee. Interview, London, 28 May 1998.

66. Idris Cox to Claudia Jones, 21 May 1963.

67. John Gollan to Claudia Jones, 17 January 1964; reply from Claudia, 21 January 1964.

68. John Gollan to Claudia Jones, 16 March 1964. Note that the Act had been passed two years previously!

69. Unfortunately the London District Committee's *Bulletin* is only available

from 1955; there is no mention of Claudia but there are a few articles on colonial independence and racial discrimination.

70. London District Committee *Bulletin*, May 1957.

71. I sent letters for publication to the *Morning Star* on 19 February 1997 and to the Democratic Left for the August 1997 issue of *New Times*.

72. Interviews, with Dorothy Kuya by telephone, Liverpool, 9 February 1998; with Winston Pinder, London, 13 October 1997.

73. Interview with Gertrude Elias, London, 2 May 1997.

74. Sam Russell, telephone interview, London, 18 February 1997; Betty Reid, telephone interview, London, 14 July 1997.

75. Interview with Trevor Carter, London, 4 May 1997. This is an unusual view of Claudia.

76. James Jackson, a senior official in the CPUSA, had also been editor of the US *Daily Worker*; Esther Jackson had been editor of the monthly journal *Freedomways*. Interview, 16 April 1997.

77. The Jacksons told me that 'the American Party never really dealt with its own racism'. However, at least it was on the agenda, whereas in Britain it was completely ignored.

78. African-American Henry Winston was a member of the Party's Central Committee and its organisational secretary. Jailed during the witch-hunts, he went blind due to prison conditions. On his release in September 1961, and accompanied by his friend James Jackson, he went to the USSR for medical treatment and to recuperate. See Nikolai Mostovets, *Henry Winston*, Progress Publishers, Moscow 1983.

79. Interview with Mr and Mrs Jackson, New York, 17 November 1997.

80. Interviews with Avtar Jouhl, Birmingham, 21 January 1998; and Taja Sahota, Leamington Spa, 10 March 1998.

81. Claudia Jones to George Matthews, 7 May 1963. The story concerned the attempt by a young West Indian to break the ban imposed by the trade union on the employment of Black bus crews in the city of Bristol. A similar ban was in place in Coventry. See Madge Dresser, *Black and White on the Buses*, Bristol Broadsides, Bristol 1986.

82. The letter for publication is with Jones to Matthews, 7 May 1963. It is very doubtful that Constantine would have misinterpreted examples of the 'colour bar'. During World War Two as a Ministry of Labour Welfare Officer, he had fought the unions' attempts to impose such restrictions. See Learie Constantine, *Colour Bar*, Stanley Paul, London 1964, p147.

83. Interview with Betty Reid, London, 29 July 1997.

The political activist

This chapter traces Claudia's multifarious political activities during her years in Britain. If the number of organisation she formed, and the number she worked with are to be taken as a guide, we can safely conclude that she felt that in order to be effective she had to move away from the British Communist Party. And effective she was – as much as anyone could be, working with historically disunited people against a recalcitrant and racist British government, as well as the intransigence of the United States government and the South African regime.

She also had to work to unite 'colonial' peoples in Britain. Why were West Indians not united? Because, until the attempts at the Federation the West Indies, British colonial administrations had done their best to foster disunity. Caribbeans were taught to despise their African ancestry. It was only the most politicised who could see that there was a common ground, not only among Caribbeans, but also between the various subject peoples of the old British Empire. That Claudia managed to bring together not only Caribbeans and Africans, but also Indians, is a testament to her political vision and personal magnetism.

As the situation of Black peoples in Britain is crucial to an under-standing of Claudia's work, a long introductory section outlines their history.

A brief history of Black peoples in Britain

Though some authors have claimed a much earlier Black presence in Britain, there is only documentary evidence from the sixteenth century. Thus the presence of Africans in Britain predates by about one hundred years their arrival in north America. As far as is known at present, there were no Black *communities* in Britain until the eight-eenth century and these apparently did not survive into the present, probably because of out-marriage.[1] For those of African descent in

Britain who were politicised, the twentieth century might have begun with the First Pan-African Congress, convened in London by Trinidadian Henry Sylvester Williams in 1900. However, 'colonials' were not wanted in Britain, not even to aid the war effort. In 1916, for example, the War Emergency Workers' National Committee passed a resolution which stated that '... having regard to the serious moral, social, industrial and economic considerations in any introduction of coloured labour [we] support the Labour Party in its emphatic protest against such introduction'.[2] At the end of the war the small port communities were attacked by anti-black rioters.[3]

There was racial discrimination in employment, wages and housing; popular racism flourished in the cinema and music halls.[4] Some forms of legal discrimination were introduced without eliciting any protest except by Black organisations.[5]

During World War Two the shortage of labour and pressure on other ministries by the Colonial Office, which had to find some way of incorporating West Indians in the war effort, led to the importation of just over a thousand Caribbean workers; a larger number served in the military and the merchant marine.[6] Though their experience was somewhat mixed, and despite many of their white fellow workers making it clear at the end of the war that Blacks were no longer wanted here, those who returned home found conditions there even worse than in war-torn and racist Britain.[7] Thus they began to return to Britain and encouraged others to follow.

However, despite official labour shortages, Blacks found it difficult to find employment. So many were unemployed that in 1949 Paul Robeson, on his first post-war visit to Britain, announced that he would attempt to lay the plight of unemployed Black ex-servicemen before the Colonial Secretary.[8] Simultaneously Mosley's (and other) fascist gangs became active once more and the colour bar began to flourish in pubs and some other places of entertainment.[9]

The 1949 Royal Commission on Population, while recommending emigration from Britain to the white Commonwealth, also stated that the much needed immigrants should 'not be prevented by religion or race from inter-marrying with the host population'.[10] Despite this advice, continuing labour shortages forced British employers to begin recruiting in the West Indies in the 1950s.[11] As this (fortuitously?) coincided with the closing of the US door to immigrants from the Caribbean, soon appreciable numbers of West Indians began to arrive.[12]

The immigrants were not welcome. Signs, now legendary, reading 'No Blacks, No Irish, No Dogs' proliferated in landladies' windows. Rents were increased for Black tenants. West Indians' qualifications, whether trade, professional or academic, were not accepted by employers, many of whom refused to employ Blacks in any capacity. Black immigrants who could club together to buy dilapidated housing – all they could afford – found that the prices would escalate when they met prospective vendors. Houses in all but the run-down inner city neighbourhoods were beyond the reach of Black purchasers.

Life for Blacks was not safe in London or elsewhere – as described by a 'Nigerian in Yorkshire': 'We have been beaten up by groups of white men several times ... When the police come ... they take the coloured boys into custody ... The police give us brutal treatment.'[13]

Hostility on the streets was fomented by a proliferation of Keep Britain White groups and imports from the USA such as the Ku Klux Klan, which addressed threatening letters to Claudia and Black and white anti-racist activists.[14] Some sections of the media took up the cudgels against Black immigrants. The *Sunday People*, according to Trevor Carter, 'fulminated against spongers from the West Indies. Thousands just want to come and loaf – sit on your back and mine and cash in on National Assistance, the health scheme and all the services of the Welfare State'.[15]

While some trade unions made public declarations opposing racial discrimination, others were silent or simultaneously suggested the need for controlling recruitment from the Caribbean. The Trades Union Congress advised on steps to be taken in the West Indies to discourage emigration. The Tory Under-Secretary of State at the Home Office also advocated immigration control as early as 1956; and Tory MP Cyril Osborne began a one-man campaign in Parliament as early as 1952. Osborne slowly gathered supporters, from all political parties.[16]

As the demand for immigration control grew in Parliament and the popular press, naturally those who had not in fact made a firm decision to emigrate felt pushed to beat the ban: in 1961 immigrant numbers escalated to 66,300 from the West Indies, 23,750 from India and 25,080 from Pakistan. An Immigration Bill to restrict the numbers entering Britain was introduced into Parliament in October 1961 and became law in June 1962, by which time about 400,000 immigrants had entered.[17]

By the 1950s the organisations formed by settlers of previous generations had collapsed, or simply could not cope with the new situation. According to sociologist Nicholas Deakin, 'the earliest kind of West Indian organisation formed by post-war immigrants were models of separate, self-help groups ... joint savings and credit schemes, Pentecostal churches, and social clubs formed usually on an island basis. But these had no political ideology or goals'.[18] Most fell into rapid decay. However, in 1958 'when the riots came, and even during the weeks of tension, various groups sprang anew into action like little streams after the first weeks of heavy summer rain in the tropics. Like these streams, which generally disappear by next spring, some of these groups lingered on over Christmas 1958; some were amalgamated, but the vast majority ... just dried up.'[19]

The riots, perpetrated by whites on Blacks, which erupted during the summer of 1958, were most concentrated in the city of Nottingham, and the Notting Hill area of the west London borough of Kensington. The causes of the riots have been much discussed, but no firm conclusions have yet been reached. However, it is likely that racist organisations active in the area, such as Oswald Mosley's White Defence League, the National Labour Party, the League of Empire Loyalists, the Union Movement and the British branch of the Ku Klux Klan played an active role in fomenting racial antipathy and in scape-goating the Black population for Britain's social ills. One example of the leaflets being distributed in those years urged whites to: 'Take action now. Protect your jobs. Stop coloured immigration. Houses for white people not coloured immigrants. A square deal for the negro in his own country. People of Kensington act now. Your country is worth fighting for. Fight with the Union Movement.' [20]

Claudia takes action: a response to the riots

There is no record of Claudia undertaking any independent political activities before the riots. It is therefore possible that it was what she considered an inadequate response by her *alma mater*, the Communist Party, which led her to participate and organise outside of it.[21] However, one must remember that even for Claudia there were only twenty-four hours in the day and keeping the *Gazette* going must have taken up many of those hours. How much time she could devote to any of the organisations is problematic, but as Notting Hill activist George Clarke told me, 'her advice and comment were as important as her actual activities'.[22]

Of the many organisations which sprang up in Notting Hill, there were two which were to last for some time. Claudia was associated with both, but what role she played in their formation is not clear. Probably the first was the Association for the Advancement of Coloured People (AACP), clearly modelled by its founder, Amy Ashwood Garvey, on her US experience with the National Association for the Advancement of Colored People. The local paper, the

Kensington News (26/9/1958, p7) described Amy as 'plump, jolly ... Recently returned from Ghana and her dress and furniture are from there ... Founder of the Afro-Centre, where she plans to establish a vocational school'. While the exact founding date is unknown, the AACP was certainly in existence by September 1958, when Dr Carl La Corbiniere, the deputy Prime Minister of the West Indies Federation, toured the riot-torn parts of Notting Hill. A meeting for him to discuss the situation with fellow West Indians was held at Mrs Garvey's home at 1 Bassett Road.[23] Claudia, clearly a friend and colleague of Amy's, whom she well might have met in the USA, was the general secretary of the Association.[24] According to the Metropolitan police reports, the AACP was 'controlled by the Communist Party and fellow travellers ... the leading personality of the AACP and the United Defence Committee against Racial Discrimination is Claudia Jones, a West Indian communist'. The AACP was still in existence in 1959 as Pansy Jeffrey, the local borough council's special social worker attached to the Citizen's Advice Bureau, reported on contacts with it that year.[25]

Amy Ashwood Garvey could not by any stretch of the imagination be counted either as a communist or even as a serious fellow traveller. Though of the other officers, Claudia and Manchanda were communists, neither David Pitt (who was soon to become a Labour borough councillor) nor Fenner Brockway, a Labour MP, had any connections with the Communist Party. Thus, the Metropolitan Police's report is far from accurate. It is interesting to note that the police knew exactly who Claudia was and described her as 'West Indian'. The United Defence Committee was probably the sub-committee set up by the IRFCC at its inaugural meeting (see below).

The other organisation that managed to outlast the immediate months of rioting was the Coloured People's Progressive Association (CPPA). It was founded by Frances Ezzrecco, a Black woman from London's East End, who was married to jazz drummer Don Ezzrecco. According to her own testimony, as she was coming home from work one evening during the disturbances, a gang of white youths chased her. 'When I got home I said to my husband: "That is it! I have had enough! We must organise our people against these attacks"... a group of us got together and the Coloured People's Progressive Association was formed. It was opened to white people as well as coloured ...'[26] Whether Claudia was one of the founding group, Frances does not state. The Association co-operated with other groups and was very active locally. For example, in March 1959 it co-sponsored a public meeting, 'How Can Coloured Workers Unite to Fight Unemployment'; in July it sent a deputation to see the Kensington mayor regarding 'housing, slum clearance, police, play space and other social needs' and in September it sent a delegation to join the Movement for Colonial Freedom's Mass Demonstration of Inter-Racial Friendship.[27] The CPPA survived at least until 1961, when the *Kensington News* reported that it was involved in mediating between landlords and tenants.[28]

> Our people had been living in England peacefully for years; now that peace was shattered when homes were stoned, windows broken and families threatened. The Black community panicked and wanted to return home where they would be safe, and leave England before things got worse. Claudia found a situation in which she was needed and was most effective. She was a catalyst; she brought people together and could inspire, inform and mobilise them. She was able to analyse situations, and through her experience and organising skills was able to advise us on how to respond to the British Government. She came up with positive suggestions to calm fears ...
>
> (Pearl Connor at the 1996 Symposium.)

At about 1am on the morning of 17 May Kelso Cochrane, an Antiguan carpenter, was murdered by six (still) unknown white assailants on a Notting Hill street. At a meeting convened by the Committee of African Organisations in response to the unprovoked murder, a new organisation, the Inter-Racial Friendship Co-ordinating Council (IRFCC) was formed.[29] At the meeting it was decided to send an open letter to the Prime Minster, stating that 'coloured citizens of the UK have lost confidence in the ability of the law enforcing agencies to protect them'. The meeting demanded that the Government should close 'racial centres' and pass a law making incitement to racial violence illegal. It was decided to seek a meeting with the Home Secretary to discuss the situation and the group's demands. The Government's response was worse than negative: the White Defence League was given permission to hold a rally in Trafalgar Square and a month later it refused to ratify the International Labour Office's Convention on Racial Discrimination.[30]

The Central Executive Committee of the IRFCC was elected in July: the chair was Amy Ashwood Garvey; Claudia Jones and Eleanor Ettlinger acted as co-vice-chairs; J. Eber, A. Manchanda and Aloa Bashorun shared secretarial duties; Pearl Connor was the treasurer; and Frances Ezzrecco was a member of the committee.[31] Though the IRFCC's official address was 374 Gray's Inn Road, which was also the address of the Movement for Colonial Freedom (MCF), it also met at

Amy Ashwood Garvey's house and at 200 Gower Street – the surgery of Dr David Pitt – which was a popular informal meeting place.[32]

The aims of the Council included 'respect for human rights and fundamental freedoms for ALL without distinctions as to race, colour, sex, language or religion; to oppose all forms of discrimination; to co-operate with other organisations to achieve [these] aims'.[33] The police report adds 'to educate the public on racial discrimination' to the IRFCC aims.[34] West Indian 'establishment' figures quickly decided to 'dissoci-ate' themselves from the Council. At a meeting with the Home Office and the Colonial Office, West Indies Federation Deputy Prime Minister Dr Carl La Corbiniere and West Indian Commissioner Garnet Gordon stated that they saw the Council as an 'African-dominated organisation with strong political affiliations ... The activities of political groups are laying the foundations of future trouble ... It is essential to time this action [of dissociation] carefully if the council was to be discredited'.[35]

Among those listed as signing the few remaining IRFCC attendance lists in existence are Ranjana Ash, Eleanor Ettlinger, John Eber, and McDonald Moses, the public relations officer of the CPPA.[36] The statement of accounts up to June 1959 shows how wide was the membership of the Council. Member organisations, or those which had paid their dues, were the MCF, the CPPA, the Committee of African Organisations, West Indians Students & Workers, the AACP, the Hornsey & Islington Inter-Racial Group, the St John Society and the West Indian Federal Labour Party. Among the contributors were D.N. Pritt, Ivor Montagu, the Communist Party, the Nyasaland African Congress, the South African Freedom Association and the West Indian United Association.

Without full documentation there are only glimpses of the IRFCC's activities. Following the open letter to the Prime Minister outlined above, on 27 May 1959 a deputation which included Claudia spent one and a half hours discussing their concerns with three Home Office officials. The delegation restated their demands: speedy action against racist propa-ganda; the trebling of the police force in the Notting Hill area; and, if necessary, new legislation to prevent incitement to race-hatred. The demands were necessitated by 'inactivity by the authorities in the face of organised attempts to stir up racial hatred by fascist groups'. The estab-lishment of its own defence organisation was to be considered if the Home Office failed to act. The deputation also proposed the appointment of a Select Committee 'with both white and coloured members, to go into the whole question of the special problems of districts such as Notting Hill where there are large numbers of coloured residents'. According to other reports the deputation also asked for the removal of policemen 'with known racial bias', and that the proposed legislation should deem racial discrimination illegal. The senior Home Office official who received the delegates assured them that the 'government was satisfied that the police were taking necessary action ... It was unlikely that West Indians would be allowed to form their own defence organisations.'[37]

However, R.A. Butler, the Home Secretary, only promised to 'watch the situation and encourage "effective integration and consider recruiting coloured policemen ... and slum clearance"'.[38] When pressed in Parliament, Butler condemned the fomentation of racial discrimination, but denied the need for a special enquiry.

> Every effort will be made to encourage effective integration ... The police discharge their duties impartially ... Any activities being undertaken calculated to lead to a breach of the peace the police have the powers to deal with ... To take action against [racial discrimination] might not be effective. That is why I do not want to step into that without a great deal more consideration.

Butler's contacts with the media 'indicate that it [the Press] is willing to take a responsible view of this matter'. After meeting with police chiefs he announced that he was satisfied with their 'handling of the situation in Notting Hill and elsewhere'. The 'root of racial tension', according to the police chiefs, lay in 'restlessness among young people and social malaise'.[39]

Within a few days of Cochrane's murder the Council sponsored a memorial meeting for him at St Pancras Town Hall. The three major political parties and forty organisations were represented. The speakers included Dr David Pitt, Dr La Corbiniere and Eslanda Goode Robeson.[40] The Council even arranged for a portrait to be painted especially for the meeting. The un-named CPPA spokesperson described the growing racial tension in the area, the 'alarm felt by the coloured people' and the 'allegations of hostility by the police'.[41]

A few days later, on 1 June, there was an IRFCC/CPPA-sponsored vigil outside 10 Downing Street to 'express a lack of confidence in arrangements for the security of coloured people'. Those participating in the vigil were given placards. Two of these read 'There is only one race, the human race' and 'Racial discrimination is illegal'; a third bore the portrait of the murdered Kelso Cochrane. Frances Ezzrecco, participating in the vigil, is reported as saying 'We want to know who will stop talking and do something'.[42]

Well aware of the positive publicity which could be gained, the IRFCC also bore much of the cost of Kelso Cochrane's funeral. About a thousand people attended the church service and 'many more accompanied the casket to Kensal Green Cemetery'. Telegrams were sent to his mother in Antigua and to friendly governments and sympathetic contacts in Cairo and Paris, soliciting support. The High Commissioner for Ghana, the Mayor of Kensington, and, despite their reservation about the IRFCC, the Premier of the West Indies Federation and Commissioner Garnet Gordon were among the mourners. The total cost of the service was £257, a vast sum in 1959, and one which excluded the cost of the burial. A fund was set up for Kelso's mother.[43]

The fight continues

Claudia, Amy Ashwood Garvey, and Frances Ezzrecco formed part of another IRFCC deputation which met with the local Labour MP, George Rogers, regarding some remarks he had made during the riots: on 2 September he had called for restrictions in immigration.[44] During the meeting Rogers stated that his remarks regarding immigration had been misinterpreted; he just wanted immigration to be a more orderly process, especially regarding housing and employment; the Labour Party was committed to passing a law against racial discrimination when re-elected.[45]

No one was ever arrested for the murder of Kelso Cochrane and attacks on Black people – now more spasmodic – continued, as did the distribution of fascist literature, which spread to other parts of London. The IRFCC issued a press release on 2 September, calling on the Government to legislate against the dissemination of racist propaganda and to continue the search for Cochrane's murderers.

At the next IRFCC Central Committee meeting, Manchanda, the organising secretary who had signed the press release, was criticised for issuing it too late to 'have any news value, especially in view of the unsympathetic attitude of the Press'. Manchanda's suggestion to attempt to make 'the racial issue an important question in the forthcoming general election', was adopted: Commander Fox-Pitt was asked to prepare a leaflet and all Parliamentary candidates for North Kensington were to be asked to a public meeting to outline their stand on racialism.[46] A two-page leaflet, 'Ask Your Candidate: racialism and the general election', was duly prepared. How many were distributed, and with what results, is not known. Rogers was re-elected.

On 11 September 1959 at a meeting at St Pancras Town Hall the Jamaican Prime Minister, Norman Manley, Carl La Corbiniere and

Fenner Brockway spoke against race hatred. The one hundred and thirty delegates represented trade unions, co-operatives and west London Labour parties. The conference called on all west London organisations to act against racialism and support the call for legislation against racial discrimination.[47]

Nothing further is known of the IRFCC. In the words of sociologists Ruth Glass and Harold Pollins, 'the meetings, marches and deputations sponsored by the Council, and the statements which were issued, gave the West Indian leaders, who had previously become known, the opportunity of becoming better known still. Now they had a public platform and could, in fact, act as spokesmen for the migrants.'[48]

The Commonwealth Immigration Act 1962

The Government's long-term response to the riots of 1958 was to fashion and then introduce a Bill to restrict immigration from the Commonwealth.[49] We do not know the undoubtedly wide range of activities undertaken by Claudia to prevent the Bill becoming an Act of Parliament. According to her comrade Trevor Carter,

> Claudia Jones with her campaigning *West Indian Gazette* and tireless work with the Afro-Asian Caribbean Conference played an important role in fostering unity and growth amongst the anti-racist lobbies against the restrictions, both at the Parliament and local community levels. When the Commonwealth Immigration Act became law in February 1962 it did not occur to her to accept defeat: she was one of the leaders responsible for organising a mass demonstration with a strong West Indian presence, including many black nurses in uniform.[50]

In November 1961 at a meeting against the Immigration Bill, Claudia shared the platform with Fenner Brockway and David Pitt. She pointed out that the Bill 'reflected the fear of unity of coloured and white workers and people. It aimed at spreading racialist divisions'. A resolution passed at the meeting called for the withdrawal of the Bill. The organisers were reported as expecting violence and their predictions were fulfilled. Mosley's Union Movement, the League of Empire Loyalists and the British National Party broke into the meeting. Shouting 'keep Britain white', the invaders threw fire works at the audience and the speakers. Ten were arrested.[51]

In January 1962 the AACC, the *Gazette*, and other Black organisations, together with the London branch of Trinidad's People's National Movement, convened a conference on the Bill at the Mahatma Gandhi Hall in Central London. The conference decided to join the MCF-sponsored march from Hyde Park to Trafalgar Square where a rally against the Bill was held.[52] Some 2000 people were said to have attended; Hugh Gaitskell, the recently defeated leader of the Labour Party, sent a message of support and John Stonehouse MP told the assembled protesters that the 'bill should be called the End of Commonwealth Bill'.[53]

The immediate aim of the Afro-Asian-Caribbean Conference, a new organisation formed by Claudia, was to unite against the forthcoming Immigration Act. The organisation probably resulted from a meeting at the Mahatma Gandhi Hall on 14 January.[54] The inaugural meeting of the Conference itself was on 18 January 1962. Norman Manley, Prime Minister of Jamaica, attended this founding meeting, which was chaired by Claudia's old colleague, George Bowrin, as a representative of Trinidad's People's National Movement.[55] The meeting decided to hold a vigil outside Admiralty House and the Home Office on 10 February and a mass lobby of Parliament on 13 February, followed by a protest meeting in the evening. This 'call to arms' was sent out to Commonwealth High Commissions and supportive organisations and trade unions by Claudia. In her circular letter on the 'iniquitous COLOUR-BAR legislation', Claudia pointed out that the 'legislation knocks down the very foundation of the Commonwealth, the majority of whose citizens are coloured ... Pandering to vicious racist elements, the Government, through this bill, is throwing the doors wide open to Fascism against whom [sic] the peoples of the Commonwealth fought shoulder to shoulder in the last World War'.[56] The result was that the representatives of India, Nigeria and the West Indies Federation issued statements deploring the racial overtones of the Bill.

According to an unannotated newspaper cutting in the Langford Collection several hundred people, including Fenner Brockway, took part in the 24-hour vigil on 10 February outside the Home Office. This was followed by a lobby of the House of Commons on 13 February, timed to coincide with the last day of the committee stage of the Bill to demand the Bill's withdrawal. At the protest meeting held after the lobby, Denis Healey, the Labour Party spokesman on colonial matters, pledged that a future Labour government would repeal the Act.[57] But it was all to no avail. The Bill was passed.

Campaigning on African, African American and Caribbean Issues

After this failure the Conference was free to pay attention to other issues. For example, there was a joint meeting with the West African Students' Union at Africa Unity House in February 1962 on 'The German problem: a threat to world peace'. The constitutional crisis in the West Indies – that is, the dissolution of the Federation due to the withdrawal of Jamaica – was addressed at a number of meetings.[58] Members feared that independence would be granted to some territories but not to all. In a press statement, a fuller version of which had been sent to the Colonial Secretary, the Conference Secretariat pointed out that the British government was yet again discussing the future of the West Indies without first consulting its people. The Secretariat called for the 'immediate convening of a Conference of elected leaders of the nine Unit Territories to study and propose safeguards essential for peaceful transition to stable and Independent Governments'.[59]

It is possible that the Conference evolved into the Committee of Afro-Asian Caribbean Organisations (CAACO) once the action against the Immigration Bill was well and truly lost. Membership is unknown, but we do know that the Communist Party did not permit affiliated Indian organisations or its members to join.[60] According to A. Sivanandan, the CAACO, 'initiated by the *Gazette* and working closely with the Indian Workers' Association and Fenner Brockway, and the Movement for Colonial Freedom, had its meetings and marches too, but concentrated more on lobbying the High Commissions and parliament, particularly the Labour Party which had pledged to repeal the [Commonwealth Immigration] Act, if returned to power. But ... after the Bill had become Act, the Labour Party, with an eye to the elections, began to sidle out of its commitment ...'[61]

Information about the CAACO, whose address was also Africa Unity House, begins in June 1963.[62] On the thirteenth of that month the CAACO held a meeting in Conway Hall in support of the struggles of the peoples of Birmingham, Alabama, 'for elementary democratic rights', and to plan a 'solidarity protest on the American Negro People's Struggle' – that is, the March on Washington for Jobs and Freedom being planned for August 28 by American 'Negro' leaders.[63] Among those who addressed the meeting were Claudia, Raymond Kunene of the African National Congress, London County councillor Dr David Pitt, trade union leader Clive Jenkins, Eslanda Goode Robeson, and a representative from the Movement for Colonial Freedom.

Earlier on 13 June nine representatives, including Claudia, Ranjana

Ash and Jan Carew, called on the US Embassy to protest against racial oppression and, in particular, the murder of civil rights activist Medgar Evers.[64] The note handed in read, 'We African-Asian-Caribbean peoples, and all democratic minded peoples of the world, expect the American Government not only to speedily bring the culprits to justice but also to take immediate steps to uproot the scourge of racialism.'

Interviewed by the *Daily Worker*, Claudia said the delegation had 'buttressed [the statement] with verbal arguments. We said we believed the professions of goodwill and offers of assistance from the American Government to the newly independent countries of Asia, Africa, Latin America and the Caribbean will count for nothing as long as 20 million American Negroes are subjected to exploitation and humiliation in the land of their birth.'[65]

On 28 August, the actual day of the March on Washington, a deputation led by Ranjana Ash was sent to the embassy. The printed statement taken by the delegates asked President Kennedy to 'end forthwith all practices of racialism in the USA [and] to implement, without any delay, the fundamental citizens' rights of the Negro people and other minorities, laid down in the US Constitution'.[66]

The solidarity march took place on 31 August, from Ladbroke Grove in Notting Hill to the embassy. The London representatives of Commonwealth governments and Black and left/peace organisations were asked for their support – unfortunately not until ten days before the march, which was too late for many to send delegations or even messages. The *Daily Worker* reported that 'at the head of the march Tobagan singer Pearl Prescod's ringing voice, almost unfaltered during the whole two hour demonstration, led the singing of what was to become the Negro anthem in the northern hemisphere, We Shall Overcome'.[67]

According to other newspaper cuttings in the Langford Collection, the three hundred marchers carried banners with slogans which called for an end to the colour bar in Britain, the end of racialism and imperialism and the repeal of the Immigration Act. Though the police cordoned off the embassy, the delegation was permitted to hand in a petition which asked for 'assurances that all necessary steps will be taken to implement ... the full equality ... to which American Negro citizens are legally entitled'.[68]

Understandably, Claudia was much concerned about the situation in the USA and lent her energies and expertise to other meetings on the issue. For example, in June 1963 Claudia addressed a meeting at the Mahatma Gandhi Hall on Civil Liberties in the USA, sharing the platform with Lord Soper and Nadia Cattouse, and on 26 November she was one of the speakers at another meeting in support of this issue.[69]

JOIN IN SOLIDARITY

with the

Hundreds of Thousands Marching

to Washington against

RACIAL DISCRIMINATION

•

MARCH

with us in London

to the American Embassy

on

SATURDAY AUGUST 31, 1963

Assemble at 3 p.m.

at the Ladbroke Grove tube station

•

JOIN US—

AND HELP SMASH BIGOTRY

Organised by the Committee of Afro-Asian and Carribean Organisations.
3 Collingham Gardens, S.W.5.

Printed by Columbia Printers (T.U.). Holborn 4442

Flyer announcing solidarity march, 1963.

Many interviewees recall that Claudia was involved in activities protesting against US involvement in Vietnam, but no evidence of this has come to light.

The CAACO sent a detailed memorandum on a range of issues to the Commonwealth Prime Ministers' Conference, which met in London in May 1964. In regard to British Guiana, the CAACO urged the Prime Ministers to 'use their influence to release all political prisoners; restore the constitutional government and set a date for independence'. The release of all political prisoners in South Africa and the imposition of economic and military sanctions was also demanded. The Committee also asked the Prime Ministers to prevail upon the British Government to release Joshua Nkomo, suspend the undemocratic constitution of Southern Rhodesia and to take the 'requisite military measures against any attempted coup by the white Smith Government'. The memorandum also included suggestions regarding British withdrawal from Aden, self-determination for the people of Cyprus and the withdrawal of the US military from Vietnam and Laos.

Work with anti-racist and anti-imperialist organisations

Claudia associated with other organisations that campaigned against racial discrimination and the colour bar. For example, Claudia replaced Essie Robeson, who was ill, as one of the speakers at a National Council of Civil Liberties conference, 'Colour Bar – Legislation and Education', on 21 November 1959. Claudia is reported to have emphasised that in the world coloured people were the majority and hence the issue of the colour bar was not a question of whites' relations with an under-privileged minority. Her speech was 'much appreciated', NCCL official L.A.D. Woodland wrote to Claudia.[70]

> In those days I was a steward for the Movement of Colonial Freedom and at many of the meetings where we were keeping order, Claudia Jones was one of major speakers. We stewards decided to organise a meeting ourselves at the Camden Town Hall opposing the racist character of the Anti-Immigration Bill ... with Claudia Jones as the main speaker ...
> (Bill Ash at the 1996 Symposium)

Claudia's collaboration with the Movement for Colonial Freedom was established by early 1959. (It is possible that she was introduced to the MCF by Paul Robeson, one of the Movement's sponsors and, as already detailed, an old friend of Claudia's.) In February of that year

Fenner Brockway wrote to her asking if any of the 'coloured persons are finding it difficult to keep up payments of fines' imposed by the county courts after the 1958 'disturbances'. He, in his capacity as MP, had tabled a motion for 'amnesty for the disturbance prisoners and fines'. Brockway wrote asking Claudia to telephone him to 'fix a cup of tea together' so that they could discuss the 're-establishment of a Caribbean Committee under the association of the MCF. I welcome the British Caribbean Association ... but with the kind of patronage it has it cannot be depended upon to adopt militant action if that ever becomes necessary'.[71]

The earliest recorded instance we have of Claudia speaking at an MCF conference is on 16 July 1959, when she spoke at the Movement-sponsored delegate conference on East and Central Africa, and on how to 'put into operation activities to deal with this problem [racial violence, which] has been delayed too long and to bring about greater inter-racial solidarity'. One of her fellow speakers was Julius Nyerere.[72] The Committee of Inter-Racial Unity was set up at the conference; Manchanda was IRFCC's representative at Unity's first meeting on 17 September 1959, when it was decided that the group's first task was a voter-registration drive among Black people.

In November that year Claudia spoke at the MCF delegate conference For Inter-Racial Unity at Islington in London, sharing the platform with the Rev. Trevor Huddlestone and Kenneth Robinson MP. The *Islington Gazette* reported much more of what she said than of the speeches of her illustrious colleagues:[73]

> If all the coloured people were thrown into the sea, it would not solve the housing problems or provide enough jobs ... One reason behind race prejudice is that Britain is an imperial country. But coloured people are now demanding their freedom and this means they are coming into a new relationship with the British people and expect to be treated as equals. That there is going to be a stable coloured population in the country has to be accepted ... I am glad that at least some of the trade unions are beginning to tackle the question in this light ... Are there good and bad coloured people? Of course there are – they are human beings.

Two months after the MCF conference, Claudia was asked by *The Guardian* to comment on Fenner Brockway's sixth attempt to introduce a bill against racial discrimination into the House of Commons: 'A racial incitement bill coming from the heart of the commonwealth would be like a tocsin ... boosting morale everywhere in the Commonwealth among those fighting against racial discrimination'.[74]

The MCF probably began its annual Africa Freedom Day concerts in 1959. Paul Robeson was the featured artist at the 1961 concert; he did not attend in 1962, but his wife Eslanda read out a message from him. While we do not know how Claudia was associated with these events, we do know that she was asked to serve as an official hostess at the African Freedom Day Ball in 1963.[75]

Towards the end of 1963 she was among the speakers at an MCF rally, on this occasion to support Fenner Brockway's tenth attempt to introduce a bill in the House of Commons to outlaw racial discrimination.

Claudia was involved with the Boycott Movement, precursor of the Anti-Apartheid Movement (AAM) from its inception in June 1959. She was a member of the first Boycott Sub-Committee, set up by the CAO.[76] (The *Gazette* had always been outspokenly critical of the apartheid regime.) In 1964, in her capacity as organiser for the CAACO, she worked with the African National Congress, the AAM and the CAO to co-ordinate a hunger strike against apartheid.[77] The press release from Africa Unity House stated that the aim of the fast was 'to rouse the conscience of the British people to put an end to the trade in blood', (i.e., British investment, totalling £1000 million) and to demand the implementation of the UN resolution condemning the ongoing trial of political activists. A part of the World Campaign for the Release of South African Political Prisoners, the fast was undertaken by Manchanda, Rashid Yousuf, Mohamed Tickely, Bryan Hamilton, Ted Stagg and M. Kojonaraja. It began on 9 April 1964 in the courtyard of St Martin's-in-the-Fields in Trafalgar Square and ended on 15 April. It was claimed that 25,000 people had stopped to enquire about the aims of the fast and that many had signed a petition for the enforcement of the UN resolution. One hundred and fifty pounds was collected in aid of the Christian Action Defence and Aid Fund.[78]

A public protest meeting organised by the CAACO was held during the fast, on 12 April. A film was shown, and there was a dramatisation of 'torture in South Africa'. First performed on 28 February, those taking part included, as narrators, Robert Lang of the National Theatre and Bari Johnson, while Nadia Cattouse, Andrew Faulds and Edric Connor were among the actors. The speakers included Claudia, the Barbadian novelist George Lamming, trade unionist Clive Jenkins and representatives of the ANC, the South African Coloured Congress and the Council of African Organisations.[79]

Claudia worked with the Birmingham-based Indian Workers Association (IWA). Taja Sahota of the IWA had met Claudia at the CPGB's International Committee, of which they were both members.

She and Manchanda helped establish an IWA branch in London, Sahota told me. Claudia also visited the home of Sahota in Leamington Spa. Aided by Mr Sahota, she attempted to persuade the Caribbean residents to form a Caribbean Workers Party. In support of this, she spoke at an IWA meeting in the city's town hall. 'She was a good speaker ... She had all the facts and figures. She also knew the situation in India.'[80]

Avtar Jouhl, who became the IWA's general secretary in 1961, recalls that they co-ordinated campaigns regarding the Immigration Bill. 'She was more experienced than we – knew how to organise, to lobby, how to book committee rooms, phrase letters to ministers ... She was focused on getting things done ... She used her experience well in the anti-imperialist, anti-colonial struggle.'[81]

Claudia was invited by the IWA to Birmingham for the Smethwick bye-elections in which the Conservative candidate campaigned on a platform of 'if you want a nigger for a neighbour, vote Labour'. She also spent three days with Avtar Jouhl and his family – helping Asian women campaigners and then with encouraging the Afro-Caribbean and Asian women to vote on election day. It was to no avail. The Conservative candidate won.

Somehow, given her numerous commitments, Claudia made time to contribute to other events. For example, at the end of 1961 she was listed as one of the speakers, with Essie Robeson and Pearl Connor, at the Africa Women's Day meeting and concert. The meeting is reported as having been called by Mrs L.J. Sesay of Sierra Leone, president of the All-African Women's Freedom Movement, based at Africa Unity House. However, Pearl Connor revealed that it was Claudia who was instrumental in inaugurating the gathering. Claudia stated that it was 'not enough to honour women; what was necessary was to translate the argument that women were equal into practical terms ... Men oftimes in speaking of freedom and independence actually exclude their wives and sisters.'[82]

On 28 June 1963 Claudia spoke at a 'What's Going on in British Guiana' meeting at Friends House in London. She was also involved with the Hurricane Flora Relief Committee, which was fund-raising for the devastated people of Tobago.[83]

In March 1964 Claudia participated in a discussion forum on 'The Kind of World the Young West Indian is Likely to Face', as part of West Indian Unity Week.[84] In May she was at the meeting of the Hampstead Branch of the British-China Friendship Association, with Liao Hung-Ying and Virginia Penn, who had just returned from over two years in China. Unfortunately, the flyer for this event does not

The only SMETHWICK Candidate who has ALWAYS called FOR THE STRICTEST CONTROL OF IMMIGRATION IS

PETER GRIFFITHS

REMEMBER THIS WHEN YOU CAST YOUR

VOTE

Printed by Smethwick Telephone Co. Ltd., 24 Hume Street, Smethwick, 40.
Published by C. E. A. Dickens, Election Agent, 68 Edgbaston Road, Smethwick, 41.

Conservative party campaign poster for Smethwick bye-election, date.

indicate the topic of her contribution. In June, Claudia was among the speakers at the South Africa Freedom Day Reception at Africa Unity House. All the speakers stressed that as world pressure had saved the lives of Nelson Mandela, Walter Sisulu and their Rivonia trial comrades, a campaign should be commenced to seek their release. Claudia is reported as emphasising 'that international solidarity must be measured not merely by sympathy for the oppressed but by how determined we are to see them through to final victory'.[85]

Unfortunately it has proved impossible to interview the people with whom Claudia shared a platform, as most have died. Clive Jenkins responded to my request for his memories of Claudia by saying that 'he really did not have anything to say other than that she was a very attractive-looking woman'.[86] Historian Eric Hobsbawm, who was a founder member of the Stars' Campaign for Inter-racial Friendship set up in the wake of the 1958 riots, wrote to me that he only has 'fragmentary memories of her, though I can still see her in my mind's eye: a strong brown face with a sharp profile, an air of power and calm assurance, and the usual non-rhetorical efficiency which was the hallmark of so many people trained in the school of the Party ... An obviously impressive person.'[87]

Activities abroad

It has been suggested that Claudia's visit to the USSR in August 1962 was due to an invitation to guest edit *Soviet Woman*. Her letter to Manchanda in which she describes the editors of that journal as her hosts supports this view. However, there is no mention of Claudia in *Soviet Woman* during the period she spent in the USSR, though other women, including women from Africa who attended the World Congress for General Disarmament and Peace, appear in both articles and photographs. Neither could I find in the journal the article Claudia told Manu she had written for her hosts.[88]

According to her report of this trip in the *West Indian Gazette* (December 1962, pp5,9) she first had a holiday 'in the fabulous Crimea'. Then she met Soviet people from all walks of life and visitors 'from other parts of the Caribbean', as well as her old African American comrade Henry Winston, who was recuperating from months of imprisonment in US jails, which had left him blind.[89]

In Moscow, Leningrad and Sevastopol she toured factories and other workplaces, schools, museums, theatres and hospitals – and she was hospitalised herself for some weeks. She was most impressed by the low rents; free education and training; the freedom and profession-alisation of women; by the desire for peace, and that 'Soviet citizens and their government make no bones about their determination to uphold the rights of oppressed peoples and support the struggles of the new and yet-to-be-freed peoples of Africa, Asia, the Caribbean and Latin America'.

This enthusiastic account is difficult to reconcile with many people telling me that during the Sino-Soviet split Claudia was firmly on the side of China; others say that while the Party was Stalinist, she was a Maoist, a grouping more closely involved in anti-imperialist activism. From the reports of her visits, it seems that she could see the positive achievements in both the USSR and China; being a true inter-nationalist she must have been against the splits within the movement.

The questions which have to be asked are: How was Claudia able to fund this trip? How did she get the invitation to go to the USSR? There is nothing at all about it in the Communist Party archives, and Betty Reid has assured me that she did not go under Party auspices: 'I would have handled it had there been a CPGB arrangement'.[90] Sam Russell is adamant that 'Claudia by then would not have allowed Betty to do anything for her. The Embassy would have arranged it.'[91] The arrangement was certainly not made through the CP's Women's Movement either, as, according to Betty Reid, Claudia was not in the movement. 'The USSR had a policy of inviting prominent people, probably on the initiative of the USSR Embassy', she told me. This statement of course begs questions about how the USSR recognised Claudia's importance, while she was being 'used' so selectively by her home Party! As she had headed the US Party's Women's Commission for some years, it is possible that Claudia had then established a relation-ship with the Soviet women's movement. She had, after all, from 1949 to 1952 devoted her activities to writing and rallying the women of the US for peace and against a third, atomic, world war ... Claudia Jones wrote many articles on this subject [and] actively helped to organise women in the peace struggle.'[92] That her relations with Soviet women might well have continued is indicated by the message sent by L. Balakhovskaya, the head of the International Department, Soviet Women's Committee, on the occasion of Claudia's funeral: 'The Soviet Women's Committee has maintained friendly contacts with Mrs. Jones for a long period of time ... we shall long remember with greatest warmth this wonderful woman.'[93]

When I asked Claudia's comrades in New York about this, it was suggested that her trip might have been arranged by the Cuban Embassy in London, as she had close colleagues there. Alternatively,

Henry Winston might have wanted to meet up with his old comrade and asked his Soviet hosts to arrange the trip.

Claudia was again in the USSR in 1963, this time to attend the World Congress of Women. There is no information on this journey except that she arrived, overland, on 20 June and flew back to Britain by Aeroflot on 4 July. The objectives of the Congress were to secure the rights of women and children; peace and universal disarmament; and national independence. There is no list of invitees, only of countries represented – which included Trinidad and Tobago. (That she represented her birthplace in Moscow as well as in Tokyo and China not only appears to confirm that Claudia did not travel under CPGB auspices, but also symbolises her estrangement from the Party.) Claudia can be seen in the back row of the photograph of the women elected to the Presidium of the Congress. Mrs Ransome Kuti of Nigeria was elected one of the vice-presidents, but Claudia appears not to have been voted onto the new Executive.[94] We know nothing of her contributions to the Congress – except that she was called upon to help Caribbean colleagues.[95]

As with her trips to the USSR, it has proved impossible to discover how Claudia came to be invited to the Tenth World Conference Against the Hydrogen and Atom Bombs meeting in Japan from 27 July to 2 August 1964. It has been suggested that she paid for the trip herself, which is hardly likely; or that the Peace Movement paid, but of this I have not been able to find any evidence.[96] Not only was she invited, but she was named vice-chair of the Drafting Committee.[97]

In the draft of an article for the *Gazette*, Claudia wrote:

> I stood with over 160 delegates from every continent of the globe to commemorate the nineteenth Anniversary of the United States imperialist nuclear bombing of Hiroshima ... Before the stone obelisk ... the bones of the 300,000 victims of this blatant crime against Japan and humanity ... each and every one of us carried a rose which we laid as we marched past ...
>
> ... Still ringing in my ears were the prolonged ovations and shouts of 'Peace!' to the delegates in the final session who unanimously adopted the following resolutions and appeals: international united action to prevent nuclear war; a total ban on nuclear weapons; support for the struggles of all the people of the world, particularly Asia, Africa and Latin America; and condemned the new war provocations by US imperialism against the Democratic Republic of Viet Nam ... These ovations were echoed and re-echoed in the huge mass meeting organised by the Japan Council against A and H Bombs of 35,000 Tokyo peace fighters;

in Osaka another 35,000 overflowed two halls, and in Kyoto a similar audience in standing ovation cheered unanimously ...

... It was the People's Republic of China who is widely regarded by Asian, African, Latin American and Caribbean delegations as leading the struggle against US imperialism and support for all national liberation struggles ...

... It was in the international conference sessions where reports showed the counter-struggles of the people of the Caribbean, Guadeloupe, and Haiti, Panama and Nicaragua; the opposition by the beacon light of the Caribbean, Socialist Cuba to Yankee imperialism ... that one learned more deeply of the principled stand of the 10th World Conference. It was in the group meetings and the women's panel where I spoke and attended with delegates from France, Indonesia, the People's Republic of China, Belgium, Hawaii, the United States and Korea, that one saw the torrent for peace which issues forth from the mothers, wives and sisters of Japan.[98]

Another view of Claudia in Tokyo is given by the Haitian delegate, Antoine Petit, who reminisced about the conference at the Claudia Jones Memorial Meeting in Peking in February 1965:

> In Claudia's attitude, her stand and her speeches, she stood up against the tendency to isolate our continent (she represented Trinidad) and even set up water-tight barriers between our peoples of Asia, Africa and Latin America. She fought actively against those ... who pretend that Latin America had nothing to do with their fight against revisionism. She, with Ahmed Kheir, played a key role in drafting the two documents which took in the principal results of our work and in which the revisionists were seriously condemned. For this reason she was chosen to read those documents, which were unanimously approved, at the final general assembly. Her firm and convincing voice was the last to reverberate through our council chamber ... In large measure, the success of the conference was her work.

In the draft of her report to the Committee of Afro-Asian-Caribbean Organisations, Claudia emphasised the difficulties that had been encountered in Tokyo in achieving unity in the face of a parallel conference called by 'the right wing of the Japanese Socialist Party'. This counter-conference wanted to ban all nuclear tests, while Communist-dominated leaders of the Japan Council Against Atomic and Hydrogen Bombs wanted to make an exception for those of Communist China and other 'peaceful forces, meaning the Communist group'.[99] She also pointed out that the Tokyo conference had drawn a distinction between just and unjust wars: the former were liberation struggles and the latter imperialist wars.

Claudia reported the 'key decisions' of the conference as:

1) appeal for international joint action to stop US aggression in Indochina;
2) common action to achieve the total prohibition of the use, test, manufacture and stockpiling of nuclear weapons, and for general disarmament;
3) dismantling [of] *all* foreign military bases and the withdrawal of foreign forces including Polaris submarines;
4) dismantling of foreign military bases and [the] withdrawal of US forces from Japan and the return of Okinawa to Japan;
5) strengthening of the relief movement for atomic victims.[100]

From Japan, and at the invitation of the China Peace Committee, Claudia flew to China with a number of other delegates. In her seven weeks there, she reported to the CAACO that she had visited five cities:

and I observed first hand with my own eyes the magnificent achievements of 15 years of Socialist Construction and its effect on lives, agricultural industry and society of the 650 million people of the New Socialist China. I talked and spoke to many of China's leaders – in government, in the People's Communes, in light and heavy industry – the ardent revolutionary men, women, youth and children of New Socialist China who are led by the Chinese Communist Party and their world Communist leader, Chairman Mao Tse Tung ... The great achievements in Socialist Construction in New China, based on its policy of Self Reliance which permeates every aspect of its society – in agriculture and industrialisation in light and heavy industry. A new morality pervades this ancient land which less than 15 years ago was engaged in a bitter, protracted anti-imperialist armed struggle to free itself from the ravages of feudalism, semi-colonialism, bureaucratic capitalism and imperialism, and achieved victory over US imperialism, the Kuomintang puppets and the Japanese militarists.[101]

In this report, Claudia outlines the arguments that she reiterated in her article in the *Gazette* of November 1964, congratulating China on the test explosion of its first atomic bomb. She maintained that China's bomb was 'solely aimed at self defence and countering the US nuclear menace' and thus 'strengthens the cause of peace ... The Chinese government solemnly declared that China will never at any time and under any circumstances be the first to use nuclear weapons.' Premier Chou En Lai, Claudia reported, was calling for a world conference, whose ultimate goal would be the 'complete prohibition and the thorough destruction of nuclear weapons'.

Claudia interviewed Madame Soong Ching Ling, the widow of Dr Sun Yat-Sen, president of the First Democratic Republic of China. Mme Soong was Vice-Chair of the People's Republic of China. (Unfortunately only fragments of the typescript remain, but much of the interview was printed in the November *Gazette*.) Mme Soong refused to discuss her own contributions; 'instead [she] engaged me in talk of my own observations during my China visit', Claudia reported. The two women discussed the agricultural communes which, with water conservancy projects and the use of fertilisers and mechanisation, was enabling 'high yields regardless of prolonged dry seasons or overabundant rains'. The communes were providing a much improved life for peasants; 'before liberation ... [they] were subjected to national calamities over and above the exploitation and oppression of ... war lords and absentee owners; the semi-colonial feudal economy left little or nothing for the poor and middle peasant'. Mme Soong emphasised that 'China is still economically backward, but we believe that the People's Communes is the answer to the concrete problems of agriculture ... A new morality pervades the land, a spirit of each helping the other.' When Claudia praised China for her 'superb fraternal aid to the newly emerging countries of Africa, Asia and Latin America and her firm anti-imperialist stand', Mme Soong 'demurred at praise of China's stand. We feel it our duty to help those countries under the heel of Imperialism. Our successes are also due to the help of people all over the world. If you succeed, it is also our success.'

The promised detailed report of her visit to China as well as 'conclusions I drew for our work in our Committee', Claudia either never wrote or they have not been preserved. Reports in the media are sparse: for example, *China Pictorial* of October 1964 merely reported that Chairman Mao had received the delegates who had arrived in China from the Tokyo conference; Claudia appears in one of the photographs of the delegates. The delegates were greeted at the airport at Peking on 17 August by crowds and slogans, according to the Hsinhua News Agency's *Daily Bulletin* of 25 August; among the list of named delegates is Claudia Jones of Trinidad. The China Peace Committee and the Chinese Committee for Afro-Asian solidarity gave a reception to the visitors from Tokyo, which was attended by Vice Premier Chen Yi. In a note in English appended to a Chinese newspaper, the photograph on an inside page is of Claudia shaking hands with the President of China.[102] Presumably, had she lived, Claudia would have written an article on her visit for the *Gazette*. She was, however, remembered and celebrated by the Europeans in Peking at a memorial meeting in February 1965, as noted above and in chapter seven.[103]

> Claudia as a communist used the spirit of the Bandung period to put forward the kinds of views that were necessary at the time, unity ... Claudia went to China, Claudia was influenced by the Chinese.[104] This was a Black woman who grew up in the conflict in the United States, who understood imperialism ... She could not have gone to China as a member of either the American Communist Party or the British Communist Party and not been influenced by the split which was happening. But she did not bring that to us. She discussed it with some of us, we all discussed it, because it was a problem for all of us, a very serious problem, and it isn't ended yet.
>
> (Trevor Carter at the 1996 Symposium)

Claudia, despite her plethora of political activities, appears in no histories of the British Left. She, like so many other Black activists, has been written out of history.

> Change the mind of Man
> Against the corruption of centuries;
> Of feudal-bourgeois, capitalist ideas
> The fusion of courage and clarity
> Of polemic against misleaders
> Who sought compromise with the enemy
> These were the pre-requisites of Victory.
>
> No idle dreamers these –
> And yet they dared to dream
> The dream—long-planned
> Holds in Socialist China –

From Yenan – cradle of the Revolution;
Of their dreams; their fight,
Their organisation, their heroism
Yenan – Proud monument to man's will
To transform Nature, and, so doing
Transform Society and Man himself!

> Written on the Plane returning from a two-day
> visit from Yenan to Peking. August 28, 1964
> Claudia Jones

Notes

1. Initially there were fewer women than men coming, or being brought to live here. This preponderance of men persisted among the newly-arrived until the 1960s.
2. Resolution by War Emergency: Workers' National Committee, NMLH: WNC 3/12. Both the TUC and the Labour Party supported the Committee.
3. See Peter Fryer, *Staying Power*, Pluto Press, London 1984, chapter 10; Andrea Murphy, *From the Empire to Rialto*, Liver Press, Liverpool 1995, chapters 1-3; Neil Evans, 'The South Wales Riots of 1919', *Llafur* (Welsh Labour History Journal), 3/1, 1980, pp2-19; Jacqueline Jenkinson, 'The 1919 race riots in Britain: a survey', Rainer Lotz & Ian Pegg (eds), *Under the Imperial Carpet*, Rabbit Press, Crawley 1986, pp182-207.
4. On how Black seamen were treated, see Laura Tabili, *'We Ask for British Justice': Workers and Racial Difference in Late Imperial Britain*, Cornell University Press, Ithaca 1994; and D. Frost (ed), *Ethnic Labour and British Imperial Trade*, Frank Cass, London 1995. On popular racism, see e.g. John Mackenzie, *Imperialism and Popular Culture*, University Press, Manchester 1986.
5. Apart from Fryer, note 3, see Marika Sherwood, 'Racism and Resistance: Cardiff in the 1930s and 1940s', *Llafur* 5/4, 1991, pp51-70; Edward Scobie, *Black Britannia*, Johnson Publishing Co., Chicago 1972, pp169-170.
6. The West Indians were not wanted by the military. See Marika Sherwood, *Many Struggles*, Karia Press, London 1995.
7. Just how appalling conditions were in these British colonies is indicated by the fact that the report of the Moyne Commission sent to the West Indies to investigate the causes of the riots of the late 1930s, was not published till *after* the war. It was believed that publication would put 'ammunition' in the hands of the Axis powers.
8. *Daily Worker*, 2 April 1949. The *Daily Worker* 9 April 1949, p5, claimed that there were said to be 3000 Black unemployed in Manchester – some 9 per cent of the total unemployed, while the proportion of Black people in Manchester would have been about 1 per cent or less. According to a

government estimate there were 26 West Indians and 125 West Africans unemployed in Manchester out of a total Black population in the city of c.3000. PRO: LAB26/226, Report of Labour Officers Conference, 20 January 1949.

9. *Daily Worker*, 7 May 1949, p3; Robert Skidelsky, *Oswald Mosley*, Papermac, London 1975, especially pp490-492. For example, some West Africans in London's East End borough of Deptford complained of the 'colour bar' imposed by some pubs and landladies, *Daily Worker*, 7 April 1949, p3; [Glasgow] *Evening Citizen*, 2 May 1949, p3.

10. Royal Commission on Population, Cmd.7695, 1949, para.329, p124.

11. There had been various schemes for importing workers from Europe; for example in May 1949 the Labour Secretary announced that he was looking for new sources of female labour in Germany and Austria for the Lancashire cotton industry and for hospital domestics, *Liverpool Daily Post*, 10 May 1949. For a summary of the schemes, see Colin Holmes, *John Bull's Island*, Macmillan Education, Basingstoke 1988, pp210-216.

12. The Walter-McCarran Act was passed in the USA in 1952. It reduced the numbers of West Indian immigrants entering the USA drastically: for example, 6723 entered in 1952 but only 1852 in 1955; in 1958, for example, 16,511 West Indians arrived in Britain. PRO: CO1031/2946.

13. A Nigerian in Yorkshire, 'Colour-Barred', *Labour Monthly*, January 1955, pp36-38. (I want to thank my colleague Sean Creighton for this article.)

14. In February 1957 the police announced that its 'files' on the KKK had been closed as the Klan had been 'nipped in the bud'. This was untrue, as evidenced, for example, by the raid on the *Gazette* offices in August 1958 and the letters sent to Clapham's Labour MP, C. Gibson, by the KKK in May 1959, warning him that if he did not 'keep quiet in the Commons, you will surely die', *Reynold's News*, 12 May 1957, p1; *News Chronicle*, 20 May 1959, p6. There are reports on the KKK in *The Guardian*, 3 May 1957, p2; 7 May 1957, p2; *Socialist Leader*, 4 May 1957, p1. According to Fenner Brockway (Labour MP for Eton and Slough) the KKK had two branches in London and five throughout the UK, *The Times*, 3 May 1957, p4; 4 May 1957, p4.

15. Trevor Carter, *Shattering Illusions*, Lawrence and Wishart, London 1986, pp66-7.

16. Osborne was knighted in 1961. See Paul Foot, *Immigration and Race in British Politics*, Penguin, Harmondsworth 1965.

17. Numbers were not recorded before 1955. The totals from 1955 – June 1962 were: 249,540 from the West Indies, 75,870 from India and 67,290 from Pakistan. See R.B. Davison, *Black British*, Institute of Race Relations/Oxford University Press, London 1966, p3. In the same period the Government spent £1.3 million on 'assisted passages' for emigrants from Britain. On immigrants from the Indian sub-continent, see Rozina Visram, *Ayahs, Lascars and Princes*, Pluto Press, London 1986.

18. Nicholas Deakin, *Colour, Citizenship and British Society*, Panther Books, London 1970, p288. (This book is based on the report of the Institute of

Race Relations, first published by OUP in 1969.) On the earlier organisa-
tions, see e.g., Peter Fryer, note 3, and Hakim Adi, *West Africans in Britain 1900 - 1960*, Lawrence and Wishart, London 1998.

19. Donald Hinds, *Journey to an Illusion*, Heinemann, London 1966, p136.
20. *The Guardian*, 2 September 1958, p5. The Union Movement was also headed by Oswald Mosley. See also Scobie, *Black Britannia*, note 5, chapters 14 & 15; Edward Pilkington, *Beyond the Mother Country*, I.B. Taurus, London 1988. The White Defence League was set up in 1959 by Colin Jordan, a schoolteacher from Coventry. (Cutting from *Daily Mail*, 31 March 1959 in PRO: CO1031/2946.)
21. The Party was not totally inactive: the local branches held a poster parade through the 'troubled area' denouncing racial hatred and discrimination, *Kensington News*, 12 September 1958, p6.
22. Telephone interview with George Clarke, London, 17 July 1997.
23. *Kensington News*, 19 September 1958.
24. A. Manchanda was the first assistant secretary; David Pitt and Fenner Brockway were respectively first and second vice presidents. Claudia is listed as secretary in two lists of organisations dated 1959. PRO: CO1031/2420 & 2545.
25. Metropolitan Police Report 28 May 1959, PRO: HO325/9; Kensington Borough Council Minutes 8 December 1959.
26. Hinds, note 19, p140. According to the biographers of Notting Hill 'activist' Michael de Freitas, the CPPA was wrecked by its own vice-chair, De Freitas (later known as Michael X), who caused a devastating internal split by objecting to the numbers of 'white' members. See D. Humphrey & D. Tindall, *False Messiah*, Hart-Davis, MacGibbon, London 1977.
27. The co-sponsor was Peter Fryer's *The Newsletter* – advertisement in *Tribune*, 13 March 1959, p3; *Kensington News*, 19 September 1958, p1; 3 July 1959, p1.
28. *Kensington News*, 13 January 1961; in its May 1961 newsletter, the Standing Conference of West Indian Organisations reported that Frances Ezzrecco was serving on its prisons committee.
29. The CAO's members were: Africa Forum, Africa League, African Society, African Research Publication, Gambian Cultural Society, Gambian Students' Union, Ghana Union of GB, Kenya Student Association, NASSAU (Ghana), National Council of Nigeria and Cameroon, ZAPU, National Revolutionary Front for the Liberation of Portuguese Territories, National Union of Kamrun Students, UNIP, WASU, West African United Front, Namibian National Party. (SOAS: MCF Papers, Box 28, AFF74). Kwesi Armah, political attaché to the Ghana High Commission, was chairman in 1960; Benjamin Machyo of Uganda replaced him in 1961 when Armah was appointed High Commissioner. In October 1960 Nkrumah gave £17,500 for a new headquarters for the CAO; 3 Collingham Gardens – Africa Unity House – was eventually bought for £42,000, *West Africa*, 22 October 1960, p1209; 19 November

1960, p1322; 4 November 1961, p1233; 11 November 1961, p1262.

30. *The Times*, 19 May 1959; *The Guardian*, 22 March 1959, 1&27 June 1959, p2; *Reynold's News*, 24 May 1959, p1; *Kensington News*, 22 May 1959, p1.

31. Unless otherwise indicated, information on Claudia'a activities is from the Langford Collection. There is a discrepancy between the list of officers in the Collection and in the list proposed by the police spies in Special Branch Report 10 November 1959, PRO: HO325/9. It is interesting to note that these three organisations were led by women. Nothing is known of Eleanor Ettlinger; John Eber was the secretary of the Movement for Colonial Freedom; Aloa Bashorun was the chair of the CPPA and secretary of the Committee of African Organisations.

32. 'Dr David Pitt made his premises in Gower Street available for meetings ... He held open political surgeries to advise and help those of our people struggling to survive.' (Pearl Connor at the 1996 Symposium.) The Movement for Colonial Freedom, one of whose founders was activist/campaigner for racial justice and MP (later Lord) Fenner Brockway, was eventually controlled by the Communist Party.

33. IRFCC Constitution in Langford Collection.

34. Special Branch Report, 10 November 1959, PRO: HO325/9.

35. Note on the meeting with the British Caribbean Association (c. 8 June 1959), PRO: CO1031/2541. The BCA was formed at the House of Commons in February 1959.

36. Ranjana Ash was a Communist Party member. McDonald Moses, having completed his studies at Ruskin College, returned to his native Trinidad in late 1959 and resumed a distinguished life in trade union work.

37. *Colonial Freedom News*, June 1959, pp3-5; *The Guardian*, 27 May 1959, p2; *Kensington News*, 5 June 1959, p1; *The Times*, 22 May 1957, p7; 27 May 1957, p10; 28 May 1957, p12; *Daily Worker*, 27 May 1959, 1&28 May 1959, p1. Social worker Pansy Jeffrey, in her evidence to the Parliamentary Select Committee on Race Relations and Immigration, stated that 'From 1959 to 1961 we at the Citizens' Advice Bureau found it difficult to believe the behaviour of the police which appeared from the stories told us by callers who came to us for advice. Then it began to seem that there must be some substance to these stories' (p234). The Government's Committee on West Indian Immigrants at its meeting on 21 May 1959 noted that 'West Indians feel lack of sympathy of the police ... complaints regarding the police bring no action'. The Home Office representative at the meeting reiterated the HO's belief that the 'hooliganism of the youth' was to blame for the riots. PRO: CO1031/2946.

38. *Kensington News*, 12 June 1959, p1.

39. See *The Times*, 5 June 1959, p7; *West Africa*, 13 June 1959, p573; *The Times*, 11 June 1959, p6. Such views will sound quite familiar to readers of the reports of the 1998 enquiry into the murder of Black teenager Stephen Lawrence by a gang of white youths in south London.

40. Ruth Glass & H. Pollins, *Newcomers*, Centre for Urban Studies, London

1960, p167; *Colonial Freedom News*, June 1959, p5; *The Guardian*, 29 June 1959, p20.

41. *Kensington News*, 29 May 1959, p1.

42. *Kensington News*, 29 May 1959, p6; *Kensington Post*, 6 May 1959; *The Times*, 2 June 1959, p7.

43. *Kensington News*, 5 June 1959, 1&12 June 1959, pp1,7; *The Times*, 8 June 1959, p6; *Reynold's News*, 7 June 1959, p1.

44. *Kensington News*, 12 September 1958, p1. The CPPA had already met with Rogers, who had told them then that he was 'not hostile' (*Ibid.*, 12 June 1959, p1). Two to three weeks after Rogers made this statement, the North Kensington Labour Party passed a vote of confidence in their MP (*Kensington News*, 26 September 1958, p1). Rogers had been one of four MPs who had seen the Home Secretary on 22 July 1959 demanding the dispersal of immigrants and the deportation of criminals, as well as legislation regarding racial discrimination and incitement to racial hatred. It seems that between July and September, ie, the period of the riots, Rogers' views had moved further to the right. (Notes on deputation, PRO: HO325/9.)

45. In a recent book Rogers is described as being one of the four Labour MPs in the pro-control (of immigration) lobby from the mid-1950s. See Ian Spencer, *British Immigration Policy Since 1939*, Routledge, London 1997; see also Pilkington, note 20, pp68, 84, 133.

46. The identity of Commander Fox-Pitt is unknown.

47. *Colonial Freedom News*, July 1959, p15; August 1959, p13.

48. Glass & Pollins, note 40, p208. A search for the papers of Professor Ruth Glass has proved fruitless.

49. See, e.g.. Spencer, note 45, pp108-134.

50. Trevor Carter, *Shattering Illusions*, Lawrence and Wishart, London 1986, pp67-68.

51. *Daily Worker*, 3 November 1961; *The Guardian*, 2 November 1961, p11; *Daily Telegraph*, *Daily Mirror*, *Evening News*, 3 November 1961. The left-wing weeklies, *Tribune* and *Socialist Leader* both carried advertisements for this meeting but did not bother to report it.

52. *West Indian Gazette*, January 1962, p1. The march took place on 14 January.

53. *West Indian Gazette*, February 1962, p16; *The Guardian*, 15 January 1962, p8.

54. The only remaining information on this meeting is the statement of accounts: expenditure, just over £21, was supposed to equal income, but in a letter to Pearl Connor George Bowrin noted that much of the promised donations had not been paid and Claudia was out-of-pocket.(Schomburg Center, Edric Connor Papers: statements dated 23, 24 and 26 Febrary 1962.)

55. The people present at the meeting were: Ronald Kunene (CAO); Ronald Armour (West Indian Students' Union); Pearl Connor (People's National Movement, Trinidad); M.D. Stanley, Messrs. Connel, Arnold and Quaile

of the UKCC (organisation not identified); Clem Byfield (W.I. Standing Conference); Claudia Jones (*West Indian Gazette*); Jan Carew (British Guiana Freedom Association. (*Ibid*: Afro-Asian-Caribbean Conference Minutes of Meeting 18 January 1962 held at the West Indian Students' Union.)

56. Hull University Archives: DCL/93/8: Letter headed AFRO-ASIAN-CARIBBEAN CONFERENCE, 31 January 1962, addressed to 'Dear brother', and signed by Claudia 'for the Secretariat'. The letter also asked recipients 'to give fraternal financial assistance'.

57. *West Indian Gazette*, February 1962, p6; *The Guardian*, 14 February 1962, p1. The Labour government did not repeal the Act. See also Edward Scobie, *Black Britannia*, Chicago: Johnson Publishing Co. 1972, pp253-256 and Spencer, note 45.

58. The West Indian Federation was brought into being in 1958, after protracted discussion between the politicans of ten West Indian territories and the British government. The people were not consulted. The terms of the Federation were vague, and seemed to promise little immediate benefit or truly representative government, as the Senate's members were to be nominated and the British Governor General held what amounted to power to over-ride the Federal parliament's decisions. Morever, it curtailed independent economic activity, which led to the withdrawal of Jamaica and shortly thereafter of Trinidad; both were granted independence in 1962.

59. *West Indian Gazette*, February 1962, p14; Schomburg Center: Edric Connor Papers, Emergency Minutes of the Meeting of the Afro-Asian-Caribbean Secretariat, 11 March 1962; Press Statement issued by the Secretariat on 12 March 1962. Claudia had addressed the federation issue in 'American Imperialism and the British West Indies', *Political Affairs*, April 1958, pp9-18, in which she argued that the new system did not present real advance towards even internal self-government; the demand should be for civil liberties and independence.

60. NMLH: CP/IND/DUTT/06/08.

61. A. Sivanandan, *A Different Hunger*, Pluto Press, London 1982, pp11-12.

62. According to Ranjana Ash, 3 Collingham Gardens belonged to the Shah of Iran, who permitted Kwame Nkrumah to use the building; the CAACO had a 'small room with a desk'. Interview, London, 14 January 1998. This contradicts the reports in *West Africa*, note 29.

63. *The Times*, 14 June 1963, p12.

64. Medgar Evers, the chief representative of the NAACP in Mississippi, was shot dead outside his home in Jackson on 12 June 1963. He was the fourth Black man murdered in Mississippi for attempting to register Black voters. The white juries at two trials could not agree a verdict on Evers's murderer – anti-semite and well-known rabid racist, Byron de la Beckwith. In December 1990, twenty-seven years after the murder, Beckwith was re-indicted. He was found guilty. See Adam Nossiter, *Of Long Memory*,

Addison-Wesley, Reading, Massachusetts 1994.

65. *Daily Worker*, 14 June 1963, p3. Other members of the delegation were Nanraya Datta of the London Majlis, R. Kunene of the ANC and three unnamed West African Students' Union representatives. Ranjana Ash represented the *Indian Forum*. There is also a brief report in *The Times*, 14 June 1963, p12. Jan Carew recalls that he and Claudia organised the delegation and the demonstration outside the embassy. Telephone interview with Jan Carew in Pennsylvania, 6 May 1998. Ricky Cambridge told me that he was also part of the delegation. London, 2 June 1963.

66. The deputation comprised Ricky Cambridge, Raymond Kunene, Evan Gibbon, A.P. Dutta, A. Ginsah, London County Councillor Fred Tonge and Claudia, *West Indian Gazette*, September 1963, p3. Ranjana Ash was still a member of the CPGB, but in dispute with Rajani Palme Dutt, the head of its International Department, over the publication of *Indian Forum*, which he had not authorised.

67. *Daily Worker*, 2 September 1963, p3; there is a photo, but no story in *Kensington News*, 6 September 1963, p1.

68. See also *West Indian Gazette*, September 1963, p16; NMLH: CP/CENT/INT/34/04.

69. Advertisements in the *Tribune*, 21 June 1963, 22 November 1963.

70. *Colonial Freedom News*, December 1959, p15; L.A.D. Woodland to Claudia Jones, 25 November 1959, Hull University Library: NCCL Papers: DCL/93/2. Co-operative organisations, Trades Councils, trade unions, the Labour Party and national and local organisations and Black organisations (including the CPPA and the IRFCC) sent representatives to the conference.

71. Brockway to Claudia, 27 February 1959. The British Caribbean Association was formed in July 1958 under the joint chairmanship of Conservative MP Nigel Fisher and Labour MP Charles Royle. It had another 67 MP members. Claudia attended some of its meetings, perhaps more in her capacity as reporter for the *Gazette* than as a member. A BCA delegation met with the Home Secretary and proposed legislation against racial discrimination, the training of the police and the possibility of the dispersal of Black settlers. Home Secretary Butler refused all, *Kensington News*, 6 March 1959; PRO: CO1031/2824 & 1032/321. (An inter-departmental committee on 'immigrants in the UK' met regularly during this period.) Pansy Jeffrey, a member of the BCA, held very similar views to Brockway about the limitations of the Association. Interview, London, 4 March 1998.

72. MCF et al circular to Dear Friend, 27 June 1959, NMLH: CP/LON/RACE/01/01; the meeting was called by the MCF, the Co-operative Party and three Trades Councils. Unfortunately both the MCF Papers at SOAS and the Fenner Brockway Papers at Cambridge University contain very little on this period – neither mention Claudia or any of her organisations. Letter from S. Plant, Churchill Archives Centre,

Churchill College, Cambridge, 11 December 1997. There are no histories of the MCF; it probably grew out of the British Centre Against Imperialism founded in February 1946 by Fenner Brockway, George Padmore and N. Gangulee. Hakim Adi & Marika Sherwood, *The 1945 Manchester Pan-African Congress Revisited*, New Beacon, London 1995, p48.

73. *Tribune*, 23 October 1959. This is an advertisement for the meeting; I have been unable to find any reports except for *Islington Gazette* 17 November 1959, p1.
74. *The Guardian*, 2 January 1960, p4.
75. See programmes for Concerts in SOAS: MCF Papers, Box 68, ACT 3, 4 & 5.
76. Letter from AAM researcher Christabel Gurney, 22 October 1998.
77. The Anti-Apartheid Movement was formed in 1960; its first meeting place was the basement of Dr David Pitt's surgery at 200 Gower Street, Euston. The CAO had also met there until it moved to Africa Unity House at 3 Collingham Gardens, Kensington. At the symposium at the Institute of Commonwealth Studies, University of London (12 December 1998) on the history of the AAM, I was told by participants that relations with Claudia were problematic because she was a communist.
78. *The Guardian*, 16 April 1964, p10; AAM *Members Bulletin* 4, April 1964. There is nothing in the Anti-Apartheid Movement Papers on this fast or on Claudia and her organisations, letter from A. Hill, Rhodes House Library, Oxford, 10 December 1997.
79. AAM *Members Bulletin*, 2 March 1964 & 3 April 1964. Colin Prescod, listed as participating in the 'dramatisation', has vague memories of reading accounts of torture. Telephone discussion, 7 December 1997. Andrew Faulds remembers the evening as 'purely readings: there was a good audience and I thought it was a very successful "do"... A goodly number of actors and performers were involved in all sorts of opposition to the South Africa regime'. Letter from Andrew Faulds, 18 December 1997. Edric Connor, Andrew Salkey and Jan Carew had also participated in vigils outside South Africa House, AAM *Members Bulletin*, 1 February 1964. The Executive Committee of the AAM agreed at its meeting of 27 April 1964 to convey its appreciation to all who had participated. (My thanks to Christabel Gurney for sending this.)
80. Interviews with Taja Sahota, Leamington Spa, 10 March 1998. Mr Sahota believes that Claudia travelled to other cities to attempt to form such a political party but that her efforts were unsuccessful as enthusiasm waned as soon as she left town. Claudia had also stayed the night with the Sahotas when she went to Stratford-on-Avon to see Paul Robeson play Othello.
81. Interview with Avtar Jouhl, Birmingham, 21 January 1998.
82. *West Indian Gazette*, December 1961 & January 1962, p5; advertisement in *West Africa*, 2 December 1961, p1335. The guest of honour was listed as Kwesi Armah, the newly appointed High Commissioner for Ghana.

83. *West Indian Gazette*, December 1963, pp3, 5. The hurricane hit Haiti Cuba and Trinidad, but was especially devastating in Tobago. According to Lyn Jones, who was the Hurricane Committee's treasurer, Amy Ashwood Garvey was also involved and the Committee met at Pearl Prescod's house. Telephone interview, London, 27 May 1998.

84. *West Indian Gazette*, March 1964, p11.

85. *West Indian Gazette*, August-September 1964, p3.

86. Letter from Christine Woodland, Archivist, Modern Record Centre (MRC), 18 January 1998. Ms Woodland had approached Mr Jenkins on my behalf as his papers are currently being catalogued at the MRC.

87. Letter from Eric Hobsbawm, 13 January 1998.

88. Claudia to Manchanda, 21 August 1962 and 31 August 1962. I looked at *Soviet Woman* from June 1962 to December 1963.

89. There is a photo of Henry Winston and Claudia surrounded by Soviet comrades taken in Moscow in the *Gazette*, December 1962, p5. Henry Winston, a member of the CPUSA's National Committee, was imprisoned in 1956 as part of the witchhunts. The doctors in prison ignored his piercing headaches until legal representations permitted a medical examination – at Winston's expense – by private doctors. He was immediately operated for the removal of a brain tumour. His life was saved but the long delay resulted in permanent blindness. He was returned to prison and not released until June 1961. He spent the period September 1961 to February 1964 in the USSR and on speaking tours in Eastern Europe. See Nikolai Mostovets, *Henry Winston*, Moscow: Progress Publishers 1983.

90. Betty Reid, telephone interview, London, 14 July 1997.

91. Telephone interview with Sam Russell, 4 August 1997. 'She was daggers drawn with the CP. If you disagreed with her, she certainly let you know clearly', Mr Russell commented. Neither Mr Denis Ogden, the *Daily Worker*'s Moscow correspondent from 1959 to April 1962, nor Colin Williams, correspondent from 1969, remember anything about Claudia Jones. Peter Tempest, correspondent from 1961 to 1969 died some years ago.

92. 'Why 6 Negro Leaders Defend Claudia Jones', cutting dated 25 February 1952, probably from the US *Daily Worker*, Schomburg Center: Civil Rights Congress Papers, Sc Micro R 7016, Pt.V, reel 6, frame 00585.

93. 'Soviet Women's Sympathy', *West Indian Gazette*, February 1965, p4.

94. *Soviet Woman* 6, 1963; p7; 1963, 7, p44.

95. An undated letter to Zunaidia Federova on Hotel Ukraina letterhead indicates that Pearl Thomas from Jamaica and Jean Pierson of British Guiana were stuck in London, awaiting their visas. Claudia understood from Essie Robeson in London that the Soviet Embassy was waiting for a cable from the Soviet Women's Committee. She asked Ms Federova: could this possibly be sent urgently?

96. There is nothing about this in the Bernal Peace Collection at Marx Memorial House or at the Commonwealth Collection at the University of Bradford. Letter from Isabelle Guillou, 20 May 1998.

97. The report in *The Japan Times*, 1 August 1964, p1, only lists 'Trinidad' as a member of the Drafting Committee. (I must thank my son Craig Sherwood for sending me photocopies of this newspaper from Tokyo.)

98. Draft of article by Claudia Jones, 7 August, written in Hiroshima on International Hotel Kyoto letterhead (Langford Collection). Much of this is printed in the *West Indian Gazette*, Aug/Sept 1964. The Japan Council Against Atomic & Hydrogen Bombs sent Manchanda a tape recording of Claudia's speech in Tokyo, but this has not survived. Manchanda to Y. Yoshida, 22 February 1965.

99. *The Japan Times*, 31 July 1964, p1.

100. Undated draft report in Langford Collection. To point (2) Claudia added: 'I believe the explosion by the People's Republic of China of its atomic bomb strengthens the cause of peace ... which ... according to China ... dashed the daydream of the US to reduce the Chinese people to slaves of nuclear overlords and is shaking US nuclear monopoly to its very foundation,' pp7-8. This is an interesting perspective, perhaps especially in the light of India's tests of atomic weapons in May 1998.

101. Untitled draft report, nd., Langford Collection.

102. Chinese newspaper in Langford Collection.

103. Telephone interview with Eric Gordon, who was in China at the time, London, 8 May 1998.

104. Bandung is the site in Indonesia of the first Afro-Asian Conference held in 1956; it is usually referred to as the Bandung Conference.

The West Indian Gazette

Donald Hinds

The *West Indian Gazette* (WIG), like a child from the insalubrious part of town, was born into a struggle and its life was destined to be short, tortuous, and somewhat bruising. The *Gazette* spent the first five of its seven years of its existence in two crowded, chaotic and untidy rooms above Theo Campbell's record shop at 250 Brixton Road, south west London. It was indeed a child of the slums; it was not born in Brixton and its parentage was uncertain. Forty years on, most of those who presided at its birth are dead.

There has always been the idea of a commercial paper for Black colonial citizens in the United Kingdom. Nearly a decade and a half after the end of the Second World War, and with the arrival of thousands of colonial citizens settling in Britain, it was decided that the time was right to launch a newspaper.

A watershed year

Nineteen fifty-seven was a watershed year for non-white members of the Empire living in the United Kingdom. It was the year when Britain and its Caribbean colonies began the experiment of a West Indian Federation, with its capital in Trinidad. It was also the year when the West African colony of the Gold Coast gained political independence and became Ghana. The year was also the tenth anniversary of the independence of India and the founding of Pakistan. Far away in the Deep South of the United States of America, the twenty-eight year old Martin Luther King was asserting that he was demanding for Black Americans constitutional rights with dignity. These times of racial divisions formed the context for all the agony and bitterness which was to follow later.

In Britain, the only network among the thousands of non-white settlers would have been through links between families and friends. When Black people made the news it was only in a sensational way. These occasions were always taken as proof by the racially prejudiced of the necessity to purge the nation of Black immigrants. In the 1950s media, the racial origin of non-whites followed their names as inevitably as the measurements of a film star's bust, waist and hips followed her name. So the white man's dream was 'blonde 36, 24, 36' and his nightmare was 'Clinton Jones, Black from Jamaica'.

A newspaper supporting non-white groups would provide a network to counter such attitudes. *Caribbean News*, published by the Caribbean Labour Congress since the mid-1950s, was thought not to be sufficiently popular. Discussions on founding the *West Indian Gazette* originally took place in 1957. The West Indian Workers and Students Association, established at this time, set up an Editorial Committee to publish a paper, probably very late in 1957 or early 1958. Claudia was a member of this committee. She was a trained journalist, and she had been actively engaged in working for improvement in Black people's conditions in the United States before she was expelled. The Committee could not fail to have been anything less than impressed by her credentials.

The *Gazette* is born

The *West Indian Gazette* burst into life, in Claudia's often repeated words 'as a one leaf flyer in March 1958'. A letter written to Claudia by the Ministry of Labour and National Service shows clearly that this government department had received from Claudia a letter dated 31 March, 'with which you enclosed a sample flyer for your new periodical West Indian Gazette ...' These might have been handbills. Jimmy Fairweather, who was the *Gazette*'s first advertising manager, and remained so until the end of 1963, remembers having seen this single leaf flyer – of the type used by the *WIG* until 1960. This flyer announced the arrival of the people's paper with a cross-section of news, and the purpose of its existence.

Could there have been a 'sample paper'; or was it to the first edition that a Mr Jameson G. Flocker, from Bow, east London, responded? We do not have his letter; Claudia's reply dated March 1958 was:

> Your prompt response to our sample paper was an inspiration to our efforts. It was only after re-reading did I realise that it was probably your daughter 13 year-old Adella, who wrote us that wonderful letter,

already acknowledged. I shall be most happy to hear from you as to how you made out with the Forerunners function yesterday evening. Also it is possible that you may be able to be a distributor of our paper in East London? Won't you write and let me know? I shall as well when I get your letter call you. It may be possible to arrange a meeting among *Gazette* readers which I or one of our staff members or members of our organisation West Indian Workers and Students Organisation could come and speak, meeting our readers directly. Again thanking you. I am enclosing a copy of a letter which shows we are seeking advertising. Since our paper was nearly sold out reaching 25,000 West Indians in all parts of London, it may be possible to interest advertisers in East London. If you will send the paper a list of possible names and addresses of advertisers, we would be glad to circularise them. And if you know of any maybe you could approach them directly.[1]

The income from advertising was clearly crucial. Claudia took this up in a letter dated 23 March to S.G. King (the future Mayor of the London Borough of Southwark):

As we agreed in our talk at the Federation Dance last evening, I am forwarding the names and addresses of the firms we have written to with a promise to send representative to collect the advertising.

As you will note, one is in North London and the others in Stockwell and Clapham. I'm afraid the other Peckham ones, Tony may be working on, and I don't wish to duplicate. But in any event, I'm sure you'll be resourceful by making direct approaches to people. Accordingly, I am sending you some letters which you might leave with, or mail to possible advertisers. If there is a local Peckham paper, will [you] mail same to me, [so that] we can circularise its advertisers. Do you think? Again, let me express my pleasure in meeting and congratulating you on your hard work. Let me know how you're making out?

Wishing you all the best...

The early days of the *Gazette*

There is no complete list of the Editorial Committee. If minutes were kept of their meetings, they have been lost. That there were disagreements at these meetings is indicated by the few remaining papers in the Langford Collection. There is evidence enough of the seriousness of these disagreements in a letter from Clyde Crevelle, secretary of the West Indian Workers and Students Association, dated 14 May 1958, when the *Gazette* was barely two months old. This letter, probably intended for distribution among all the Committee, gives the clearest insight into the working of the early days of the *WIG*. Two members of the Committee, law students 'Murry and Sylvia' had offered to withdraw (for unknown reasons). Crevelle tried to persuade them to stay:

> I do not think that this matter should end like that, and a solution must be found.
>
> I personally do not feel happy about how things have been going in the Organisation, and on the paper. You may have observed that we seem to work at an emergency all the time. And that is bad. The *Gazette* is not yet what we would like to see it, and that may be the position for a number of issues to come. This however, need not happen if the Editorial Board should mould itself into a smooth, efficient machinery. To accomplish this is not an easy task. There will be disagreements, there will be high handed measures which must be dealt with, there will be hoarding of responsibilities which cannot be tolerated.
>
> The Executive Committee has appointed ... Claudia to be the convener of the Editorial Committee. She was charged with exploring the possibilities of producing a paper ... Claudia made a report ... and it was decided that a flyer would be issued. After this was done and the work was prepared for the issue of the paper, Claudia presented another report on the *Gazette* in which the Editorial Board recommended that she be the Editor. This was agreed upon.
>
> The EC's attitude is that the Editorial Board should run things. By that we mean that decisions should be taken collectively, and in a democratic manner ... The EC's representative who in this case is also the Editor, is there to see that the Organisation's policy is reflected in the paper. What I am trying to say in all this is that all members on the Editorial Board should exert the same rights. The only time there would be intervention from the EC is when there is a failure of agreement. The Editor's role on a journal is never quite clear. The EC hopes that as time goes by the Editorial Board would lay down some standing orders on this.
>
> I know that your interest in the Organisation was primarily in the Newspaper. I know that the paper meant much to you. You have a stake in it as much as anyone else and leaving it has really caused me some displeasure. Now I am not saying that you are wrong. What I am saying is that you should come back to the Editorial Board and have the matter raised and an understanding arrived at. I am therefore asking you and Sylvia to attend the next meeting of the Editorial Board, at which I hope

to be present and to take part in the discussions. I shall also try to get George Bowrin, the Chairman to attend on this occasion.

Claudia will send out motives [notices] to the next Board meeting.

I do hope that you are both doing fine.[2]

While this civil war wage raging an enemy of both sides struck. The Ku Klux Klan (KKK), an avowedly anti-Communist and anti-Semitic organisation, took up the cudgels for racial primacy. The Klan wrote to 'The Editor of the West Indian Gazette':

My Dear Mr. B. Ape,

Kindly post two copies of your paper to the above address every month until order to cease. Possibly you are wondering why we have so-far failed to pay attention to your audacity in setting up this filthy hack-trash of a paper? Pray good Sir, We The Aryan Knights miss nothing, close attention has been paid to every issue of this rag, and I do sincerely assure you, the information gleaned has proven of great value to the Klan. May we take this opportunity to wish your **** paper every success whilst you are able to continue printing it.

Aryan Regards,

A. Whiteman[3]

To attempt to ensure that no more copies *were* printed, the Klan trashed the *Gazette's* office.[4]

The Klan letter and the attack on the office of the *Gazette* brought some sympathetic mail. For example, Alistair Graham (of whom nothing is known) wrote to Claudia that he was:

shocked to hear of the abusive letter ... It seems that the forces of racial hatred and fascism are rearing their heads again ... The fact that you have been a target for abuse shows that you are doing good work ... Have you seen the slime sheet *Black & White News?*... This is such a poisonous paper, I am seriously wondering whether a copy shouldn't be sent to some MPs to see if it can't be suppressed.

He concluded by asking whether he could call on Claudia when he was next in London.

There was an AGM on 29 June 1958. This is puzzling since neither the *Gazette* nor the West Indian Workers and Students Association had been operating for a year.[5] There is little doubt that a cataclysmic row took place between May and July 1958. Perhaps it raged throughout June, despite the old Caribbean saying that 'June was too soon for a

Ride with the Aryan Knights
KU KLUX KLAN OF BRITAIN

We are peaceful, lawabiding and tolerant.
Secrecy is our defence against those who desire
to mongrelize our proud heritage.

Communism Enslaves, Jewish Usurers Invented it.
England Awake, Keep Britain Pure and White.
Put the Traitors to the Sake.

Anti-Communist : *Anti-Semitic*

KING KLEAGLE, KLAVERN NO. 1, PROVINCE OF LONDINIUM, IMPERIAL REALM OF ALBION,
ARYAN KNIGHTS KU KLUX KLAN OF GREAT BRITAIN.
C/o Box 5062, Waco, Texas, U.S.A.

The Editor,
'West Indian Gazette
250, Brixton Road,
London.S.W.9.
August.18-58.

My Dear Mr B. Ape,

Kindly post two copies of your paper to the above addressevery month
until ordered to cease.

Possibly you are wondering why we have so-far failed to pay
attention to your audacity in setting up this filthy hack-trash
of a paper?, . Pray good Sir, We, The Aryan Knights miss nothing,
close attention has been paid to every issue of this rag, and I do
sincerely assure you, the information gleamed has proven of great
value to the Klan.

May we take this opportunity to wish your ------paper every
success whilst you are able to continue printing it.

Aryan Regards,
A,Whiteman.

Copy of original letter sent to the *Gazette* office. From Ruth Glass 1960,
see note 3.

hurricane'. Metaphorically, one did rage and it wreaked havoc among the members of the West Indian Workers and Students Association. The absence of minutes heightens the imagination and scope for conjecture. There are those who say that the Association had been set up by a disgruntled group from the Caribbean Labour Congress, which had broken away and taken the idea of the *West Indian Gazette* with them. This led to a struggle for power in the break-away organisation.[6] The tireless Secretary on 2 July sent a stern memorandum to Claudia, headed *Committee of Investigation in the affairs of the West Indian Gazette, official paper of the West Indian Workers and Students Association.*

> As you aware no doubt aware of the decision of the AGM on Sunday 29th last re the *West Indian Gazette*. I have been instructed by the above committee to obtain from you the cash book receipts and other statements of accounts of the newspaper. Bearing in mind the understanding you gave at the said meeting, I expect you would arrange to deliver these documents as quickly as possible in order to facilitate the speeding up of our work.

From this date the correspondence becomes somewhat rancorous. In response to Crevelle's letter, Claudia took legal advice, asking John Morris of Wilkes & Co., who had chambers above the office of the *Gazette* at 250 Brixton Road, to deal with the matter. Morris concluded that the Association had no claim to the documents. In reply, Crevelle stated that:

> This newspaper is owned by the West Indian Workers and Students Association ... I may inform you that she [Mrs Jones] made a report to the Annual General Meeting of the Association on 29th June suggesting that a limited company be formed to take over the newspaper and saying that she had already consulted Solicitors (presumably your good selves). It was pointed out that she had no right to take such a step without authority by many members and none had been given and in view of the disquiet expressed a resolution was carried by 36 to 3 to set up a Commission to investigate Mrs Jones' behaviour, and it was in consequence of that resolution that I wrote to her for access to the relevant documents.

Morris responded that he 'cannot agree that Miss Jones is not the owner of the *Gazette* ... Should you still maintain that our client is not the owner of the above, you are at liberty to take any action you ... may deem fit.' Claudia would not be handing over any property or documents. Unfortunately, no further correspondence has been preserved, but Claudia was left in undoubted command of the *West Indian Gazette*.

Sam King recalls the publication of the first issue by the Coloured People's Publishing Company, established by Claudia as owners of the *Gazette*:

> Our first print run was somewhere in the order of ten thousand. I took one thousand and distributed them all over the country. You see I still had my RAF contacts and we were still in touch. I accounted for nine hundred and ninety-five copies. I was immediately made Circulation Manager. That was typically Claudia. She was a doer and she recognised other people's efforts.

Life at the Gazette

The office of the newspaper was always the focal point of many activities. It was truly the cultural centre for Blacks in Britain. It was a place alight with optimism for both the individual and the community as a whole. The *Gazette* community was unique. It attracted a far broader cross-section of Black personalities than any of the High Commissions, and the atmosphere was less formal. Which other organisation had the status to attract international personalities like Paul Robeson and his wife Essie; the actor William Marshall; politicians of the calibre of Norman Manley, Carl La Corbiniere, Phillys Alfrey, David Pitt, Fenner Brockway, Cheddi Jagan; writers like George Lamming, Jan Carew, Andrew Salkey, Namba Roy, Sam Selvon, and John La Rose? All of these at one time or the other visited the *Gazette*'s office and others remained in close contact, giving unstintingly of their time. No Black newspaper since has had such an alliance.

Claudia loved and understood people, more than she did the balance sheet. She was completely at her most superb at the microphone telling the audience just what they wanted to hear and what they should hear and sometimes they were not the same; she should be seen in her surgery, counselling, or writing letters; as in one written to a Mr Sinclair of Burton Road, SW9 on 5 February 1959:

> Miss Thomas from the National Council for Civil Liberties gave me an urgent call asking that you immediately call her at home tonight. Please call me to let me know that you have taken care of it.
>
> The problem is this; we have a campaign on. Lawyers have been assigned to the case by the National Council for Civil Liberties and they are at a loss not having heard from you, and your friends. Miss Thomas

asked me to emphasise to you the importance of your being present
otherwise the very fate of the hearing may be meaningless.

Please call immediately. If there is any question about your, and your
friend taking off next Monday, 16th February, we should plan a community affair to raise the funds ... PLEASE LET ME HEAR FROM YOU
EITHER TONIGHT or in the office tomorrow a.m ...

Whatever the problem was, it was being addressed. Something the
High Commissions were unable to do. The Black community had
someone to whom they could bring their concerns. Quite often the
problem was solved by having someone to listen to it. After all this was
the whole purpose for the founding of the *Gazette*:

West Indians in Britain form a community with its own special wants
and problems which our own paper alone would allow us to meet ...
West Indians wanted an organisation to represent their interests ... [and]
welcome efforts to unite and to further British-West Indian unity...[7]

Staffing problems

The *Gazette* never could afford to take on paid staff. In the summer of
1958, Theo Campbell introduced Donald Hinds to Claudia. By the
autumn Hinds' title and job description, according to the *Gazette*'s
mast-head, was that of City Reporter – in American usage he was a
roving news reporter. Early in 1959, Ken Kelly, a young intellectual
from Trinidad who wrote crystal clear prose, and like Hinds was busily
writing his first novel, joined the *Gazette* and was designated Staff
Feature Writer. Neither Hinds nor Kelly was paid. Outside of their
commitments to the *Gazette*, Kelly worked as a typist for a news
agency and Hinds as a London Transport bus conductor. The fact that
the *Gazette* could not pay salaries or expenses meant that its writers
had to look elsewhere if their rents were to be paid. But no one could
avoid Claudia's magnetic personality, and everybody had a
Micawberish attitude to the *Gazette*. This was in a large part due to the
numerous letters of support which poured in from well-wishers, and
especially from the growing Black community which hailed the
Gazette as the people's paper.

Hinds was probably the only person to have been issued a *Gazette*
press pass. He was also to become the first *Gazette* reporter to be sent
abroad on a story. In the summer of 1959 he was sent to Vienna to
cover the Seventh World Conference of Youths and Students. This was,

to all intents and purposes, a communist festival sponsored by the Soviet Union. Was it Claudia's contribution to the young Jamaican's education or was it truly a journalistic assignment? It was probably intended to be both.

In the same year Hinds recalls going to the *Gazette*'s office still wearing the trousers of his bus conductor's uniform. Minutes later he found himself, still in his conductor's trousers, with Claudia in a taxi heading for Westminster. The bewildered young Jamaican was within half an hour climbing the plush red carpet of Lancaster House to the Nigerian Resume Independence Conference.[8] Dazed by the enormity of it all, he can still recall, some forty years after the event, a stinging rebuke delivered by Chief Awolowo to a British official who had mentioned Nigeria's poverty: 'Poverty is not peculiar to Nigeria'.

The *Gazette* had the support of a group of young women, some still in their teens, among them: Della McKenzie; Diana Grant-Somers; Brenda Tigh; Olive Chen and Carmen Spencer. The turnover of willing helpers was high as their personal circumstances did not allow them to commit themselves on a voluntary basis for a long period. There were times when there were not enough helpers to keep the office running.

Hinds was told he would be the first paid member of the *Gazette*'s staff when the paper could afford it. But it never could, and only three names from the original team of 1958 remained on the mast-head of the *Gazette* by the time of the paper's demise in the summer of 1965: Jones, Manchanda and Hinds. The former was the founder, Manu was Managing Director and Editor, and Hinds was still in post as City Reporter.

Financial problems

A circulation of 50,000 among a population of a quarter of a million and growing was not impossible, but the *Gazette* never achieved it. The circulation peaked at 30,000 during the winter of 1958, but by early 1959 that figure had fallen drastically. Not even the murder of Kelso Cochrane in May 1959 had much effect, and the circulation settled back at 10,000.

The financial situation seemed insoluble. For example, the paper's printers presented a bill of one hundred and twenty-two pounds ten shillings for the 1958 Christmas edition of the *WIG*, with a note at the bottom of the page stating that the 'November account must be cleared, before a start can be made on December issue'. On another occasion, Ken Kelly recalls having gone to collect the paper from the printers, only to be turned away because an outstanding bill had not been settled. In its relatively short life the *Gazette* had many printers!

By 1959 Manchanda, then the *Gazette*'s Business Manager, complained that the Coloured People's Publishing House was heavily in debt and was getting more and more so. On 3 March 1959 he wrote a letter to Claudia which he 'delivered personally by hand':

> With due respects I wish to bring to your kind notice the following for your information:
>
> Despite my repeated requests to you that we should establish the functioning of the West Indian Gazette as well as the Coloured People's Publishing House Ltd on proper business lines and normal company methods, you have obstinately insisted onto carry on in a very chaotic, most inefficient, uneconomic, unsystematic and un-business like working both of the West Indian Gazette and the Coloured People's Publishing House Ltd; with the result the company is under heavier debt every day.
>
> In view of the need of a paper like the West Indian Gazette, it has had a most encouraging response, and no body would deny the hard work you have put in. But just hard work is not enough nor are the good intentions. Many a company or public organisation has come to naught for lack of proper business methods, or more concretely, financial methods of working.
>
> In view of the above facts and your insistence to not to share any responsibility in either running of the *Gazette* or the company, you left me no choice but to disassociate with the both. Hence I am getting in touch with the solicitors so that the necessary steps can be taken in this regard.
>
> Wishing the best of luck
> I remain yours faithfully.

Despite this threat, Manu remained with the paper. According to Donald Hinds,

> The cost of putting out the paper was high and always increasing. Its advertisers were overwhelmingly the small businessman who wanted the West Indian trade. Some of these were West Indians launching out into business. Advertising revenue was not always paid, at least not regularly. The agents who sold the papers were never prompt in returning their receipts. This meant that the paper was always hard up ...[9]

Undoubtedly Claudia understood the economics of running a newspaper. She, like most of those who worked under her, often wished that the burden of the *Gazette*'s chaotic finances could be lifted from her shoulders, for it was in the hurly-burly and turmoil of the politics, the demands for social progress and dignity, stemming the haemorrhage from the wounds caused by racial hatred, that she was at her best.

There is an undated memorandum written by Claudia, which, to judge by the style of the letterhead, might date from late 1958. Whatever the date, the anxieties of running the *West Indian Gazette* remained constant throughout the seven years of its existence.

The present status of the *WIG* may be summarised as (1) having established the need for a paper for Afro-Asian-West Indians in the UK with emphasis mainly on the West Indians, who are the most numerous of the coloured population in Britain (2) having contributed to developing a sense of identification with the struggles of colonial and ex-colonial peoples everywhere for peace and freedom (3) showing the relationship of the coloured people to their allies who fight for similar aims of peace freedom and equality and self determination for culturally oppressed peoples. However, the problem of sustaining a paper of this kind with a progressive policy in lieu of the level of political and social consciousness and the whole mentality of newly arrived migrants – pre-occupied with their own problems of settling in to the community – presents numerous problems re the sustaining of a paper of this kind affecting its growth and expansion.

These problems are manifold: (1) they are the question of regular circulation of the message of the *WIG* to a wide cross section of West Indians. This question is fully complicated in lieu of a lack of organisation among West Indians. The problems of insularity and lack of a unity perspective; the question of the lack of support; the transient nature of the population etc. They also include (2) the problem of the high cost of production of newspapers of this kind and the almost sole reliance for financing of such a journal on advertising revenue. The question of the policy of the paper – a people's paper and the reliance for support among the migrants themselves, the business interests whose market is largely among West Indians now resident in England.

The failure to establish a working team that takes responsibility for every aspect of the paper's growth, circulation and editorial work is one of the chief weaknesses to date. This is not to say that attempts have not been made to form a core of persons who basically hold common advanced views about the need for such a paper – with such a policy; secondly the fact of the turn over of the teams of people who have worked in the past has been due to (1) attitudes which hold that they can only work on the basis of immediate remuneration materially; (2) that they urge compromise in the paper's policy and (3) that those who have shown understanding and loyalty and sacrifice to a degree soon reach the glut facing individual and personal ...

Here the memorandum suddenly ends. Since it had run to the end of the page, it is a fair assumption that the second page has not been preserved. Claudia was always explaining the *Gazette* to those who would listen. Among her papers can be found three lengthy memoranda on the role of the paper and its commitment to the Black community. Besides the above, there was one written sometime in 1962, and the third written shortly before her death in 1964 for the American journal, *Freedomways*.

When Claudia wrote that 'the failure to establish a working team that takes responsibility for every aspect of the paper's growth, circulation and editorial work is one of the chief weaknesses to date', this was not a condemnation but a cry for help. Claudia was a woman in her mid-forties, but with a history of debilitating illnesses, of tuberculosis, resulting in one good lung and a heart condition. Running the *Gazette* was not an easy task. It was not the time of expanding Black businesses. The Black entrepreneurs of the time were mainly to be found in hairdressing and very occasionally in corner shops in rundown areas. So although in her 1962 memorandum she was to state that the *Gazette* attracted five pounds of advertising in its first issue and was attracting three hundred pounds per month four years later, it was merely editorial licence employed to talk up business.

In 1962 while Claudia was in Moscow, the *Gazette* was left in the care of its General Manager, Manchanda. While the *Gazette*'s supporters had always allowed themselves to be charmed by Claudia and rarely questioned her motives, they did not respond readily to the didactic Marxism of Manchanda. Some say that it was because he was an Asian, but by then the *Gazette* had moved on to take the sub-title *And Afro-Asian-Caribbean News*. The international out look of the paper made it impossible to pander to petty racism. However Manchanda, who had frequently criticised what he termed Claudia's chaotic style, was now able to review the situation from the Editor's chair. He wrote to Claudia on 30 October:

> Thanks for your letter of the 25th instant, and the so-called collective discussion, or is it 'collective criticism'. In fact, it is not collective yet as your comments are one person's comments hence one can't call them collective, unless you are the collective.

However, this letter is not an attempt to reply to your letter. This is only to give you some news of the happenings here.

First Shock – Theo Campbell has been quietly or rather surreptitiously establishing relations with the *West Indian Observer* ... this paper has been printed by fascists CPU press (sic). These people brought out their *Daily News* during the newspaper strike and later to break the Postmen's strike they used to run vans for delivery of mail ... When Theo was warned about it he said he did not care for trade unions. The address of this paper is now 250 Brixton Road, SW9 – very significant. He even dispatches this rag from here now. Our readers will be mistaking it to be our paper... Of course I have disclaimed any connection with it. Theo's name is still on our mast head as Sports Editor, will you remove it on your return? ...

Now shock (no.2?) David Miller [sic] of Carmen's refused to sell our paper because of our support for Nkrumah, Cheddi and Castro, this he thinks is supporting the 'Reds'. However, I wrote to Carmen, she has not replied. David wrote: 'They believe in capitalism and they are proud of it'... More when you return.[10]

Re: November issue. As I told you on the telephone, I am doing a special feature on BG. Incidentally, Guyana is the new name they have chosen for their country. *Thunder* has been using it for quite a few months. I got some material from Jane ... Donald comes to the office some time, but he is too busy with his family...[11]

Gazette activities

It is perhaps somewhat misleading to separate the *Gazette*'s social from its political activities, as the 'social' always had a political purpose.

Social events

There were many distinguished visitors to the *Gazette* or to events organised by it. In September 1959 the *Gazette* reported an evening with the Robesons. Under a huge banner with the legend *THE PEOPLE*, the photograph shows a smiling Claudia Jones next to Paul Robeson.

Robeson's speech was reported in full in the *Gazette*. To many it was enough that the great Robeson was present; the speech was a bonus:

> My warmest greetings to you, my brothers and sisters of Africa, of the West Indies, of Asia and of Great Britain. A very, very warm hello. We are surely happy to be with you.

It is not by chance that we come here under the auspices of the *West Indian Gazette*. This has become one of my favourite newspapers as I am sure it is of yours – a paper courageous, deeply human, concerned with a decent life for us all – Black, Brown, White, and Yellow; a paper calling upon us all to realise that a new day has come, that the dawn rises on a glorious chapter of human history; a time when we all can and must be free ... This very fact, realisable future, demands the understanding, sympathy and unceasing labour of us all, throws upon us tremendous responsibilities. Let us not fail ourselves, our children and generations yet to come ... How proud we must always be of our mothers and sisters, newly-born Harriet Tubmans and Sojourner Truths, struggling without stint without sparing any sacrifice ... I am proud to be on this platform by the side of a dear, dear friend Claudia Jones...[12]

The *Gazette*'s own City Reporter added:

Hundreds of West Indians, Asians and other friends will long remember the two unique evenings [the other was at St Pancras Town Hall] in which the *WIG* paid tribute to the Robesons, but we of the *WIG* staff feel it is the Robesons who did honour to *WIG*, by their presence at our receptions.

The queue of nearly 1000 people who could not get in due to a sell-out of seats at Lambeth was an example. But most important, was the feeling of love, respect and admiration displayed by those who met Paul and Eslanda Robeson: they shook and felt their hands and heard Paul's great voice raised in speech and songs ... All songs were against oppression.

We honour them among other reasons, because of their great courage, but their honour to us imbues us with greater determination to give them – not only our continued love and respect – but our faith that that for which they have dedicated their lives comes to pass – he fights – we may term it for human dignity.

In response to the 1958 'disturbances' the *Gazette* began to organise carnivals, modelled on the annual event in Trinidad. The first, held in February 1959, was a great success.[13] Apart from organising these and giving receptions, the *Gazette* produced its own talent contests. While these were open to all races, their prime purpose was to present West Indian talent to the public, which at that time could not see Caribbean people as anything other than hewers of wood and drawers of water. The *Gazette*'s talent contests and carnivals attracted many personalities from the world of British show business who either acted as judges or gave guest appearances. Among the best known were Cleo

Claudia with, from left to right, Paul Robeson, Amy Ashwood Garvey, Eslanda Robeson, the Mayoress and Mayor Calderman. *Estate of A. Manchanda. Photographer unknown.*

Laine and Johnny Dankworth, Nadia Cattouse, Corinne Skinner, The Mighty Sparrow, Edric Connor and Pearl Prescod.

Philanthropic causes

When natural disasters struck, such as Hurricane Flora in October 1963, the *Gazette* was quick to put on a benefit concert, selling tickets at five shillings. These all-star variety concerts boasted the usual show business folks who gave of their time again and again. 'Because Claudia asked ... No one said "no" to Claudia. There were times when I was not really asked, but told', stated Nadia Cattouse, the actress and singer from British Honduras (Belize). The concert was under the patronage of Sir Learie Constantine.[14] The benefit Concert Committee members included Nadia Cattouse, Claudia Jones and C.L.R. James and the sponsors were Edric Connor, Pearl Connor, George Lamming, Dr David Pitt, Andrew Salkey, Sam Selvon and The Rev Dr Donald Soper. The programme, which was sold for one shilling and six pence, had a tear-off section with the following instruction: 'If you can see this double ... then maybe ... You will be the lucky winner of the case of RUM! Tear off this bottom part of the Raffle ticket and place it in the drum in the Front Hall'. The *Gazette* always reflected the real personality of the West Indian, that seriousness should not always succeed by suppressing happiness.

Political events

According to Jimmy Fairweather, who was advertising manager of the *Gazette* soon after its founding and for the next five years, Claudia:

> was at her best when there was trouble! To see her in action during the Notting Hill riots was to be inspired. No one knew just how many committees she was on, how many meetings she spoke at, how many delegations she led or was on. Race hatred, and the menace which followed in its wake, generating fear, was something that Claudia had had to deal with in the United States. Her presence, her speeches were powerful and demanding yet without rancour. Her tone was conciliatory and with dignity. Her anger, no, her anguish, I think is the better word, was dignity personified.

So when racial disturbances flared up in the summer of 1958, there was a Black community leader, in Claudia Jones, and a newspaper of quality, in the *West Indian Gazette*. Racial tension had been continuous. It was there when Blacks joined a queue; when they boarded a bus and sat next to a white person; the verbal insults were as customary as 'good morning, good evening, and thank you very much'. Blacks worried about whether the shopkeeper would serve them, or pretended they were not there. Blacks could be invisible. On other occasions they were depicted as being the country's worst nightmare: they were taking all the houses, all the jobs, and at the same time they were crowding into single rooms until the buildings were ready to burst at their seams. Blacks did not have jobs and were burdens grafted onto the Welfare State and yet they were depriving whites of job opportunities at the same time.

Claudia repeatedly pointed out that the problem in Britain was that no one was ready to stand out and declare him or herself as racist. This was different to the situation in America where a Dixiecrat would openly prophesy that 'segregation would be maintained here down in Dixie'. But British groups insisted that they were not prejudiced, but that they thought that it would be better if Blacks were repatriated and something was then done by the British Government to help these colonies.

The newspapers in their handling of the 'disturbances' not only reflected the bigotry of their leadership, but gave voice only to the 'official' explanations of events. For example, the *News Chronicle* declared that it was all the doings of white hooligans and West Indian criminals. *The Manchester Guardian* on 26 August 1958 reported the Chief Constable of Nottingham as having said: 'The attacks made by "teddy boys" in the past fourteen days were responsible for Saturday night's outbursts. The coloured community, he said, apart from a few isolated cases, was very well behaved.' Donald Hinds, wrote in 1965:

> During that period the *Gazette* was repeatedly a best seller, having topped its printing order of thirty thousand more than once. Its premises along the Brixton Road were near one of the largest concentrations of West Indians in Britain. Its cramped offices were a beehive of activities which rivalled the West Indian High Commission Office in Mayfair.
>
> From there [the *Gazette*'s office] a deputation left to the Home Office, where it made a strong representation to the Secretary of State about the indignities that coloured people, especially in the Notting Hill district, were being subjected to. Other deputations went to Local Government Offices, and local Police Stations. People fearing for their life and property would come, waiting impatiently to pour out their troubles. They had little use for the Migrants Service Division of the High Commissioner's Office. What they needed was a godmother, not diplomatists. That was the role Claudia Jones played best.
>
> The office was always crowded and disorganised. At times it was very difficult to tell whether a paper was being put together or the woman who had had her house stoned, and painted over with 'nigger get out' was being convinced that to sell and go home to the Caribbean was not the best thing to do. Very often both things were accomplished, only the paper came out two weeks after its deadline.[15]

Perhaps West Indians were too quick in cleaning the taste of the summer of 1958 from their mouths, for in the middle of May 1959 the murder of Kelso Cochrane was to become the single biggest blow to hit West Indians in Britain since the dance hall scraps in the wartime years.[16] In her editorial of November 1959, Claudia was weary but she still believed that unity could defeat rising racial tension:

> In some respects it is amazing how short people's memories are. A charitable view might ascribe this to the fact that the human mind tends to reject unpleasant facts. But much as we would like to forget unpleasant facts, we cannot fail to observe that the aftermath of Notting Hill is

continuing in insidious ways. In the past several weeks in Britain West Indians and other peoples of colour have been victims of racial prejudice and colour bar practices. Take the recent case of Joseph Dill Simon of Notting Hill, formerly of Portsmouth, Dominica, who was walking quietly with a friend to catch a breath of fresh air, on an evening in October, when he was summarily shot in the wrist, at the corner of Talbot Road. He said: 'I know the police do not believe me, but a white man fired at me, because I am coloured.'

The atmosphere of Notting Hill, in which scrawled signs with ugly epithets BAN THE NIGGERS are chalked up is the milieu in which race hatred is being actively fanned by the fascists to whom it is their stock in trade.

The root of race hatred

In 1963 Claudia drafted an editorial on how she saw the menace of race hatred in Britain:

> Racialism is now a serious threat in Britain. The effect of Tory policy on Commonwealth immigration is to encourage racial division. The Fascists are exploiting this to preach racial hatred. This is a direct challenge to the basic principles of democracy, to working class unity, and to all those who believe in racial equality.
>
> No one denies that until July 1962 the number of coloured immigrants to Britain was increasing. This was the Tory excuse for the Commonwealth Immigration Act. In the next 16 months up to October 1963 the Act reduced immigration to 60,000 – less than half the total for 1961...
>
> *Root Of Race Hatred*
> Imperialism is the root cause of racialism. It is the ideology which upholds colonial rule and exploitation. It preaches the 'superiority' of the white race whose 'destiny' it is to rule over those with coloured skins, and to treat them with contempt. It is the ideology which breeds Fascism, rightly condemned by the civilised people the whole world. This racialist ideology has also made serious inroads among the British people, even in the ranks of the working class and in many trade unions. Faced with rising unemployment and the shortage of houses it is an easy temptation for many workers to fall into the trap of blaming coloured immigrants for this situation ...

In 1964 Dr Martin Luther King, on his way to Oslo to collect his

Nobel Peace Prize, called to see Claudia. Her comment on that meeting was to be the content of her last editorial:

> Dr Martin Luther King, widely regarded as a 'moderate' in his native America, where he is a leader in the mounting Negro people's struggle for equality and freedom, had some excellent, and for some, very radical things to say when passing through London on his way to Oslo to receive his Nobel Peace Prize.
>
> What he said on racial discrimination caught the nation's headlines, and intrigued the overwhelming majority of Commonwealth citizens from Asia and the Caribbean. As well it might. For his visit came in the midst of a debate on renewal of the Commonwealth Immigration Act, challenge to its renewal was virtually absent either by the Labour Government or by the Tory Opposition which introduced it. Yet, undoubtedly this colour-bar act has accelerated racialism in this country and has led to the imposition of a second class citizenship status of Commonwealth coloured citizens in Britain.
>
> We take it that Dr King's main whiplash was against racial discrimination. Hitting out at the Commonwealth Immigration Act he told Britain: *While I cannot speak on specific issues, there are some things which we have learned in the United States that, I think, have some relevance here. As far as housing is restricted and ghettoes of a minority are allowed to develop, you are promoting a festering sore of bitterness and deprivation to pollute your national health and create for yourselves a serious situation. Second, equal opportunity for education, training and employment must be made available without regard to class or colour, if the nation is to prosper in spirit and truth. Third, the presence of immigration laws based on colour are totally out of keeping with the laws of God and the trends of the Twentieth Century. It will eventually encourage the vestiges of racism and endanger all the democratic principles that this great nation holds.*
>
> We will not now quibble about Dr King's reference to the 'vestiges' of racism, or, as a few of our intellectuals seem to be pre-occupied with 'meditating about their navels', whether or not the American Negro struggle in all its aspects parallels our situation here. We can agree that there is enough that is similar from which to draw certain lessons. One such lesson is the necessity to uphold a principled stand on every issue of discrimination facing our people – even if some of our proclaimed friends do not, and even if all struggles are not won at one fell stroke.
>
> In this connection, it is interesting to note that in most of the press coverage of Dr King's warnings, stress was laid not on its essence, i.e. his criticism of racial discrimination, but rather on the so-called issue of

'growing ghettos'. Of course, Dr King could not have known that there are some, who, pleading their friendship with Commonwealth immigrants, seek to obscure the main issue of racial discrimination by counter-posing the so-called question of 'growing ghettos'. Of course, there is an underlying method in their madness. If the root causes of racial discrimination are obscured, the 'scape-goat theory' remains untouched and can, like Damocles sword be hung over our heads again and again. Discrimination, however, is man-made and is based on the exploitation for profit at the expense of colonial and newly-independent peoples as an integral part of the imperialist system, which oppresses other nations using Racialism to disrupt working-class unity. Ghettos of course, are abhorrent and should be fought. But the best way to fight these is to ban discrimination in housing.

Recently, the Rev Stephen Pulford, 69 year-old Rector of the Church of England, near Ross-on-Wye, Hertfordshire, said that coloured people should be given return tickets to their own countries from Britain. He presumed the slogan raised in the Smethwick election campaign: 'If you want a nigger for a neighbour, vote Labour' to be an accurate gauge of the feeling and fears of the British people as a whole. In true Southern Dixiecrat fashion, invoking the name of God, he talked about opposition to mixed marriages, repeating the worn out racialist clichés 'that coloured people come to Britain to batten upon the welfare state', and that 'this country is already overcrowded and Britons are queueing up for houses' etc . This minister made these points in a letter to a local newspaper in Leyton, where the British Foreign Secretary, Patrick Gordon Walker, defeated at Smethwick, proposes to stand for his Commons seat.

There has also been a recent rash of suggestions as the proposals to 'Buy-for-Whites' houses in Smethwick, hearteningly condemned by Labour councillors in Smethwick, and the proposal for built-in racially restrictive covenants to presumably overcome the problem of overcrowding for which it is alleged, Commonwealth immigrants have a special penchant. Then there are the prevalent views which seek to muddy the waters further by counter-posing inter-national differences among Commonwealth citizens as being synonymous with White supremacy.

What is all this but an attempt to divert the concern from the spawners of racialism itself onto the heads of Commonwealth citizens from Asia, Africa and the West Indies? The so called issue of 'ghettos' has been blown up far beyond all proportion. Commonwealth citizens, if they live together in the same street or house, only doing what most people with similar cultural and traditional backgrounds normally do in family groups, then that constitutes a ghetto. Why should people, except those of an apartheid mentality, fear this? More over, people do so usually after having the bitter experience of being faced with colour-bar adverts and refusals to give them housing if it is available. The attempt by the racialists to buy houses does not have as its aim the overcoming of overcrowding. If it did, they would fight for a proper housing programme to build the homes needed for all Britons. Its aim is to break up and squeeze out Commonwealth citizens who by banding together have been enabled to purchase houses or rent them at the most exorbitant 'colour-tax' prices and rentals.

Suspicion is therefore rife as regards the 'holier than thou' attitudes of those who would distort the essential warning made by Dr King which finds an echo in the hearts of all Commonwealth citizens. Some of those who are pre-occupied with 'ghettos' are the main perpetrators of racialism. Accompanying this trend is the usual concern voiced by them about fears of unity of coloured Commonwealth citizens, and the implication of such unity as related to what is termed 'Black supremacy'.

The shoe is on the other foot. The lessons of the American Negro struggle are that whatever advances towards equal rights and integration have been made, they have been accomplished in unity and struggle. As Paul Robeson observed recently on the militant Negro struggle, 'We can't say Great God Almighty we're here at last, but we're moving'. Commonwealth immigrants too 'can move' if they but heighten the trend for unity and organisation.

That is why Dr Martin Luther King's answer had to be a dual one, namely, the necessity for all decent Britons to challenge every case of racial discrimination and for the Commonwealth citizens to organise and unite – the better to effectively challenge the disabilities confronting us.

The last years of the *Gazette*

By the end of 1962 and the beginning of 1963, the magic circle of the *West Indian Gazette* was showing signs of fracturing. Ken Kelly had an article published in *Punch* but opportunities for freelancing for non-white writers in the early 1960s were almost non-existent. Kelly went to stay with German friends Hinds had made when he went to the Youth Festival in Vienna in 1959.[17] Donald Hinds now had a wife and two daughters. His career as a writer flickered along with the fate of the *Gazette*, and the occasional broadcast on the BBC's 'Caribbean Programme', which too was shrinking. Many of the young women who provided secretarial help at the *Gazette* and acted as hostesses at receptions were occupied with more permanent situations. Della McKenzie, Carmen Spencer, Cherry Lawman and others joined a dance troupe and left for an extended tour abroad. Relationships with Theo Campbell, who owned the premises at 250 Brixton Road, did not improve and the *Gazette* found new premises off Coldharbour Lane in Brixton. The dissolution of the Round Table was under way.

In 1964 Claudia described the *Gazette* to readers in the USA as having served as a catalyst, quickening the awareness, socially and politically, of West Indians and Afro-Asians in Britain, for peace and friendship between all Commonwealth and world peoples:

> It has campaigned vigorously on issues facing West Indians and other coloured people, whether against numerous police frame-ups, to which West Indians and other coloured migrants are frequently subjected, to opposing discrimination and to advocating support for trade unionism and unity of coloured and white workers. West Indian news publications have attempted to emulate the path of the progressive Negro (Afro-Asian, Latin American) fight against imperialist outrages and indignities to our peoples. The *West Indian Gazette and Afro-Asian Caribbean News* has served to launch solidarity campaigns with nationals who advance with their liberation struggles in Africa and Asia. The present circulation and readership of the *West Indian Gazette* would be larger, but for the usual welter of problems faced by most progressive journals. A campaign of support for financial aid among its readers and friends has recently been launched to help its expansion to a weekly and to establish its own printing plant. It counts among its contributors and supporters many West Indian writers (who live in Britain), trade unionists and Members of Parliament.[18]

Claudia was admitted to St Stephen's Hospital, Fulham, in early December 1964 where Donald Hinds visited her towards the middle of the month. Before going into hospital, Claudia had dropped a note through his letterbox. It was short and to the point: 'Where are you? Have you forgotten us?' He was anxious about her health but he also wanted to talk to her about his new daughter born on 19 November. He also wanted to talk about the writing of his book, *Journey to an Illusion*. She was happy on both accounts. The conversation soon turned to the *Gazette*. It was going to be late again especially if she was to be kept in for another week. She was hoping that she would not be. She was most jovial, and the conversation soon took a side turning: she told him a joke which was somewhat *risqué*. This was only out of the ordinary since unlike the army of other helpers he addressed her as 'Miss Jones', never as 'Claudia'. Although he was now a father of three girls he still held this woman some seventeen years his senior in something approaching awe. Perhaps Claudia was acknowledging the fact that he was no longer the young man she had greeted with the words 'so you want to write?' on that June day in 1958 when Theo Campbell had introduced him to her.

One day, during that awkward period between the Christmas holidays and the new year Hinds went into the *Gazette* office in Station Road, Loughborough Junction, an excuse at the ready. The synopsis of his book was due, inevitably he was behind with his *Gazette* column! The office was quiet. Ricky Cambridge, the new boy on the block, was alone and answering the telephone. He turned with the saddest face imaginable: 'Claudia is dead!' he said.

Notes

1. A hint of the *Gazette's* finances, while it was being set up from Claudia's home -110 Narbonne Avenue, Clapham – can be gleaned from the scraps of accounts which have been preserved. An invoice dated 24 February 1958 for a rubber stamp and a pad, appears on an undated list headed 'Manu's [Manchanda's] accounts', which details total expenditure of twenty seven shillings on stationery and an income of forty shillings from advertisments and nine shillings for 54 issues sold at two pence each. Total income, forty-nine shillings from which Claudia's expenditure on airmail of one pound, one shilling and three pence had also to be deducted. This left a surplus of nine pence.
2. Unless stated otherwise the source of all manuscript material is the Langford Collection.
3. Ruth Glass, *Newcomers*, Centre for Urban Studies, London 1960, p180.
4. *Daily Worker*, 28 August 1958, p1.
5. Sam King was a young activist from the middle of the 1950s. He recalls the many political groups which were around at the time consisting mainly of students: 'There were many chiefs, but very few Indians. They tried to recruit the migrant workers. That is why they founded the so called West Indians Workers and Students Association. I went along to the meetings but there were very few workers, indeed. The first meeting (September 1957) was held in a small hall in Victoria. Most of the other meetings were held at a flat in Baron's Court, the home of a Jamaican barrister, who eventually went back home and became quite famous. I remember that everybody wanted to lead. Only Claudia did any work in the organisation. The names on their letterhead made it look impressive. George Bowrin and Vince Bowles were from the Trinidad Oilfield Workers Trade Union were in London on trade union scholarships. I remember that so-called Annual General Meeting when the final break between Claudia and the

West Indian Workers and Students came. It was a hot sticky Sunday afternoon at the end of June 1958. The vote went against Claudia. I voted with her. I was convinced she knew what she was doing, and she was doing it! A few days later she had the paper registered as owned and published by the Coloured Peoples Publishing Company.'

6. The stationery of the Association shows that at some time in its ten months of existence, Vin Bowles acted as Secretary and at that time Clyde Crevelle was Treasurer. The address of the organisation had moved form SE11 to one in W14. The President and Honorary President were two well known West Indians whose names would add prestige and lend weight to any Caribbean organisation at that time: Bowrin was President; the Honorary President was none other than the indomitable Amy Ashwood Garvey, first wife of Marcus Garvey.

7. Excerpts from the *Gazette* quoted by Glass, see note 3, p210.

8. The conferences between colonial nationalists and the British Government regarding the shape and timing of independence were all held in Lancaster House.

9. Donald Hinds, *Journey to an Illusion*, Heinemann, London 1966, p165.

10. David Roussel-Milner ghost-wrote his mother's beauty column for the *Gazette*.

11. Janet Jagan, president of Guyana.

12. Both were African-American women; Harriet Tubman rescued many Africans from enslavement in the South via the 'Underground Railroad' while Sojourner Truth spoke out for the equality of all women.

13. See chapter 6.

14. Sir Learie Constantine (1901-1971) of Trinidad, moved to Britain in the 1930s to play cricket for Nelson, Lancashire; he also continued to play for the West Indies. During the war he served as a Welfare Officer in the Ministry of Labour; after the war he qualified as a lawyer. In 1954, he returned to Trinidad, becoming chairman of Eric Williams' People's National Movement. Having returned to London as independent Trinidad's High Commissioner (1962-64), he decided to stay in Britain and served as a governor of the BBC and as a member of the Race Relations Board. He was knighted in 1962 and made a life peer (the first Caribbean to receive that honour) in 1969. The author of a number of books on cricket, Constantine also wrote *Colour Bar* (London 1954), part autobiography, part political tract.

15. Hinds, see note 9, pp164-165.

16. See chapter 4.

17. Kelly went on to pursue a career with the *Rundfunk* in Frankfurt, writing playlets. Some of these were published under the title '*Der Minister Und Seine Sippe*'.

18. 'Caribbeans in Britain', *Freedomways*, Summer 1964.

Carnival
Colin Prescod

Dear Friends – I am sure that you will want to know that our FOURTH ANNUAL CARIBBEAN CARNIVAL will take place on Friday evening, March 16 1962 at Seymour Hall, Seymour Place, W1, from 7 to 11.30pm.

The carnival promises to be the most exciting and colourful in years. Heading our caste of artistes this year will be – The Mighty Sparrow, king of calypsonians, in person, whom we are flying over to perform at our Carnival; The fabulous Dixielanders; Curtis Pierre and his Trinidad Steel Band have also been booked and will be there. Elaine Delmar etc. The talented choreographer Boscoe Holder is arranging the choreography, and a Carnival Fiesta with a new slant will form the evening's programme. Dancing, at least three hours, is planned this year. Mr Pat Castagne is to produce our show for us this year. And lots more.

By 1962 the *West Indian Gazette* was clearly conscious of the fact that its annual Caribbean Carnival celebration had become an important cultural event for Caribbeans settling in Britain. As of late 1958 the *WIG* had assembled and worked with an organising Carnival Committee to stage a joyous event that at once echoed the carnival festivals of the Caribbean and served to bring British Caribbeans and their non-Caribbean friends together in a spirit of defiance against the kinds of division that had marked the riots of the summer of 1958. They could not have known then that they were founding what was to come to be described in the 1990s as the largest street event in all Europe. And they could not have known then that at the end of the century the founding-rights of this festival were to become a major bone of cultural and political contention.

The evidence now assembled demonstrates that Claudia Jones was in fact the great founding spirit of what has become London's Notting Hill Carnival – now having celebrated its fortieth anniversary and regularly attracting, over two days every August Bank Holiday, about two million participants. Of course a variety of factors and additional inputs will have accounted for the phenomenal growth and popularity of the carnival over these four decades, but we are interested now in the fact that the remarkable Miss Jones once again had her unfailing finger on the button of yet another socio-political invention – not because she herself was an inveterate carnivalist, although one might argue that she had Trinidad's carnival in her blood, but because in her politics she had always been aware of, as she put it, 'the role of the arts in bringing people together for common aims'.

In 1959 Claudia had reached out to the friends she held dear in artistic circles to stage an event that would symbolise a spirit of bouncing back after the saddening street rioting events of Nottingham and Notting Hill in the summer of 1958. It was not the first or the last time that she would marshal cultural performers to bring an additional dimension to an organised response to political events. Throughout her time in Britain, she regularly mounted staged performance events which focused audiences on the big international struggles for justice – from apartheid in South Africa to civil rights in the USA. Clearly, she recruited support from and cultivated close friendships with musicians, actors, singers, dancers and choreographers, both Black and White. From her correspondence she appears to have been in active contact with every single Caribbean or African artist of note who lived or passed though Britain. The people whose names and photographs are featured in the brochures and programmes printed by the *WIG* for these various events attest to this. And of course, exactly because she was not restricted by the racialisation of an imperialised world, she held dear any white as well as Black artists who would join her cause, just as she was interested in registering in that first London Carnival souvenir programme a photograph of a Kathakali dancer as reflecting the East Indian influence in the West Indian Carnival.

Although not all of the artists whom she gathered around her went on to become famous, a remarkable number of names still have some resonance today. Cleo Laine, actor and jazz-singer, Edric Connor, actor and magnificent baritone, Cy Grant, musician and performer, were with her from as early as 1959, as was the British film star, Yvonne Mitchell. And by 1962 the Carnival Queen judges that she had assembled included the young British playwright John Osborne, the well known actor Earl Cameron; the exciting young Trinidadian visual artist Althea McNish; the very specially talented emerging Guyanese writer Andrew Salkey; and the emerging giant in British theatre Joan Littlewood. And, to illustrate the manner in which for Claudia culture and politics mixed seamlessly, in 1962 also serving as a Carnival Queen judge was her friend and comrade from the USA, Essie Robeson – as significant an activist then, as her husband Paul, both still today largely under-celebrated.

It is perhaps here, in her culturalist vein, that we get the clearest sense of the fun-loving, vivacious Claudia Jones and her joyful liberationist spirit. As Corinne Skinner-Carter, actor and performer, recalled at the 1996 symposium: 'Claudia, with all her seriousness, was a real party-goer, she would come and spend long hours with us, *liming* as we called it, talking about politics, but in between talking about politics she could be rather a lot of fun.' Corinne also recalls the first time she met Claudia who was then staying with her friend, Mikki Doyle, in Putney, London.

> I thought it would be a very severe, austere person that I was going to meet. I was invited to go there to meet her, to press her hair ... Today they use chemicals to straighten. In those days we used what they call an iron comb, and we straightened the hair, in the fire and the grease ... I was presented with this rather handsome, elegant lady, and I was shocked, because communists were supposed to have two heads ...

Corinne found Claudia to be 'full of herself, full of everything, full of life'. 'She had this charisma about her that she could make people do things that they never knew they could do. She pulled things out of people that they had thought could never be done'.

Quite clearly Claudia had an ability to galvanise action around the causes that she espoused, but it would be as well to recognise that in the prime time of her activism in Britain, she was working with very willing spirits. This was the time of universal anti-colonial struggle; when the peoples of the Third World were self-consciously their own liberators. And this was the politicised cultural climate of internationalist anti-colonialism within which all the artists collaborating with her in the 1950s and 1960s had been nurtured. They were all looking for focus and leadership and Claudia provided these aplenty. The *WIG*, Claudia's central organising medium down the years, is packed with evidence of the variety of cultural events which were in fact rallying points for political demonstration and mobilisation. Many of the very same artists who participated in Claudia's carnival events would be found performing readings and dramatic re-enactments at anti-apartheid rallies in townhalls and other venues. And the same people could be seen in street marches and demonstrations, organised by Claudia, against injustice. Claudia led in 1963 the London demonstration held to coincide with the momentous Martin Luther King civil rights march on Washington, arms linked with the singer-actor Pearl Prescod, both of them belting out an amplified 'We Shall Overcome'.

Carnival – the early years

> Claudia as you know, was the great leveller. First I must say, carnival in itself is a great leveller of people, it's a thing in Trinidad that brings all nations, creeds, colours, everybody together and I think Claudia can be referred to as carnival, because she brought everybody together, in whatever sphere of life that they were in, she brought them together.
>
> (Corinne Skinner-Carter, symposium 1996)

In the Notting Hill area of west London the 1958 riots were started by mobs of white people making sporadic attacks on unsuspecting Blacks and they ended when Black people said 'enough is enough' and organised a fight back. The police belatedly intervened and put an end to the fighting by driving the roving mobs off the streets – but this occurred only after weeks of terror, where Black people went out on to the streets in fear of attack, and then only in groups for their own protection. The most generally accepted version of what took place credits Oswald Mosely, already notorious as an avowed fascist, and his henchman Colin Jordan, a west London organiser of fascist and frustrated elements in the local white population, as key instigators, if not organisers, of the attacks on Black people.

The Paddington, Notting Hill, Ladbroke Grove areas constituted in the 1950s a centre of new, post World War Two Black community. For some time before the arrival of the Caribbean workers, the area had developed a reputation as one of London's most run down and dangerous neighbourhoods; it contained large pockets of dilapidated housing. It was only in conditions like these that Black people could hope to find accommodation as a result of what was called then the 'colour bar'. Here the Caribbean workers found similarly marginalised, and therefore sympathetic, white working-class people who would share and sub-let their already poor and overcrowded living spaces. And here there were unscrupulous and sometimes criminal landlords and landladies, already with bad reputations in the local newspapers. Amongst these was a man called Rachman whose activities threw up the concept 'Rachmanism', epitomising the very lowest and most vicious form of exploitative landlordism. But here too, as history would have it, Mrs Amy Ashwood Garvey, radical pan-Africanist, first wife of Marcus

The Caribbean Carnival 1959

Sponsored by West Indian Gazette

CLAUDIA JONES, EDITOR   *A. MARCHANDA, MANAGER*

TELEVISED BY B.B.C. TELEVISION

Director Cabaret Programme: *Choreographer:*
EDRIC CONNOR   *STANLEY JACK*

Decor: *Souvenir Journal Cover Motif:*
RHODA MILLS   *LAUREL ANDERSON*
CHARLES GRANT

Stage Manager:
TREVOR CARTER

Carnival Committee

NADIA CATOUSE	*ESTELLE LEWIS*	*IVAN CHINN*
THEO CAMPBELL	*GAY JULIEN*	*O. SERGEANT*
PEARL CONNOR	*LENNOX PAUL*	*FLAVIA DAVIS*
A. CODLING	*R. SERTIMER*	*ESTHER GITTENS*
PAULA BEAUBRUN	*LA FLORA LEVY*	*ANN WOODING*
GEORGE DRUMMOND	*DAISY M. TAYLOR*	*SHEILA CLARKE*
McDONALD STANLEY	*DAVID DAVIDSON*	*ROY HENRY*
PAUL ENGLAND	*LAUREL ANDERSON*	*LYN JONES*
	JUNE BADEN-SEMPER	

Artists

CLEO LAINE	*THE SOUTHLANDERS*	*BOSCOE HOLDER TROUPE*
MIKE McKENZIE TRIO	*THE MIGHTY TERROR*	*PEARL PRESCOD*
SEPIA SERENADERS	*FITZROY COLEMAN*	
CORINNE SKINNER-CARTER	*TRINIDAD ALL STARS AND HI-FI STEEL BANDS*	
WEST INDIAN STUDENTS DANCE BAND	*RUPERT NURSE & HIS ORCHESTRA*	

BERYL McBERNIE, O.B.E. Pioneer W.I. folk lorist. Founder Little Carib Theatre.

The organisers and artists of the 1959 Carnival as listed in the souvenir programme

Front cover of the first Carnival programme.

Garvey and close friend of Claudia Jones, had her residential and
activist base, at No1 Bassett Road in Ladbroke Grove. Another
member of Claudia's close circle of friends, the singer and actor Pearl
Prescod, also lived in the Ladbroke Grove area, one street away from
Bassett Road. So Claudia Jones knew and regularly visited the area
within which the Notting Hill riots took place and where just months
later, in May 1959, young Kelso Cochrane would be murdered in the
streets because he was Black. This was the area where, by a string of
connected coincidences, the Caribbean Carnival celebrations that she
initiated and nurtured would take root to generate Europe's biggest
twentieth century street festival.

The genesis of the Carnival

In November 1958, just months after the riots, a Caribbean Carnival
Committee was set up under the sponsorship of the *West Indian
Gazette*. The Committee must have worked swiftly and efficiently,
since on Friday 30 January 1959 it was able to mount what was
announced as the Caribbean Carnival, at St Pancras Town Hall in
central London. The souvenir brochure published at the time
announced that the carnival was organised by the *West Indian Gazette*,
that the carnival cabaret was directed by Edric Connor and that
between 10.45pm and 11.25pm the carnival cabaret would be televised
by the BBC. The programme was transmitted but, unfortunately, the
BBC appears to have no film or tape record of the event in its archive.
    The 1959 carnival souvenir publication also included the following
statement – 'A part of the proceeds of this brochure are to assist the
payment of fines of coloured and white youths involved in the Notting
Hill events.' And there speaks the politics of Claudia Jones. She had
called her friends and comrades to form the Caribbean Carnival
Committee as part of a complex strategy – social, cultural and political.
In her brief introductory statement to the 1959 Carnival souvenir
brochure, which she gave a grand title, 'A people's art is the genesis of
their freedom', we have a wonderful example of Claudia's particular
lucidity, as well as something uncannily prophetic.

> Rarely have the creative energies of a people indigenous to another
> homeland been so quickly and spontaneously generated to such purpose
> as witness the work of the Caribbean Carnival Committee 1959, set up
> last November under the sponsorship of the *West Indian Gazette*.
>   It is as if the vividness of our national life was itself the spark urging

translation to new surroundings, to convey, to transplant our folk origins to British soil. There is a comfort in this effort not only for the Carnival Committee and the West Indian Gazette and for the fine artists participating in our Carnival who have lent of their talents here, but for all West Indians, who strain to feel and hear and reflect their idiom even as they strain to feel the warmth of their sun-drenched islands and its immemorable beauty of landscape and terrain.

There is of course another cause to be assessed to their response to those who have filled St. Pancras Town Hall. That reason is the event of Notting Hill and Nottingham – an event which was the matrix binding West Indians in the United Kingdom together as never before – determined that such happenings should not recur.

If then, our Caribbean Carnival has evoked the wholehearted response from the peoples from the Islands of the Caribbean in the new West Indies Federation, this is itself testament to the role of the arts in bringing people together for common aims, and to its fusing of the cultural, spiritual, as well as political and economic interests of West Indians in the UK and at home.

A pride in being West Indian is undoubtedly at the root of this unity: a pride that has its origin in the drama of nascent nationhood, and that pride encompasses not only the creativeness, uniqueness and originality of West Indian mime, song and dance – but is the genesis of the nation itself. It is true to say that [this] pride extends not only to what the West Indians have proudly established in the culture of the Caribbean but to [what they have contributed] to the treasury of world culture.

For me and for the management of the *West Indian Gazette*, and to all of the Carnival Committee I say a deep thank you. It would be unfair for me not to tell you that we have still another determination, that is, to make the *WIG* Caribbean Carnival an annual event. In that endeavour, we know we can count not only on the artists and the decor, the committee heads, our friends and neighbours but many who we have not yet reached.

Claudia may not have dreamt up a carnival celebration all on her own but she certainly led the adoption of the idea. For Trevor Carter, another of the early carnival organising participants, 'the spirit of the carnival came out of Claudia's political knowledge of what to touch at a particular time when we were scared, we were people in disarray' (see Symposium). Supporting this assessment of her role, David Roussel-Milner, whose mother, Carmen England, was another of the early Carnival supporters, recalls Claudia saying the reason for Carnival was to go out into the streets and show the white natives that West Indians were a cultured people, who were prepared to share their culture with those white people, and therefore to heal the wounds. And Pearl Connor believes that, 'Claudia was trying to calm the fears. Everybody wanted to run away, leave. This fear was in the area and she was thinking about how to do something about it, (see Symposium). Corinne Skinner-Carter, one of the volunteers and performers in the early carnival years, recalls that,

> Claudia was really a mixed person, in the sense of mixed ability person, that she could be talking politics one minute and she could be doing something else the other minute. She thought the best way to bring all these people together is in a carnival. And she brought all these important people, like Pearl Prescod, Peggy Seeger, Ewan McColl [both popular left wing folk-singers of the era], Paul Robeson – a whole cross section – Nadia Cattouse, Cy Grant, Edric Connor. Before the carnival, she had meetings with us. She organised what we should do for carnival, what should be done for carnival, the committee where we talked about what we were going to do.

In addition to the costume displays, the song and dance performances and the jump-up that provided the main entertainments of the Carnival, a central feature of all the early Carnivals, and one borrowed from the popular festival in the Caribbean, was the Carnival Queen beauty contest. Indeed, announcing the January 1959 Carnival in London, the *WIG* introduced the crowning of the carnival queen as a highlight of the evening.

Corinne Skinner-Carter has a really sophisticated take on this element of the early carnivals:

> She [Claudia] also started – I know that the women nowadays would drop their hands in horror – also started beauty contests – a Black beauty contest. And this was before Black Power days. This was before we all knew that we were beautiful. We might not have known it but she knew that we were beautiful and she started this beauty contest. And the first year there was a girl called Fay Craig that won this beauty contest, and I'm telling you, Fay Craig was Black, I mean really Black. But pretty. But without Claudia we would not have known that, because then we used to judge everybody's beauty by the European standard.

What a conundrum this must present for some schools of late twentieth century feminism. But for Claudia Jones, a revolutionary in and of her time, engaging with popular culture and its institutions was clearly central to moving with the people as well as moving the people along. Of course in the late 1950s and early 1960s most people, including radicals, would have accepted female beauty contests, largely uncritically. But, for Claudia, the idea of installing real, dark black, Black, as beautiful, using a low-culture institution like the beauty contest, was a brilliant move in its time – and knowing Black audiences delighted in this insertion of African features into the aesthetics of standards of physical beauty. The contests were a very popular feature of the Carnival, attracting business sponsorship, as well as providing a career vehicle for some of the contestants.

The spirit of Carnival

While Claudia lived, for each year beyond 1959, her *West Indian Gazette* sponsored and organised a Caribbean Carnival – all of the celebrations being held in London, indoors, in the British winter, timed to coincide with the carnival in the Caribbean. The venue often changed, giving more exposure to the performers. In 1959 the carnival took place at St Pancras Town Hall; in 1960, at the Seymour Hall; in 1961 at the Lyceum Ballroom; in 1962, by which time the souvenir brochure announced that the Carnival was organised by the *West Indian Gazette* and *Afro-Asian-Caribbean News*, the celebration was again held at the Seymour Hall with some elements touring to Manchester; and in 1963, it was back at the Lyceum, again touring to Manchester.

Among the acknowledgements of support in the twenty-four page 1959 Caribbean Carnival brochure, is the line – ' … to Dr Bor, of Kew Gardens, for his help in facilitating our securing of palms for our tropical décor'. There's a wonderful poignancy to this entry. It gives us a touching glimpse of these people of the tropics, begging and borrowing homely props to comfort their winter sojourn in a hostile land. This passing reference to decorative palms from Kew also tells of the spirit of audacity of Caribbean settlers in Britain – a spirit joined by Claudia Jones and her *WIG*. When they wanted something, they went to the top and to the heart of the establishment, if necessary. In order to lever influence, they engaged with people in the establishment, at the forefront of popular culture and at the centre of public life. The result, in the Carnival movement as in the broader social arena, was that some of those approached were recruited to the social and political movement that would, given time, gradually transform the sociology, at least, of Britain. One consequence of this is that, in spite of economic, political and historical divisions and differences between its citizens, Britain's cities have none of the social apartheid that still marks the USA to this day, in spite of its momentous mid-century civil rights shifts.

The point is that late twentieth century British Blackness, initially defined by Caribbean presences in the main, but soon joined by Asian settlers, has insisted on transforming the social scenes shared with British Whiteness. This has meant, in a sense, a change in the culture of contemporary Britain. Carnival, or rather, the Carnival, epitomises the success of this intervention. And at the heart of this intervention is an insistence on engaging with the natives, at the everyday, living, communal, human level. It is this taking of the culture by the scruff of the neck, so to speak, that has simply blown away the concept of race relations as characterising what it is that ails Britain's new Black populations. There is definitely a problem around race and racism in British society, but particularly in our very mixed, cosmopolitan cities, there is no race relations problem – if that means a problem about Black and White people, from different so-called 'races', relating to each other. They work, play, live, love, make babies, families and live in the same communities. There is no race relations problem because with their audacious and insistent attitude, the Black people who came to settle in Britain have simply refused to be cowed into the kind of social and residential ghettos that have resulted from living alongside white racist hostility in so many other societies.

Now, in spite of the fact that she was born, and to some extent, bred in Trinidad, it is difficult to know exactly how much Claudia Jones would have been a dedicated carnivalist, identified with the whole of the complex spirit of the carnival. The carnival is of course a celebration of the masses, an event which would be attractive to a socialist revolutionary. But there is also risk and daring in the carnival. And there is also danger and decadence. In its fullness, the carnival is a bacchanalian affair, characterised by excess. Where its ritual works, it achieves a kind of temporary zone of freeness in regard to normal rules, restrictions and respect for persons. Its uninhibited sense of exhilaration, its pursuit of the feeling of freeness and its explicit programme of subversion, all are attractive to the revolutionary spirit, but surely, with a cautionary proviso for a Marxist schooled to be suspicious of spontaneity and anarchic tendencies. And as it turned out, the intention to use carnival as one of the tools that would change the culture of hostility facing Black settlers was to be overtaken by the very fullest expression of cultural and political subversion that is part and parcel of the spirit of a true carnival. It was this spirit that would emerge in the

London carnival riots of the mid-1970s. These were expressions of public reaction to heavy-handed policing of the by then massive, free-for-a-day carnival festival that had taken to the streets of Notting Hill. But Claudia Jones could not have predicted that this level of militant confrontation with the authorities would emerge out of her support for a modest intervention at the level of arts and culture.

The first London Caribbean Carnival celebration was conceived as simultaneously a harmoniser, re-establishing some sense of shared community after the riots of 1958, and a transformer, intended to change even as it embraced those who might have stood in opposition to the new Black working-class presence. In that first carnival brochure, Claudia expressed a hope that the event might be 'the leaven to weld still more firmly the brotherhood and unity of West Indians and other peoples of colour, as well as the friendship for all peoples ...' She would have been familiar with the insistent, dancing, joyous spirit of the carnival. And it was to join this spirit that she marshalled her friends and acquaintances, the musicians, calypsonians, mas-makers, bandspeople and entertainment stars. The carnival assembled and toured what would have been the first steel-bands seen by most Britons. By 1962, the Carnival celebration at Seymour Hall London featured the Mighty Sparrow – to this day, acclaimed, along with Lord Kitchener, as the greatest of calypsonians. In that year the *WIG* organisers toured Sparrow to perform at the Manchester Free Trade Hall. Other notable entertainers appearing in the Carnival celebrations of the early 1960s and not yet mentioned included – Boscoe Holder's and Allistair Bain's dancing troupes; calypsonians Mighty Terror and Lord Ambassador; musician Fitzroy Coleman; singers Elaine Delmar and Jackie Edwards; actor and comedian Horace James; singing groups, the Southlanders and the Dixieland Quartet; and band-leaders Rupert Nurse, Curtiss Pierre and Ivan Chin.

Support for the early Carnivals also came from the embassies and High Commissions – in 1959 from the Commission for the West Indies, British Guiana, and British Honduras, joined in 1962 by the Commissions for Ghana, Sierra Leone, Haiti, Nigeria and India; and in 1963 the High Commissioner for Trinidad and Tobago, Sir Learie Constantine, attended the celebrations alongside Jamaica's High Commissioner, H.C. Lindo, C.M.G.

We begin to have a sense of the network of resources that she was able to command by looking at those leading figures, Black and White, from the worlds of theatre, literature and progressive politics, who supported Claudia Jones and her *WIG* collaborators (General Manager, A. Manchanda, always listed) in organising the carnival.

So when, in 1965, after the death of Claudia Jones, the white local community activist Rhaune Laslett approached Andre Shevington to engage some carnival elements to bring to the Notting Hill Fair parade, he was able to tap directly into an already existing London based Caribbean carnival. The carnival with its steel band men and costumed mas' players simply emerged from its nursery halls and took to the streets. And man, did it take!

Claudia's death, burial and legacy

Death

Around 1963 or 1964 Claudia moved into a two room flat on the ground floor at 58 Lisburne Road, Gospel Oak in north London. Living on the top floor of the same house were two young men also associated with the Communist Party. One was an Indian student of accountancy. The other, Eric Levi, was of Jewish-Syrian-Egyptian descent, who had migrated to Britain from the USA in 1958. The middle floor was occupied by people outside of this political fraternity.

As Eric saw no signs of Claudia on Christmas morning 1964, or on the day after, he knocked on her door. There was no answer. He knocked again later in the day; still no reply. Now worried, he broke one of her windows and clambered in. Claudia, book in hand, reading glasses in place, was lying in bed, dead. She had died of a massive heart attack, aged only 48.

Eric immediately informed the Communist Party and some of Claudia's comrades, such as Mikki Doyle and Ranjana Ash. He also sent a telegram to Manu, who was then in China.

What happened next is unclear. It seems that Mikki Doyle tried to appropriate Claudia's body and belongings in the name of the Party. According to Eric Levi, 'the Party wanted to have her buried quickly ... The Party believed the decision regarding the funeral was between her and them'.[1] However, Claudia had a first cousin (or a nephew?) in London at that time who tried to prevent this interference with Claudia's remains. When Mikki would not listen, this relative, Mr Cumberbatch, took out an injunction to prevent the CPGB making arrangements for the funeral and to postpone the funeral until Manu's return from China. In a letter written in 1982, Manu claimed that Claudia's 'fake friends ... these comrades [against whom] Claudia waged a relentless struggle to the end, to expose their betrayal to (sic) the national liberation and working class movements ... rushed to cash in [on] her great political prestige'. Elsewhere he wrote that 'Micky (sic) Doyle of the CPGB (with the connivance of her Party comrades), pretending to be a "close friend"... took possession of her mortal remains as well as other assets ... Only [through] the court action did I get back from Micky Doyle Claudia's material assets.'[2] What, however, Manu appears not to have got back was the manuscript of Claudia's autobiography, which both Nadia Cattouse and Donald Hinds remember having seen or listened to Claudia read from; Ricky Cambridge also remembers that Claudia was working on an autobiography.[3]

On his return from China Manu obtained, through Letters of Administration, control of Claudia's papers. Manu then bought a burial plot next to the grave of Karl Marx in Highgate cemetery. In the name of the *Gazette* and the Committee of Afro-Asian Caribbean Organisations Manu arranged for Claudia's cremation at the Golders Green Crematorium on 9 January 1965.[4]

Burial

On that 'wet and cheeerless' day friends and comrades of Claudia assembled at the chapel of rest at the corner of Hoop Lane and Finchley Road. The funeral procession, 'led by a huge banner with figures of African, Indian, Chinese, European men and women, representing the whole human race, with a slogan "WORLD PEOPLE UNITE FOR FREEDOM AND PEACE", symbolised the aims for which Claudia Jones fought and died.' The coffin was borne on the shoulders of both Black and white pall bearers ... The procession was led by Mr. A. Manchanda, Dr David Pitt, George Lamming, members of the diplomatic corps from Africa, Asia, West Indies, Cuba, and leaders of the Committee of Afro-Asian Caribbean Organisations.'[5]

> I count as one of my greatest experiences being there at the funeral. It was the first really big Black funeral I think that ever London saw, and we walked with her coffin up to the crematorium. The place was of course full. And Paul Robeson had a recording I remember. It was a wonderful day, and we celebrated her life. We didn't mourn, I think we've all mourned since for a long long time, but at that time we didn't mourn so much, here was a great woman who was passing. Not mourn-

ing her person so much as mourning her politics. Mourning her contribution.

(David Roussel-Milner, 1996 Symposium)

In the Crematorium Hall, Pearl Prescod led the tributes by singing 'Lift Every Voice and Sing'. Then came speeches by Dr Pitt, John Williamson of the CPGB, Raymond Kunene (of the African National Congress) and Manu. Finally a recorded message from Paul and Essie Robeson was played to the mourners, of whom there were so many that loudspeakers broadcast to those who could not get into the Hall. The sad day closed with the singing of 'We Shall Overcome', led by Nadia Cattouse.[6] Paul Robeson's message was:

> It was a great privilege to have known Claudia Jones for many years, and to have worked with her on many occasions. She was a vigorous and courageous leader of the Communist Party of the United States and was very active in the work for the unity of white and coloured peoples, and for dignity, and equality, especially for the Negro people and for women. She was an important leader of the Youth Movement, and was active in the trade union struggles during the 1930s and 1940s – a crucial period in contemporary American history. She was a regular and popular contributor to the *Daily Worker*.
>
> The death of Claudia Jones is a great loss to us on this side of the Atlantic, and to you on your side. Many friends and comrades here grieve for her and are saddened by her loss. We send you our sad and sympathetic greetings, and it helps us to know that her work will continue through the Committee of Afro-Asian-Caribbean Organisations which she had built. She will surely be pleased with such a Memorial.

Essie, terminally ill with cancer, said:

> We women are saddened by the death of Claudia Jones, and will remember with deep appreciation the fine and useful work she accomplished in her lifetime.
>
> We salute her with love and respect and grief.[7]

By the time of the cremation Manu had formed the Claudia Jones Memorial Committee, based at the *Gazette*'s offices in Brixton. Paul Robeson agreed to be the chairman. In the name of the Committee Manu arranged for Claudia's ashes to be interred on 27 February at

CLAUDIA JONES
MILITANT NEGRO
ANTI-IMPERIALIST LEADER

Funeral and Cremation
Programme

Saturday 9th January 1965

Claudia's Funeral and cremation programme.

Highgate cemetery in a grave registered in the name of the Committee.[8] Later on the same day there was a Memorial Meeting at St Pancras Town Hall, at which Manu had arranged for a recording made by Ruby Dee of Claudia's speech to the American court in 1953 to be played. Paul Robeson sent a recorded appreciation of Claudia. A film of the funeral was also shown.[9] The speakers at the meeting, which was chaired by Raymond Kunene, were the Algerian Ambassador L. Khelifa; Peggy Middleton of the London County Council; the novelist George Lamming; Fenner Brockway, and Frances Ezzreco, now vice-chairman of the Standing Conference of West Indian Organisations. Musical tributes were from James Phillips, Isabel Lucas and George Webb; Peter Blackman read his poem 'To Claudia'; Bari Johnson read Langston Hughes's 'Let America Be America Again' and Martin Carter's 'Death of a Comrade' was read by Earl Cameron.[10] The event was closed by James Phillips leading the singing of 'We Shall Overcome'.

The February *Gazette*, edited by Manchanda, was a special memorial issue. Among the tributes printed were the following:

> I think of her as a kind of twentieth century Harriet Tubman, always in the vanguard of the march of oppressed peoples towards freedom – in the United States, in the Caribbean, in Africa, in Asia – wherever she might be, wherever she might help advance the struggle by word or action.
>
> (Alphaeus Hunton, Secretariat of the *Encyclopaedia Africana*, Accra, Ghana)[11]

> Progressive America will always cherish the memory of Claudia Jones. For two decades hers was a passionate voice for truth and justice resounding in our land. Eloquent orator, talented journalist, inspiring organiser, she believed devoutly in the historic inevitability of Communism's triumph and was an ardent fighter for the cause of the working people. Above all she was a tireless crusader for equality and freedom for the Negro People of the United States and for national liberation and independence of the peoples of the Caribbean. Her leading work in the youth, women's and Negro People's movement in the United States brought her honor from progressive people, but persecution at the hands of the authorities ...
>
> (Gus Hall and Henry Winston, CPUSA leaders)

> Claudia was the driving spirit behind the hunger strike staged in protest against the Rivonia trial in South Africa. During that period Claudia was associated with every protest against the political trials and torture in

South Africa ... All who were associated with her ... were deeply impressed by her vitality and sincerity. She will always be remembered by those who rebel against injustice and oppression.

(Barney Desai, President, Coloured Peoples' Congress of
South Africa)

The death of Claudia Jones has deprived the liberation movement all over the world of one of the most dynamic and most militant fighters. It is difficult to think of anyone who in recent years has remained so incorruptible in spite of all the insidious influences of artificial independence. Claudia belonged to the forefront of the struggle against imperialism, colonialism and fascism.

(Raymond Kunene of the African National Congress)

It is still impossible for many of us to realise that Claudia Jones is not with us. For so many years she seemed always to be with us. There was never an occasion when one was speaking for human equality or for the freedom of peoples or for the emancipation of peoples everywhere that Claudia didn't seem to be present. She was lovely in herself and she spoke with such persuasive charm that she carried not only conviction but stirred others to activity.

I shall always remember how she spoke to our trade union members in my old constituency of Slough and how deeply moved workers from our factories were by her appeal. They often asked me to bring her back. I wish she had been able to do so. I think it would have made the difference of the 11 votes by which I was defeated.

The way she published the *West Indian Gazette* was typical of her devoted service. She carried it on almost alone ... It was a continual expression of the equality of peoples and did very much to encourage the West Indian community in Britain despite the humiliation which they sometimes received and to stimulate British people to begin to understand their difficulties and the need for cooperation with them.

(Fenner Brockway)

... She was a symbol of inspiration to all anti-colonial movements.

(Kwesi Armah, High Commissioner for Ghana)

Politics resided in every nerve of Claudia's body... Militant for her cause, she was also gracious in her relationships. The lioness could disagree like an angel. Here was a great source of her strength: a certain flexibility of mind and a generous heart.

(George Lamming, Barbadian novelist)

We shall long remember with greatest warmth this wonderful woman, this tireless fighter for the triumph of the brightest ideals, and peace and friendship among nations.

(L. Balakhovskaya, head of the International Department, Soviet Women's Committee, Moscow)

Claudia was a good woman. She cared. She worked hard. I had enormous respect for her ... Though I never showed it, I was always extremely proud of her. Most West Indians in Britain were also uncertain about making it public. Claudia didn't really need us at all. Yet she was thankful for our spasmodic support and our half-hearted co-operation. She was strong, independent and forceful ... Claudia died without a country, without our love and without the comfort of knowing that we cared. I will long admire her strength. I will always miss her.

(Andrew Salkey, Jamaican-born novelist)

Claudia's death was widely reported, but only in the left-wing press abroad. For example, the editorial in the British Guianese *Mirror* of 10 January 1965 called her 'a freedom fighter with her voice, she also used her pen for the cause she so dearly loved, the freedom struggle'; the Hsinua News Agency's *Daily Bulletin* of 13 January 1965 (p15) noted that 'all the speakers paid tribute to her unyielding struggle during the past 30 years against imperialism, colonialism and racial discrimination.' The CPUSA's *Public Affairs* (February 1965) called her a 'vibrant and dynamic organiser, an eloquent speaker and writer who evoked confidence and enthusiasm among all who knew her, winning the love and respect of tens of thousands throughout the land ... She was endowed with an enquiring mind and a militant spirit ...'

A memorial meeting was held in Peking on 21 February 1965, sponsored by a 'Committee of British and American friends of Claudia Jones'. Among the speakers were Rose Smith, founder member of the CPGB, who said:

Refusing to recognise any obstacles she literally worked day and night to organise coloured workers in Britain and unite them in struggle with British workers ... Called to task by a leading member of the CPGB for making a statement contrary to the Party policy (on China), and not daring to expel this class fighter, the Party representative asked her if she wanted to resign. She answered in true Claudia tradition: 'No! You can kick me out if you like, but I have no intention of resigning'.

Florine Adams of the United States, stated that:

Claudia recognised fully that the liberation movement of the people in colonial and dependent countries is inseparably intertwined with the struggle for peace ... Through thirty endless years of confrontation, obstacles and searching tests, Claudia was forged and steeled as a full-fledged heroine in the citadel of imperialism and racism.

Tang Ming Chao, of the China Peace Committee:

Defying every difficulty and hardship she told the British people the truth about China ... Comrade Jones was a proletarian internationalist. Her whole life was that of a revolutionary and militant fighter. She devoted her life and energies to the struggle against imperialism, colonialism and revisionism, and for national liberation and the defence of world peace.

The meeting closed with the adoption of a message to the forthcoming London memorial meeting.[12]

The headstone affair

The Memorial Committee issued a fund-raising circular 'to establish a befitting memorial and also to help in the continued publication of her fighting journal'. However, not enough was raised for even a headstone. The *Gazette* itself survived only for another two issues. Claudia's grave was ignored for almost twenty years. In 1982 an article in the *Camden New Journal* (17 June) stated that 'pensioner Bill Fairman' had come across her grave 'accidentally'. After discovering 'who she was and what role she had played in the black community', Mr Fairman decided to tend her grave. He also 'contacted old friends of Claudia Jones to help raise money for a headstone in her memory'.

Unravelling the history of the headstone reveals as confused or manipulative a situation as that at the time of Claudia's death. In fact, Mr Fairman, a communist, had first turned to the Communist Party's newspaper, the *Morning Star*, but his letter had apparently not been printed.[13] Fairman and his comrade Bob Ellis had been tending the neglected graves of both Karl Marx and Claudia Jones, and wanted the Party to ensure their future maintenance. Fairman now turned to the Afro-Caribbean Organisation (ACO) at 335 Gray's Inn Road, whose secretary was Winston Pinder, also a Party member.[14] The ACO issued a fund-raising flyer and formed the Claudia Jones Memorial Fund and a committee to administer the funds raised. A gravestone was ordered and arrangements made for a ceremony on 26 September 1982, at

In Memory Of'
CLAUDIA JONES

(LATE EDITOR, WEST INDIAN GAZETTE & AFRO–ASIAN–CARIBBEAN NEWS)
MILITANT FIGHTER FOR FREEDOM OF ALL PEOPLES

Saturday, 27th February, 1965

INTERMENT OF ASHES

HIGHGATE CEMETRY, SWAINS LANE, N.6 10–30 a.m.
(BUS 210 15 minutes walk ARCHWAY TUBE)

PUBLIC MEETING

ST. PANCRAS TOWN HALL, EUSTON ROAD, W.C.I 12–30 p.m.
TRIBUTES IN : SPEECH ■ SONG ■ POETRY

L. Khalifa, Algerian Ambassador; Kwesi Armah, Ghana High Commissioner; Lord Brockway; Mrs. Oliver Tambo; Dr. Yousef Dadu; Dr. David Pitt; George Lamming; Raymond Kunene; Dr. Ranjana Sidhant; Francis Ezzreco; F. Bryant; A. Manchanda
Earl Cameron; Nadia Cattouse; George Webb; Isabel Lucas; Barry Johnson; Ewan McColl; Peggy Seeger; The Singers

CLAUDIA JONES' historic speech in U.S. court, before she was sentenced to one year's imprisonment, specially recorded by Ruby Dee, famous Negro Artiste.
FILM OF FUNERAL
CLAUDIA JONES MEMORIAL COMMITTEE, 13, Station Avenue, London

Printed by A.A. Publishing Co.,(T.U.) CLErkenwell 3924

Poster announcing the memorial meeting.

which Dr David Pitt would unveil the stone in the presence of Camden's mayor and other civic dignitaries.[15] However, these plans had to be postponed as by 4 October only £500 of the required £800 had been raised, and Manu had interfered with the ACO's plans.

The ACO met with Manu, but apparently some disagreement arose, probably over the appropriation of the name 'Claudia Jones Memorial Committee', as well as over lack of initial consultation. Manu had, after all, formed a committee by that name in 1965 and he owned the plot in which Claudia's ashes had been buried.[16] Manu put the matter into the hands of solicitors, who informed the ACO on 24 September 1982 that 'the Secretary of the Claudia Jones Memorial Committee [Mr Manchanda] withholds his permission for the erection of a Headstone upon the late Ms. Jones' grave ... or any other interference with her grave'.[17] He also called a meeting of those members of the original Committee who were in London.

It is probable, judging by his enquiries to the ACO regarding the composition of their Claudia Jones Committee, that Manu was suspicious that either the Committee or the ACO might have had more than close connections with the Communist Party.[18] According to Manu, 'On the pretext of honouring her memory, they [the Afro-Caribbean Organisation] have exploited the great international prestige of the late Claudia Jones, to serve their own sectarian political ends. For this they have been using variously different organisational names to collect money from people who cherish her memory.'[19]

In September 1983, Fairman, Pinder and the ACO were apparently in a position to erect a headstone. However, in his last preserved letter regarding this issue to Pinemarsh Limited (the owners of Highgate cemetery) dated 10 January 1984, Manchanda asked by what right Fairman had approached the company regarding a headstone. Clearly the matter rumbled on, perhaps, unless further evidence comes to light, until Manchanda's death on 27 October 1985.[20]

Claudia's legacy

Today Claudia is virtually unknown. She has been written out of history, even of Carnival.[21] There have been some efforts to keep Claudia's memory alive. These include the London-based Claudia Jones Organisation, an Afro-Caribbean women's group involved in education and social welfare, which lays a wreath at Claudia's grave every year.

In December 1978, the very first issue of *The Black Liberator*, 'a theoretical and discussion journal for black liberation', reprinted Claudia's 1964 article 'The Caribbean community in Britain' from the African-American journal *Freedomways*. In their introduction, the editors stated: '... Claudia's death (in December 1964) deprived us of one whose individual energy, ability and organisationally mediated commitment would, beyond question, have helped to advance our struggle to a point well beyond its current empasse ... [We] reprint sister Claudia's text [in order] to pay tribute to her memory. We do so to bring it to another audience. We do so, also, to give an opportunity to re-appraise both where Black theorising about our struggle had reached in 1964 and how it has moved on in the decade and a half since then.'[22]

In 1985 Buzz Johnson wrote and published *I Think of My Mother': Notes on the Life and Times of Claudia Jones*, which, while recounting Claudia's life devotes only eleven pages to her years in Britain. However, the book is a valuable compilation of some of Claudia's writings, published both in the USA and in Britain. There are four pages devoted to Claudia in Beverley Bryan, Stella Dadzie and Suzanne Scaife's *The Heart of the Race*, published in 1985 by Virago Press.

In 1986 Alex Pascall proposed to the Community Centre in Powis Square, which is near the site of Kelso Cochrane's murder, that statues should be erected to the memory of both Cochrane and Claudia Jones.

Sometime in the 1980s, Camden Black Sisters, an organisation set up in 1979, published a pamphlet, *Claudia Jones, 1915-1964: A Woman of Our Times*, researched and compiled by Jennifer Tyson. In their introduction, Yvonne Joseph and Louisa Jean-Baptiste wrote:

> We learned more and more about this great, brave Black Woman, who like Sojourner Truth and other great heroines, determinedly carved a way forward through all obstructions. We recognised in Claudia the strength and the courage of Black Women struggling all over the world. This booklet is a tribute to Claudia Jones and to the millions of Black Women whose lives can no longer continue to be denied.

In January 1989 London's Royal Court Theatre staged Winsome Pinnock's play about Claudia, 'Rock in the Water'. *The Guardian* newspaper heralded the play with a long article on Claudia by Michele Hanson, which concluded with 'Claudia was always poor, extraordinarily unselfish, tolerant, full of love for everyone and worked herself more or less to death for the benefit of others. Just the sort of person nobody ever hears about.'[23] *The Sunday Times* (22.1.1989, p9) reported that the play was 'an important act of recovery in that few will have heard of Claudia Jones ... The 19 scenes give little sense of her ideas so we do not know precisely what she was imprisoned for'. The theatre critic of *The Times Education Supplement* (13.1.1989, p33) found that the play, presented by the Royal Court Young People's Theatre, did not give 'a clear picture of the woman behind the facts'.

An attempt was made by the Camden Trades Council to keep Claudia's memory alive and to recognise her work by establishing annual lectures in her name. The first of these was given in October 1990 by Arthur Scargill, president of the National Union of Mineworkers.[24] Responding to my questions about this, Mr Scargill replied: 'Unfortunately I never knew her personally, although from friends and comrades who did I have gathered some sense of her extraordinary personality as well as her total commitment to Socialist principles!' It has not been possible to discover why the lectures were abandoned or how they were instigated.

But these legacies come nowhere near doing Claudia justice. She was much more than this, much more.

She came to Britain straight from jail, after a lengthy period of persecution in the United States. She came with a history of tuberculosis and heart trouble. She came expecting to be embraced by the British Communist Party and found herself unacknowledged, rejected almost. She came with no friends or colleagues in Britain except fellow exiles from the United States who sometimes proved to be false friends.

Claudia came with years of campaigning, speaking, organising and editorial experience in the United States Party, that had given her authority and an undoubted 'presence'. Virtually forsaken by the party which had been her 'home' in the USA, how was she to use her experience to find avenues to express her political commitments? She found herself in a country where not only did she not know anyone, but where the majority of Black peoples were recent arrivals who had not yet formed any coherent political organisations. Yet she found the courage to turn to the nascent communities of West Indians and other colonial migrants to create a forum, a platform, and as many organisations as the political exigencies of the times demanded.

It has not been possible to discover the exact nature of the problems between Claudia and her other 'natural' political home in Britain, Caribbean Labour Solidarity and its newspaper, *Caribbean News*. Could the Party itself have partly engendered this? Was her perspective too broad for a narrowly focused group?

Claudia could perhaps have found refuge and support in the group around the veteran activist George Padmore. But probably her continuing membership of the Communist Party prevented a realistic contact with the anti-Stalinist Padmore, who was, by then, perhaps also too narrowly focused on West Africa for Claudia.

Thus Claudia had to start from scratch in not very auspicious circumstances: in a racist Britain where she had no support, no family, no friends, no colleagues. Not only that, but her health was precarious. She had no income, no home, no passport, and no contacts outside a Party headquarters that rejected her. Nevertheless, start she did, and how magnificently. She published a monthly newspaper. Marrying art and politics, she began carnival, beauty contents and talent quests. She persuaded apolitical artists to contribute their talents to political events she organised. She brought people who had never before co-operated together into organisations. She even managed to inveigle Party members into supporting some of her activities. Her office became a necessary port-of-call for visiting Black politicians and was an advice centre for beleaguered Black people. Nevertheless, her continuing affiliation with the Communist Party alienated some people.

When she eventually obtained a passport, and despite her ill health, she travelled widely, contributing in every country she visited: in the USSR, in Japan and in China.

Interestingly, on her last trip abroad, she reclaimed her Trinidad origins by stating that she was representing that country. Does this indicate a rejection of Britain as well as the British Communist Party? Or was this move a reaction to her rejection by the Party? Or is it an affirmation of not only her origins but also of Trinidad's recent independence?

Of the many people I interviewed for this book, no one claimed to be Claudia's friend. Did she have friends in Britain? Maybe not. She was used to a different level of political discourse, a different commitment among her friends – Black and white – in the United States. That could not be replicated here. She might have been too committed, too 'senior', too experienced and too much a woman with her own mind for those she met in Britain. Her determination kept her alive and kept her active twenty-four hours a day. She died undoubtedly exhausted by what had become a superhuman effort.

Claudia was magnificent – and a woman alone.

Notes

1. Telephone interview with Eric Levi, 23 June 1997. Mikki Doyle was 'proprietorial; she and Manu fought over Claudia's papers', Ranjana Ash

told me. (Interview, London 14 January 1998.)

2. Manchanda to Bill Fairman, 3 August 1982; undated draft of letter to Pinder et al, c. late August 1982; Langford Collection. (Henceforth unless otherwise indicated, all Claudia's and Manu's correspondence and material relating to the funeral are from this collection.)

3. Telephone interview with Ricky Cambridge, Oxford, 17 May 1998.

4. Statement from J.H. Kenyon, Funeral Directors, 9 July 1982; Claudia Jones Memorial Committee flyer, 5 January 1965.

5. *West Indian Gazette*, December 1964, p8. Among those bearing her coffin were members of the Indian Workers Association.

6. *Ibid.*

7. Buzz Johnson, *I Think of My Mother: Notes on the Life and Times of Claudia Jones*, Karia Press, London 1985, p175.

8. Letter from Highgate Cemetery, 5 June 1998.

9. It has not been possible to locate this film.

10. Isabel Lucas was a singer; Peter Blackman was a communist, a friend of Paul Robeson's; Bari Johnson was an actor and singer who returned to Jamaica in 1970 as a producer for the Jamaican Broadcasting Corporation; Earl Cameron is an actor.

11. Hunton was an African-American, who had been a member of the CPUSA and a leading figure in the New York-based Council on African Affairs. See Dorothy Hunton, *Alphaeus Hunton: The Unsung Valiant*, New York 1986.

12. Hsinhua News agency press release #022129, 22 February 1965.

13. Manchanda to Fairman, 3 August 1982. Mr Fairman had shown Manu, during Manu's visit on 11 July, a copy of his letter to the *Morning Star*. Neither Fairman nor Ellis is still alive.

14. Afro-Caribbean Organization to Manchanda, 4 January 1983. In 1983 the secretary was Maxine Brown. In an interview on 13 October 1997 Mr Pinder told me that the Afro-Caribbean Organisation did not restrict its membership to communists. He claimed to have joined the CPGB through Claudia's influence and to have visited her regularly when she lived in north London, partly to inform her of the progress of the ACO. It has not proved possible to establish the date of the founding of the ACO; Mr Pinder stated that its papers have been destroyed.

15. Minutes of meeting of the ACO's Claudia Jones Memorial Committee, 2 July 1982.

16. Letter, 'To Whom It May Concern', from J.H. Kenyon, Funeral Directors, 9 July 1982.

17. Geo. J. Dowse & Co to ACO, 24 September 1982. Mr Pinder in an interview, London, 13 October 1997, was unclear as to whether he had received letters from the solicitor, and claimed that the grave site was owned by Mikki Doyle. This is contradicted by the existing documentation.

18. Manchanda to Pinder, 25 October 1982, asking for list of members of the ACO 'concerned with the preparation of putting up the grave stone' and

for a statement of the amount of money collected in this connection.

19. Manchanda to E. Herman, Superintendent, Highgate Cemetery, 8 September 1983.

20. Highgate Cemetery, in a letter date 5 June 1998, advised that it had no information regarding by whom or when the memorial stone had been installed.

21. See David Roussel-Milner, 'False History of Notting Hill Carnival: a review of Professor Abner Cohen's "Masquerade Politics"', *The Association for a People's Carnival Newsletter*, no.7, 1996.

22. The editors of the *Black Liberator* were Ricky Cambridge, Cecil Gutzmore and Colin Prescod.

23. Michele Hanson, 'A true woman to her people', *The Guardian*, 10 January 1989. I must thank Cris Le Maitre for giving me a copy of this article.

24. Telephone interview with Nicola Side, London 9 February 1998; letter from Arthur Scargill, 31 January 1998. It has proved impossible to discover more about this proposed lecture series, its inception and demise.

Symposium on Claudia Jones
28 September 1996

Session 1: My friend Claudia

David Roussel-Milner My brothers and sisters, we have come here together today at this seat of learning to make a mark on the wall of history. We have come to carve a name on that wall, the name of a great African woman whose contribution to the history of Black people entitles her to a very important place in that history. But we are going to have to carve her name very deeply, because seats of learning such as this have so often denied a place on that wall of history to Black people, and particularly to Black women, even to the extent of obliterating as many as they can of such names from that wall...

Some of you may have read in last month's newsletter of the Association for a People's Carnival, my review of Abner Cohen's book entitled *Masquerade Politics* (London 1993). This book, which has been promoted as the bible of the Notting Hill Carnival history, is not just full of unfortunate mistakes; it is stacked with lies. And who is the author of this travesty of historical truth? An emeritus professor of anthropology from the School of Oriental and African Studies, a sister college within this seat of learning, the University of London. Of indoor Mardi Gras carnivals in London promoted by Claudia Jones each year from 1959 to her untimely death during Christmas 1964, Abner Cohen sneeringly writes,

> It transpired that some time after the 1958 race riots Claudia Jones had arranged a big party for West Indians somewhere in London and that a competition between individual masqueraders was held at it. Victor Critchlow said he had attended that event and had won the first prize. He even displayed a photograph showing himself in his usual suit but with a hat in the shape of the Eiffel Tower on his head.

Cohen does not seem to be aware that the photograph was taken in 1962 at the Seymour Hall on the edge of Notting Hill, and that it included the great Black cricketer and diplomat, Learie Constantine, as well as Claudia herself. As for the single big party, is that all Cohen can say of the six annual events supported by hundreds of English people as well as West Indians in the wake of the 1958 race riots? Arguing that until the middle of the 1980s the white social worker, Rhaune Laslett, 'had been acknowledged as the founder, the initiator, the first organiser of the carnival', Cohen scoffs at first generation West Indians, presumably including some of us here, who 'suddenly discovered that it had been a West Indian woman, Claudia Jones, who had somehow started the Carnival'. Like Hume, Cohen had with a stroke of his own empirically incompetent pen dismissed all that some of us have as personal knowledge of the hard work and heartaches of the true founder of Notting Hill carnival, the woman who, when I was a young man, was my journalistic and political mentor and whom I counted as my friend, Claudia Jones.

Pearl Connor Thank you. It is a privilege to be here with you all today to celebrate the life of Claudia Jones, one of the most charismatic Caribbean women I ever knew. Like me she was born in Trinidad, but her early life experience of poverty and hardship in the United States, to which her parents emigrated when she was eight years old, drew her into the ranks of the struggling underclass where she had her grounding. She developed into one of the most effective women fighters for human rights in America.

We came across each other in 1958 when I was in the process of establishing a theatrical agency to represent Afro-Asian and Caribbean artists while Claudia was planning the launch of the *West Indian Gazette*. She had made an early commitment to change things for Black people in America and joined the Communist Party which gave her the support and backing she needed, but this marked her out for victimisation and eventual deportation from the United States, which was in the grip of the Cold War.

Many of us had experienced colonialism in our own countries and were fighting desperately for independence, lobbying Members of Parliament and government officials. We were joined in this activity by the West Indian and West African students who were very active and militant at their headquarters in Earl's Court. The League of Coloured Peoples was working hard at issues affecting Black people who had settled here. Dr David Pitt, later Lord Pitt, made his premises in Gower Street available for meetings in which Claudia and many of us took part. David held open political surgeries to advise and help those of our people struggling to survive. Claudia found a situation in which she was needed and became most effective. She was a catalyst; she brought people together and could inspire, inform and mobilise them. She was able to analyse situations, and through her experience and organising skills was able to advise us on how to respond to the British Government.

There were not many Black women involved in the political struggle or working actively in the community at that time; Claudia determined to mobilise as many Black women as she could. She established the Black Sash Movement at the Africa Student Centre in Earl's Court and presented awards for special achievements by women. I was one of the fortunate recipients. Her wishes were to build up Black women leaders in the community who would carry on the struggle and organise others in defying the harsh immigration laws that were being enacted ...

Many of the immigrants who came to England in the 1950s had left their homes because of hardship; they found a post-war Britain in need of their services. Enoch Powell, then Minister of Health, sent off to the Caribbean to recruit personnel for hospitals, while other Ministries recruited staff to run the buses and the railways. Many were drafted in for menial tasks like street cleaning, which the British work force had rejected. I don't know who was sweeping the streets before we arrived, but we did a very good job, very efficiently, and we became very competitive, insofar that there was a backlash when the English people began complaining and wanting their jobs back.

We were all in search of financial stability and wanted to educate our children and assist our families back home. But our success had an unexpected effect, encouraging families to rush in to join us, thus throwing open the floodgates to immigrants who were seen as a blot on the British landscape and caused fear amongst the local people. The British Government now began to look at the situation with new eyes.

Claudia made contact with our people in Brixton and Notting Hill; she connected up with Amy Ashwood Garvey, whose husband Marcus Garvey propagated the ideas of Black consciousness, just as Steve Biko came to do more recently in South Africa. Mrs Garvey lived at 1 Bassett Road in a house known as the Afro People's Centre. It was there that many of us met when the race riots exploded in the Grove, and Kelso Cochrane, a Black man, was murdered. The *West Indian Gazette* was already a going concern before the riots and proved of great importance in analysing British press reports ... Claudia had had experience of Jim Crow, the Ku Klux Klan, lynchings and overt racism in America.

Claudia was on the scene to mobilise Black opinion and advise on how best the problem could be tackled. She came up with a positive suggestion, to calm fears and restore harmony in the community: with Mrs Garvey and many supporters she organised a carnival celebration at Porchester Hall, Bayswater, inviting as many people as possible to attend. This was the beginning of what was to become the Notting Hill Carnival.

As a journalist and political activist, Claudia linked the *Gazette* with the struggle for independence in the Caribbean and Africa, and struck out against the harsh apartheid regime in South Africa. She linked her political stance with the artistic and cultural achievements of our people, and soon had the co-operation and active support of writers like George Lamming, Jan Carew and Andrew Salkey, and Black publishers like New Beacon Books and Bogle l'Ouverture. Many performing artists joined in to support her efforts, like Pearl Prescod, Nadia Cattouse, Carmen Monroe, Ram John Holder, Horace James, and Edric Connor, my deceased husband, and myself.

Most outstanding among the supporters in the arts was Paul Robeson, that great Black singer and actor who had been persecuted in the United States for his beliefs. Paul had many discussions with us in London when he was appearing in *Othello* in 1959 at the Stratford Memorial Theatre, just one year after the riots. He had been very active in supporting Claudia in her stand against the authorities in America that were determined to extradite her. Another of Claudia's political allies was Martin Luther King, the civil rights leader and man of peace. In 1963 when the Civil Rights Movement was at its peak and he marched on Washington, Claudia organised a march on the American Embassy in Grosvenor Square in London to coincide with that event. Many of us who supported the struggle joined in that march.

Claudia supported efforts by Edric and myself to seek union representation for Black artists and to have conditions of employment improved, wages upgraded, and contractual arrangements brought into line with the standard rights of their British contemporaries. Just as she had promoted the rights of Black workers in America, so we were promoting the rights of Black artists in Britain.

When Martin Luther King passed through London on his way to receive the Nobel Peace Prize in 1964, Claudia arranged a private meeting at her home with David Pitt, Edric and myself, to discuss ways and means of assisting him. Little did I realise how soon after this they would both be gone from us.

Bill Ash What I'm going to say is quite general and very much about Claudia as a friend. From the time of Claudia Jones' arrival here, expelled from the United States by rampant McCarthyism, till her death at the end of 1964, no one in this country seriously involved in struggles against racism, fascism or imperialism could have failed to get to know her and to work with her.[16] She founded the *West Indian Gazette*, she was responsible for organising the Afro-Asian and Caribbean Committee, she was active in opposing the racism in Notting Hill when Kelso Cochrane was murdered, and she planned a huge Notting Hill march in 1963 in solidarity with the civil rights struggle in the United States. Indeed I always think of the Notting Hill festival as being in part a celebration of all Claudia Jones has done for the people of Britain.

She knew and worked with all the African leaders in the fight against imperialism, she visited the Soviet Union, China and Vietnam where she was received as the spokesperson for the world anti-imperialist struggle. All this in addition to numerous conferences and protest meetings at which she spoke here in London.

Rajana Ash We met shortly after she had arrived in Britain, at, I think, a concert by the Indian musician, Ravi Shankar. And that was the most amazing thing about Claudia: never before, or since, have I come across a person as deeply committed politically, far more than any of us, whose cultural appreciations were worldwide. If only today, confined as we are to our narrow ethnic groups, we could cross boundaries as she did, what a wonderful world we could make of it, at least culturally if not in political terms.

Our sympathies were very close to the struggle for African countries' indepedence. There had been many, many solidarity organisations, and there were so many more protests and marches which called all of us from our different groups to march. It was for strengthening that, that she formed a solidarity committee called the Committee of Afro-Asian and Caribbean Organisations. We were very grateful to the Ghana Government which had given the Earl's Court building, already mentioned by Pearl, at 3 Collingham Gardens; that became a centre, and the Committee was given a room and premises, so many of the meetings were held there.

And sisters and brothers, as we sit here, we simply cannot imagine what London was like in those days. The struggle for freeing – which wasn't successful – Dedan Kimathi, the great Mau-Mau leader; the struggle for the independence of Guyana; the struggle that Cuba was waging; the struggle of Vietnam; Malaya; Cyprus; Aden: these are all names we have forgotten. Each one of them was fought for; each one of them involved the British Government killing; all that has been forgotten. Claudia was always ready. That woman was not well, but she did it all. Something that we must remember, is that she made us think about uniting struggles which could so easily have been divided. Within the Communist Party she fought to put the national liberation struggles raging in three worlds on the agenda. It was so easy for people fighting their struggles here to forget about these and not to see the connecting links; indeed half of them didn't even know where these places were.

Enrico (Ricky) Stennett I arrived as a young man in England in 1947. On my arrival, within weeks I began to meet quite a few people who were active in political struggles, people that most of us seem to forget. I would like to remind this meeting today, because I think it's very important that we remember all the people who fought battles, street battles and other battles in England, for the survival of the newcomers. I don't know if anyone here remembers Robert Matthews, a man with no fingers, but a man who night after night walked the streets of London trying to help the unfortunate people that were arriving into a country which was racist and which took all race advantages possible.

When Claudia Jones arrived on the scene we were glad because of the fact that until her arrival women in politics, in Black politics in England, were not many, in fact very, very few. I heard the name of Amy Garvey mentioned; she was a friend of mine. Yes, I used to gather there as well, you know, to listen and to speak, and she also made a lot of contribution. Claudia Jones however was a beacon, a light. She arrived at the same time as Cliff Lynch; I don't know if any one of you remember Clifford Lynch. They both arrived in England about the same time, and Clifford Lynch died last year. He became a member of the African League that I was a member of at the time, and we both supported Claudia Jones in the *West Indian Gazette*.

Before the *West Indian Gazette* we had what was called the *African Voice* (possibly *African Arrow*). I don't know if anyone here ever knew of that paper, but it was a paper that we sold on the street. We were inadequate, however, because we were not writers, we were not publishers, but this lady comes along and she taught us a lot.

Had Claudia Jones not died, I believe with her leadership we could have done quite a lot. But with the death of Martin Luther King we saw what happened in the United States of America, where the struggle seems to have died – the same thing applies to Claudia and to us here. She is not dead as far as I'm concerned, she will never die. Neither will the Black people that I know who have led the struggle. These people will never die, because as long as the struggle is to be fought their name shall be a light before us.

Trevor Carter I think somebody was talking about Claudia as an extremely serious person, but on another dimension a very simple soul who related to not only the politics of people but also the personal lives of people. To coin a phrase, she was somebody on whose shoulder one could rest one's head.

I remember one incident of her as a friend, but it's highly political. When I arrived here in 1954, like everybody else I was called up for National Service. As students you were deferred for two years if you so desired. I got my deferment for two years because, as Ranjana [Ash] was saying, at that time the serious wars were going on, it was Aden, it was Guyana, it was Cyprus, it was Kenya, and it was Malaya: five. So many of us, especially those of us who were in the Communist Party, found it very awkward to join the National Service or be called up. Some of us went to court and lost and had to go into the army. In 1956, I can't remember if you were there Ranjana, but we were at a Party school at Hastings doing Stalin's book, *The Colonial Question*. Of those of us who were in the Party, I remember Claudia was there, Betty Ambatielos was there and so were Tony Gilbert and Kay Beauchamp.

I was very worried at the time because I got the final call-up to say that I had to go and do my National Service. I didn't want to, obviously: there were moral and political reasons for not going into the British forces at that time. But there was also the financial reason: I think we used to get ten bob a week in the army then, or something like that, and Corinne, my wife, was home in Trinidad at the time, so were my parents, my brothers, sisters, and you couldn't really squeeze that ten bob to send home some things. So, in my worry I spoke to a comrade called Stan Levinson who was the oldest youth at that time. He was in charge of the youth festivals and the cultural things and the youth work in the country, a Young Communist Leaguer and Stan said, 'Well there's something called the International Brigada', which was building the stadium for a sports festival which was going to be held in 1956 in Leipzig. And he said, 'You can go there'. Because I was a member of the World Federation of Democratic Youth, I was a council member, so I had privileges, I suppose. Anyhow that was in my mind, but before I did anything I had to get permission from the Party to do it, and as Idris Cox was one of the lecturers at Hastings, I said to him, 'Look Idris, I have a chance of going to the GDR to get away from the army'. And Idris replied, 'Comrade, the policy of the Party is that we all do our national service and, like the French party, organise in the National Service to get the soldiers on our side'. I was very worried. So I went to Claudia, and Claudia with that mischievous look on her face said 'Don't be worried comrade, Raji Palme Dutt is coming on Friday to give a little fiery speech, you will speak to him'. So I did, with all sorts of trepidations of course, this is Rajani Palme Dutt! I explained to him what happened, I said what Idris Cox said, and he did his thing. And as Ranjana was saying, there was goodwill from the CP but there was a lack of understanding, and Raji said to me, 'Comrade, I am the vice-chair of this Party, I say that you shall go. The problem with this Party, they do not understand the colonial comrades'. And the following day I was on a plane; I ended up at Tempelhof airport in Berlin, and for some months I was in Leipzig.

Pearl Connor We were fighting for Caribbean independence, but Claudia was involved not only with the diaspora but with the whole of Africa as well. There was also the issue of Guyana, but after the Caribbean we got involved with Ghana, with Nigeria, with Kenya. All these people were coming here, Tom Mboya from Kenya; Nkomo was coming out of Rhodesia; we had, from Tanzania, Julius Nyerere. They were always lobbying in the House of Commons. We met Tom [Mboya] before he was assassinated. There was all this talk going – people thought he was a CIA man. There was Nkomo – Nkomo was the man that they were nurturing. I mean the British Government had a way of operating with us; colonialism was really marvellous, it was operating right inside here, in the centre of the Raj, and so they had us, they were manipulating people. We had to be informed, to have an informant. And when Claudia came, she was able to mobilise, to get people together, people who never really felt they had to come out; she was able to bring people out in support. Claudia was a very knowledgeable woman, she had a lot of good information which we didn't have.

Claudia was a catalyst, she pulled together that force and made us much more effective than we had ever been before with this British Government here.

David Roussel-Milner We had some of the meetings for what I think we used to call the London Carnival Committee at my mother's flat in Chalk Farm. I remember my mother was the chair of the Queen's Committee, and on one occasion Claudia handed me a tape measure and asked whether I would like to measure up the girls. Of course I was delighted, being in my early twenties, all these beautiful girls around!

Except that my mother was hopping behind me and grabbed it and said 'Oh no you don't!'

But I remember Claudia as somebody who had a tremendous, fantastic influence on my life and changed my way of thinking, who made me realise just what I had been doing as a commando in Egypt, how I had been in support of a British Raj which I didn't understand, and the implications of that. And obviously at the present time with the fortieth anniversary of the invasion coming up in the next few days, I'm very conscious of what was going on at that time.

Symposium on Claudia Jones 28 September 1996

Session 2: The political activist

Trevor Carter I remember the first time I heard a reference to Claudia Jones in my lifetime was in the late 1940s. My father was reading the *Evening News* in Trinidad, he turned to my mother jocularly, and said, 'I see your cousin is in trouble again in the United States'. And there was a photograph, a small photograph on the front page of the *Evening News*, and it was talking about a problem during the McCarthyite period. My imagination at that time was on the margins of political thought – although I was one of those fortunate people who was recruited to something akin to a communist party or Marxist party in my sixth form at my school, a modern secondary school, by a bloke called J.E. Moore. He was in a Marxist organisation, that Pearl will know more about, because Pearl was in the Youth Movement, and carried banners and all that, in those days. He was in this organisation with John La Rose, Cris LeMaitre, Rojas, and other people whom I can't recall now.

But it did coincide with the little reading that one was able to do at that age, both my age – my chronological age – and the times, given what the libraries had or what was selling in the bookshops. But one was reading a bit of the post-war personalities: Ralph Bunche most of us would remember from those days – he was a Black person working on the Palestine thing at the time for the United Nations. And of course there was Paul Robeson, everybody knew him.[4] There was also Richard Wright, on whose seminal book, *Native Son*, I think all of us grew up.[5] And of course there was Haile Selassie ... he had chased the Italians out – well not really, but he did make a speech at the United Nations, sitting on a bench. Then there was Marian Anderson, one of the best contraltos that the world knew. But we were split, because on race grounds we were loving and supporting her, but on political grounds we had a problem because she was speaking for the United States at the times of the height of colonialism. So, those were the thoughts around which Claudia came into my consciousness.

Those were the foreigners. But nearer home, we had Norman W. Manley, Richard Hart and Bustamente in Jamaica, we had Uriah Buzz Butler in Trinidad, we had Cheddi Jagan in British Guiana, we had Gairy of Grenada, we had Beryl McBurnie, who was the cultural revolutionary at the time for us in Trinidad; and C.L.R. James was already important. To many of our age one of the most important books was *The Black Jacobins*, because we in the Caribbean learned West Indian history from that history book I think by Gutteridge, where the story of Haiti was half of a page, but quarter of the page was a picture of Toussaint, and so before James we just had these few words.

The world was small for us, we were island people, and we didn't know what was going on in Jamaica or even in Tobago!

Again, I want to put Claudia, the knowledge of Claudia, in another context, because I travelled to this country and I joined the Communist Party. So my political life began in this country particularly with the advent of Claudia. But I must not omit another person very important to my education, Billy Strachan, who was known in the telephone directory as Flight Lieutenant William A.H. Strachan. But the most important thing that was happening at that time, to us, in our souls and our feelings and our consciousness, was the spirit of Bandung and of the Bandung heroes, Chou En Lai, Nehru, Nkrumah, and Sukarno. So that was the context in which we were thinking.

When I was coming here I got something from the archives of the Communist Party which was a letter from the American party to the British party, introducing Claudia ... You cannot talk about Claudia without talking about Claudia the Communist Party member. We cannot talk about the cultural person without talking about Claudia's days in the US Communist Party. You can't talk about Claudia the universal person without talking about Claudia the Communist Party member. That is important.

You cannot talk about Claudia without talking about two important aspects of the history of the Communist Party, that is the struggle around the Scottsboro Boys and the Peekskill incident. And for those of you who might not remember, the Scottsboro Boys were nine Black youngsters, who looked at a white woman and were charged with rape. Claudia and the Communist Party mounted their defence. You can't talk about Claudia without talking about the Peekskill incident. There is a little book about it, I think it's around still, *Peekskill Incident*, written by Howard Fast. Why I raise this business of the Peekskill incident, is because it was a narrative that is important to all of us. In the hard, heavy, angry, nasty days of the McCarthyite period, Paul Robeson in his eternal heroism decided to sing in Peekskill, which is a place just north of New York. And he spoke, he sang there, and the fascists, the racists, the KKK, decided that he shouldn't sing, but he went ahead, despite the threats. The movement, the wide movement of trade unionists, communists, anti-racists, anti-fascists, decided that he *was* going to sing. And the fascists came and they threw stones and bricks. And our good friend, Mikki Doyle, lost an eye.

Of course, we in the Communist Party organised support for Claudia while her court case was heard in the USA. The day she arrived here I went to meet her with Billy Strachan. Some of you might know that the wounded veterans were given a little car by the Government. It was a little thing; it was a motorcycle within a bit of a canvas thing like a tent. It was for one person, but because we were broke in those days I used to travel around London sitting at Billy's side at the bottom of this thing. So we went to the station to meet the train from Southampton. I remember driving through the smog, because it was real smog and you couldn't see ten yards in front of you. But there we met Claudia. And then we went back to the place where she was going to stay in south London.

I have to tell you of my first image of this person. Here was a woman – and you have to think about my mind being a small, in a way colonial mind, that was just becoming fertile – and this woman looked so successful! In Trinidad I had only ever known of two successful Black women. And Claudia had that appearance, the appearance of a woman who knew where she was going: everybody's headmistress or the leader of the Girl Guides, that leader sort of person. But I also had contemporaries in this country, people who stood out, and it's not because I am sitting next to Pearl but your name is here first, Pearl. There was Winifred Atwell. There was – not because I'm sitting next to you, David – but there was your mother, Carmen England. Not because I'm sitting next to you, there was Ranjana. It's not because you are here Colin; there was your mother, Pearl Prescod.[18] So, these were the women I knew, but as Pearl was saying earlier, as Ranjana was saying earlier, we were all limited to a certain extent.

Claudia came in a period of anti-colonial struggle. We were doing our thing as far as the Caribbean was concerned, but the most important thing about having come to this country was that gradually we became one soul. The period was the height of immigration from the Indian subcontinent, Africa and the Caribbean. The essence of the politics, though we didn't have a name for it at that time, was the growing Black Consciousness movement. For those of us who were in the Communist Party, it was a class-before-race situation. But growing out of the movements in the United States, Africa, Asia, the Caribbean, Latin America, there was this consciousness, race consciousness, a Black consciousness. Claudia towered over us, and she towered over us by her American experience.

Those of us whose background was communist, especially for those of us who received most of our political education and experience in this country, there was no experience of Black struggle to fit into. When we arrived we had to create struggle. Every step we made was struggle; every job we went into we were confronted with 'You are the first Black man I have ever met', et cetera, et cetera. Racism was in the consciousness and the psyche of the society and there was the problem of racial discrimination.

Claudia was a leader, she was a leader of the only Western communist party that was steeped in the Black experience, a party which had the advantage of being informed and led by brilliant Black men and women. The best example we have of that is the father of them all, W.E.B. Du Bois. Claudia was able to see very quickly above the small island and continental chauvinism that was an element of our young British Black communities. Many of us from Trinidad had never seen or heard a Jamaican accent in our lives – we were only thrown together by immigration. There were little controversies about which island was larger and which island was smaller, and who spoke the best English and all that kind of nonsense. And then we had the continental business, people from India. Those of you who read Naipaul's *An Area of Darkness*, will know what I mean.

But the most important thing about Claudia was her heroic contribution after the 1958 Notting Hill and Nottingham race attacks on the Black communities. And Claudia was able to be stoic about it, because we, besides seeing a few American films on the issue, knew nothing about being racially attacked. But Claudia came from a culture that understood that – in America they were not only attacked but also lynched and killed and burnt. And she was able to rise above that and give some leadership.

Claudia also recognised something about the lack of political experience and conviction in this country, that even finding people to sell all these papers was very difficult. As a Jamaican man said to me in front of the Westbourne Park tube station, where I was selling *Caribbean News*, and he was pushing a pram with a baby in it. I said, 'Would you like to buy a newspaper sir?' He looked at me. I said, 'Come on, come on brother, buy a paper'. He said, 'Look brother, I look only at the ads for a place to live'. You see that was our problem in those days. But Claudia rose above that, and Claudia recognised that problem. What Claudia went for was what today Stuart Hall and Paul Gilroy would call the cultural thing. Claudia recognised that as being revolutionary. As John La Rose wrote to Billy Strachan in 1956, 'The most democratic institution in the Caribbean was carnival'. And all the time I thought carnival was just something where people 'jump up' and all that sort of thing. But when John described it as the most democratic institution, I understood something, something that I had grown up with. I don't think Claudia did, because she left when she was six or eight-years old. So she knew nothing about carnival, but she saw the value of it. She understood there had been the Black cultural struggle in the United States, and that the Harlem renaissance sort of exposed that to the world. So in 1959 we had the first carnival in St Pancras Town Hall.

The most important thing about Claudia was her strength in bringing people together. We fought the battle in many places: some in the Communist Party and in the Caribbean Labour Congress; Matthews did his thing in Hyde Park; the students did their thing at Hans Crescent and Collingham Gardens. Some of the people in the theatre, like your husband Pearl, Edric Connor, and Cy Grant, they did their thing in their place. Claudia brought all of us together. All of those people now are significant people in the cultural and political world. Take Cy Grant for example. He was a solicitor. And he was in the theatre. Cy Grant was our answer to Harry Belafonte. It wasn't just a stupid thing, because what Cy was trying to do was to bring to the public an aspect of culture that the public knew nothing about. Cy Grant brought to popular culture the kind of calypso that talked about what the problems were that we were going through.

Gertrude Elias I met Claudia the first time in 1958 when she addressed a meeting of the British Communist Party together with Palme Dutt. I was immensely impressed by her as one of the most knowledgeable, brilliant women I had ever heard. Then I lost sight of her. A year later I bumped into her in Oxford Street, and I asked, 'Are you Claudia Jones? Why is it that one never hears you in London? Are you perhaps addressing meetings up north?' 'Oh,' she replied, 'nobody cares who I am, nothing. Look, I'm starving and I haven't got a nickel on me.' So I said, 'Let's have lunch'. I still had a pound or two, and we bought some fish and chips, and there we were, sitting in a small place in Soho talking for three hours. She told me about her life. I was tremendously impressed, knowing that most of the so-called leading members of our movement wouldn't even spare a minute for you, and there was this woman, absolutely pouring out what she had gone through. She was totally oblivious of her own achievements, which were very great. For example, during the Korean war she said to the American Negroes, 'You shouldn't go and fight now for the United States, who didn't even give you what they promised to you during the Second World War when you were fighting and dying in Europe against the Nazis. You must know that all prejudice against Black people re-appeared within five minutes after the American Negro contingent returned to this country.' Claudia mobilised American women to stop all traffic in Washington and New York to prevent the soldiers going. She said to them, 'Black and white women, don't let your sons and your husbands and your lovers go to be slaughtered again in Korea'. Mobilising All-American women to fight for their men had a tremendous effect on the American establishment. It had never happened before that a Black woman came out to fight for both Black and white men and women.

She was not a Black nationalist, she was a humanist, a universalist, she wanted to fight for peace and for life for all people, the human race. I was amazed when I saw a film about her life on television where she was shown as a feminist, as a young woman fighting for women's rights. She fought for human rights. Her struggle against war was massive and tremendous.

For Claudia, it was a period of hope; it was a period which did not cultivate mutual hatred.

Pansy Jeffrey In 1958 the race riots took place in Nottingham, followed by the one in Notting Hill. In September 1961 I think it was, I was appointed by the Mayor's Committee of the Royal Borough of Kensington and Chelsea, and the London Citizens' Advice Bureaux, as a West Indian social worker with my office in Ladbroke Grove Citizens' Advice Bureau. Among my jobs was to sit on committees concerning the West Indian community. One of these organisations was the British Caribbean Association; there I met Claudia Jones. At one of our meetings which we extended to a sort of social as well as a discussion, she was sitting with Baroness Barbara Castle and some other people, and I was invited to meet her. The meeting was interesting. I discovered immediately that she was special to the cause, easy, knowledgeable, with no trace of arrogance, just out to make a useful contribution to the cause with a number of

interesting ideas which did not remain ideas but were put into practice. She was a fighter. Our work together was very interesting for
me.

We met several times at her home, and I found her a teacher
supporting any project you wanted to introduce. Her knowledge was
not only in the world of community work and politics, but also in
other avenues. One particular evening, I met her at her house, she was
entertaining Jan Carew. We were somewhat late in our discussions, and
so the supper was a little behind, and she taught me to cook potatoes
in five to eight minutes; I've used this recipe to this day. She had a sense
of humour, which was helpful.

We met one day at the house of Amy Ashwood Garvey in Ladbroke
Grove. Mrs Garvey was a member of the Mayor's Committee in
Kensington. It was she who appointed me. For some unknown reason
I had on a red winter coat. Mrs Garvey seemed to be unhappy about
this colour. This was the 1960s. I was at a loss. Later Claudia remarked
to me, 'Ignore Amy, ignore Amy's remarks. She loves to behave and
look after you as a mother.'

Claudia encouraged me, and I encouraged our Caribbean brethren
and others who were interested, to buy the *West Indian Gazette*. There
was very important information in this paper, and it was the only one
as far as I can remember for the Black community. It was housed in
Theo Campbell's record shop, another stalwart in his own way.

Ranjana Ash I want to say two things about Claudia's political work.
She was superb at being able to accept major differences in outlook. We
haven't come to the present plight of the international working-class
movement without major divisions. There were two crucial issues. One
has already been touched on: the relationship between the working-
class struggle in the metropolitan countries, Britain, France, the USA,
and the struggles of the people out there in the 'third world'. They had
the same enemy, but they were being fought in different ways and with
apparently no relationship whatsoever. Claudia was forever trying to
bridge that huge gap, not through theoretical discourse but through
practical action and her inimitable way of being able to draw upon a
world of political experience.

There was also a huge split in the international communist movement: there was the Russian Communist Party line, and there was the
Chinese Communist Party line, and these were major divisions.
Claudia understood the significance of those divisions. It's quite wrong
to say that she was unaware of them, she knew only too well what each
side was saying, but she did not want to split the communist move-

ment, and I think this should be remembered by all of us who weren't that clever.

Donald Hinds I've always wondered (perhaps there's a bit of controversy coming up here) about the two great West Indians that I have been privileged to see and talk to, C.L.R. James and Claudia Jones. I thought that there wasn't as much unity as I would like to have seen between the two. I was looking through copies of the *West Indian Gazette*, and in December 1962 Claudia reviewed C.L.R. James's *Party Politics in the West Indies*. I think it's worth reading, because she was very critical of James's book. Later on someone told me that this was probably because they took sides in the difference between Trotsky and Stalin. Well it's worthwhile looking. We're being very nice to Claudia; we can also bring in just a little controversy.

Joseph Mogotsi I am from South Africa. When I came here in 1961 I came with a group of musicians and artists. It was then that I realised how we, the Black South Africans, were being left out of the political situation in the world. But as I went around, and I looked about, I met this wonderful woman, Claudia Jones, for the first time. I was not introduced to her but I had noticed this woman; every time we had a show she was there outside issuing these pamphlets, and I said to myself, I wonder where this woman comes from. And eventually I had to introduce myself. I said, 'Look, I am Joe Mogotsi of the Manhattan Brothers, and I have been in this country under pressure. How can you help?' And she said, 'Well, welcome, my brother. One day South Africa is going to fall. You people have been left out of the politics, but we are here to bring pressure on the South African situation.'

Claudia was one person I admired, one woman I have always thought of every day of my life, I say to myself, what a woman, what type of a woman is this who will be going out on her own? Because whenever she was issuing these pamphlets I never saw someone around helping her; she was there on her own issuing all these pamphlets on South African apartheid. I feel that a lot still has to be done, because from that time I haven't seen that type of woman outside any place, any embassy, talking about the pressures of the day.

David Roussel-Milner I remember asking Claudia one day what was it that made her so politically active and aware. She told me that having arrived in the United States when she was about eight years of age, and her mother having to work so very very hard, living in quite a degree of poverty, she went to her priest and said, 'Now why is it that we people have to live like this?' And her priest said, 'Well that's the way God ordained it so that's the way you have to accept it'. And this set her thinking, and instead of following the religious way, she followed the political way.

I count as one of my greatest experiences being there at the funeral. I think it was the first really big Black funeral that London ever saw. We walked with her coffin up to the crematorium. The place was full. Paul Robeson sent a taped message. It was a wonderful day, and we celebrated her life. We didn't mourn; we celebrated a great woman who was passing. I think we've all mourned ever since, not mourning her person so much as mourning her politics. Mourning her contribution.

Symposium on Claudia Jones
28 September 1996

Session 3: *The West Indian Gazette*

Donald Hinds One of the terrible things in life is to have to confess that you are present somewhere and you really didn't know the full importance of it. It's like my pupils at school are busy doing their course-work on the Long March, and a woman who was on the Long March said, 'We didn't know we were on the Long March, we just knew that we were marching westward, westward, westward, all the time'. And I wish, listening to the debate this morning, that working with Claudia Jones had made me appreciative of how truly great her standing as an international person was. I have to confess that it didn't.

I came to the *Gazette* about the third issue, in 1958. I was working on the buses then, I think it was the No.109 and I was on my way from the Embankment to Purley. I got as far as Burton Road and Brixton Road when Theo Campbell, whose name has been mentioned earlier, came on the bus; he was the man who opened, I think, the first Black record shop in London. He had a handful of *West Indian Gazettes* and I'd never heard of it, which is not really surprising as it was just about the third issue. He said, 'Would you like to buy one?' I said, 'Yes, more than that, I'd like to write for it'. So Theo said, 'OK, come down to the record shop and I'll introduce you to Miss Jones'. And as soon as my shift was finished, down I went to the record shop. Theo took me upstairs where the *West Indian Gazette* was and introduced me to Claudia, and I told her, 'a great idea', but above all I wanted to write. And after about twenty minutes or so she said, 'So, write. Go and get me an article'.

So I went out in the streets of Brixton with a copy of the *Gazette* in my hand, showing it to many people and asking them what they thought about it, was it a good idea to have a paper for Black people, and the answer was yes. I wrote up my story, took it back, she read it, smiled and said, 'Oh, I think you can write'. The article never appeared. It's the first of two articles I wrote which never appeared in the *Gazette*. I'll tell you about the second one because I probably made one of the greatest mistakes ever. I heard that Amy Jacques Garvey [Garvey's second wife] was passing through London with Marcus Garvey Jr, so I dashed over, interviewed her, wrote a very flattering thing about this very lively woman, and brought it back, handed it to Claudia. She read it and said, 'It's a lovely piece Donald, but ...' And I thought, but? And she said, 'We're not going to publish it'. And I thought, this is censorship gone mad. And she looked at me and she saw how disappointed I was. She said, 'Think, why am I not going to publish this?' I said I couldn't think, and she said, 'Right'. She took a copy of the *Gazette*, turned to me and said, 'Look'. And one of the members of the editorial board was Amy Ashwood Garvey [Garvey's first wife]. And so that article was never published; the first one wasn't censorship but the second one was.

I'd never worked in a newspaper office before, so the *Gazette* was for me exactly what as a struggling writer I wanted. Claudia never taught me to write, she just said, 'Write'. And of course she would edit my work, any article I brought in. But some strange things happened to me. I was working on the buses ... you had to do some other job to survive, as I wasn't really salaried staff on the *Gazette*; no one was, not even Claudia. So, if I was on late shift I would turn up at the *Gazette* and do some work and then I would dash home, get my conductor's jacket on and go off to work.

So this one time I came down and she said, 'Oh I'm glad you're early, come on'. We jumped into a taxi, I said, 'Where are we going?' 'You will see'. And before long I was bounding up the posh red carpet of Lancaster House going to the Nigerian Resume Independence Conference. And that's the sort of thing I was propelled into, that was the sort of thing that the *West Indian Gazette* did extremely well. We covered that; I still can hear the voice of Chief Awolowo echoing in my ears. I was so green as a reporter that I grabbed the first chair and sat down, and then I noticed all the other reporters up and down had speeches on their knees and were making corrections and adding bits, and so was Claudia. So I turned to Claudia and I said ... (I never said Claudia, let's get it straight, she was always Miss Jones to me. Not that she insisted, because others who were as young as me called her Claudia, but to me she was always Miss Jones.) So I turned to Miss Jones and said, 'Why haven't I got one of those?' And she just gave me a gentle nudge and said, 'You are sitting on them darling'. I was sitting

on these speeches! So, there it was, I've been able to boast to generations of Nigerians that I was present at their Resume Independence
Conference.

Someone mentioned Claudia's reviewing of James Baldwin's book
The Fire Next Time.⁴ Again turning up at the *Gazette* I was marched
off to a hotel in Bloomsbury to interview James Baldwin and to review
his book, *Another Country*.

I don't think I really grasped the true fact that I was in the presence
of history. Otherwise there are questions I would have asked Claudia
and perhaps things I could tell you, which I can't now. I know that
Claudia was writing her autobiography. Whatever happened to that? I
know that it existed, I know she read extracts to me, and after her death
it disappeared. I don't know who to point the accusing finger at. As it
is such a valuable document I can only hope that whoever has it will
allow it to surface.

The *Gazette* never really paid its way. Whenever I read some of the
Black papers now I am seized with envy and jealousy at the amount of
money that they seem to have. We were so short of cash! Shortly before
his death Ken Kelly was reminding me of going all the way to Tooting
(in South London) to collect an issue of the *West Indian Gazette*, and
we hadn't carried the full £100 the printers were charging for the issue.
We couldn't get it. The printer said 'No, £100 or you can't have it'. I
don't want to look back at it as a sort of great romantic thing. Quite
often if you see some of the copies of the *Gazette*, it will be 'November
and December', a combined issue, not because we didn't have enough
news for the November issue, but we couldn't afford to pay for it, so
it had to be run together. Jimmy Fairweather, who is sitting at the back
there, he was made responsible for selling our small ads, and as we were
reminding each other a while ago, it was sometimes pretty easy to sell
the space, or to credit the space; collecting the money was another
thing.

One of the things I learnt about, and I am astonished at how I
survived given how little political education I'd had, was the clash
between China and India. Being a typical colonial I obviously backed
India and it was going to be India right or wrong. Going into the office
and really spouting off and then having on my right Claudia Jones, and
Manchanda on my left. How did I survive that? Well I know how I
survived that, it's because they were both so gentle with me. And it was
about that time that Claudia thought about my education needs, and I
was packed off to Vienna to cover the seventh World Festival of Youths
and Students. I think I probably hold the record for being the *West
Indian Gazette* reporter that went furthest from home. I thought

perhaps I might have scraped through my A-levels in political awareness then. That was a great experience, and so was coming back and writing it up.

1959 was the year when Kelso Cochrane was murdered. The Notting Hill and the Nottingham riots had taken place the year before, and by the spring we thought that things were not getting better but getting back to where they had been; and then Kelso Cochrane. Anyone who saw Claudia during those days, rushing from conference to conference, from meeting to meeting, and so on – it wasn't to make publicity out of Kelso Cochrane's death and his funeral, but to make an awareness. I think people became suddenly aware of what was afoot.

David Roussel-Milner mentioned the meeting about carnival in his mother's flat. I was lucky to be one of the people in the room... Claudia asked, what can we do? These last two years left a really nasty taste in her mouth. Roy Henry, or somebody said a carnival, and we all started laughing. Claudia said, 'No, let's think about it seriously'. And before long Edric Connor was drafted in. She had a marvellous way of ringing up people and telling them what they were going to do. I don't think Claudia ever *asked* anybody to do anything. You suddenly realised that all at once we had these truly amazing West Indian women, Pearl Connor, Pearl Prescod, Corinne Skinner, and Nadia Cattouse, Carmen England. There I was sitting in my little corner and watching all these people coming in, and being given their jobs to do, whether they liked it or not ... Edric Connor had sort of mapped out the rehearsals, what was going to be done and so on. I'm always amused when people hear of the Notting Hill carnival as if that's where it started, in Notting Hill, but it didn't start there, it started in the room above Theo Campbell's record shop in 250 Brixton Road. That's where it started, and from then on it started going on and on.

Who but Claudia Jones? Who but Claudia Jones really could bring Paul Robeson in a concert to Brixton, in Lambeth Town Hall? I was doing my O-levels then and I told my English teacher, and she said, 'No, you mean the really truly great Paul Robeson?' I said, 'Yes'. And she wouldn't believe it until I showed her. I sold her a ticket, and she came back the following day and said, 'My sister still won't believe this unless she gets a ticket'. So, I had to get her another ticket. This was something else.

Having said that, I don't want to give the impression that I or everybody was there for Claudia whenever she wanted us, because, there's no point in giving excuses, everybody had their own agenda. Nobody was paid for doing anything for the *West Indian Gazette*. Those who were politically aware knew that it had to be done. I'm not sure whether I knew that it had to be done, but I knew that a West Indian paper was needed, and also there was the carrot that if the *West Indian Gazette* did get on its feet I was going to be the first full-time employee.

I was going through some of the old copies and noticed an article by Ken Kelly about a day in the life of the *West Indian Gazette*. I can't remember it because it was a long time ago. We're all sitting around, Ken wrote, and Claudia was saying, 'Oh dear, I certainly need a holiday, I've got to go away, I need a holiday', which was quite a dream I suppose. And the phone rang and Claudia said, 'Donald, you get it this time', because according to Ken the phone had rung something like fourteen times during the last five minutes. So I think we were reasonably busy. Ken charted a day in life of the *West Indian Gazette*, and showed how involved we all were and how in a way we thought it was so necessary.

After her death, a man bravely tried to carry on the *West Indian Gazette* tradition, but there were only two other issues. A lot of us had come to associate the *Gazette* with Claudia. They were almost inseparable, it was so much a part of her. If we'd carried on, a new paper should have been started.

If there ever was a spokesperson for the people from the Caribbean at the time, it definitely was Claudia Jones. She was the one that the BBC and other news organisations would seek out. So did West Indians: it was there on the steps of the *West Indian Gazette*, that I bumped into La Corbiniere who was something in the West Indian Federal Parliament, Norman Manley, and several other people from the Caribbean. They had come to London on official business, but they would end up in the offices of the *West Indian Gazette* talking to Claudia. And so would the person who was being put out of his or her flat, and Claudia could do it quite easily, switching from the person who was being evicted in Brixton to Norman Manley or whichever visiting fireman is passing through. A truly amazing person.

Billy Strachan The *West Indian Gazette* developed from the *Caribbean News*. Within the Caribbean Labour Congress London branch, there was a young man who was very bright, highly intelligent, called George Bowrin, B-O-W-R-I-N. He was very bright, he was sponsored by the Oilfield Workers of Trinidad to come and study law here. We had to struggle to keep the Caribbean Labour Congress London branch alive, with nobody being paid, no salaries, no money. None of what there is today, all sorts of grants going from local authorities for Black people, and all sorts of things like newspapers being given subsidies. We didn't have any of that, as Donald Hinds pointed out.

We were running *Caribbean News*. It was being printed by a good comrade who was a printer, and he charged us next to nothing for printing it. We had to go and collect it, so it was even cheaper. My three sons used to sit there at night, because the paper came straight off the press, sit on the floor folding them over and making them into form, like a newspaper. And so the *Caribbean News* was working. A great struggle to keep it alive, a great struggle to get it amongst people, particularly the Black people, particularly even more so the Caribbean people. We had great difficulty in making it.

George Bowrin then took the view that we were too narrow and too sectarian in our approach, and that is why all the ordinary people were not supporting it. I disagreed with that view. Put it in the record, I disagreed with that. Unfortunately Claudia agreed with George Bowrin against me. So as a result of that disagreement, I decided that as I had worked very hard I'd stay on the committee but I'd no longer be secretary and no longer run the paper. So immediately I did that the *Caribbean News* died, slipped away unfortunately, because that printer wasn't printing it for nothing for anybody else, he printed it free because of my relationship with him.

Trevor Carter He was in the Communist Party.

Billy Strachan I agree, but it was also a personal relationship. But Trevor is right, it was because we were all Communists. There was no difference between the Communist Party and Claudia at that time, there were no differences at all.

But as a result of that I no longer stood as secretary. George Bowrin was elected as secretary of the Caribbean Labour Congress, because nobody stood against him. It had one meeting, and never any more. The Caribbean Labour Congress London Branch disappeared off the face of the earth.

Claudia took on the *Caribbean News* and one issue came out. Then it collapsed because no longer was the printer doing it for nothing. Then she went and set up the *West Indian Gazette*. And she got associated with Manu Manchanda, who was a close colleague of hers, an Indian ex-Communist Party member. He had his differences with the Indian Communist Party, they didn't agree with him; he had differences with the British Communist Party, they didn't agree with him. And then there came the point that he became a great Maoist, and a great supporter of the Chinese Communist Party. And some of you may remember the very glossy bookshop that was set up in Camden Town of which Manu was the manager.

He was away to China at the time when Claudia died. It's very different speaking right off the top of my head, but I wanted to explain that there was no Communist Party difference with Claudia. In the dispute with George Padmore, Claudia herself never supported Padmore strongly, in my personal experience with her. What happened unfortunately is that we all walked on our separate lines or went off on our separate lines, and we were not prepared to make any compromise. I say that applied to me, and dare I say it applied to Claudia; but it applied to a lot of other people too, unfortunately.

Pearl Connor Post-war there were all these organisations that people could belong to; there was general confusion. We were really very proud of George Padmore. We were proud of him because of his association with Ghana, with Nkrumah, and the Pan-African Congress. We were not thinking too much about international communism, and Russia, and Mao and all them people that you guys got to know so well. We just knew that he was our man, a Caribbean Black man who had good sense, and who had a lot to do with Nkrumah coming into power. He was our own man. And that to us was more important than who was left, didn't join, gave up, or got kicked out. We had a branch of the People's National Movement here and George used to be there sitting down with us. I didn't know about his other involvements. George was there supposedly operating for Caribbean independence. So that we have this confusion which we tried to get away from, because on the international level, I knew where Russia was, I think, on the map ...

Billy Strachan It's not as big as Trinidad.

Pearl Connor Not as big, no.

Although we had a limited area and small population, our individuality was the most important thing to us. Padmore was an international in our whole arena, he went out into the world, he was able to move into Africa, which we were all looking towards with hope.

All these falling-outs and so that happened – and they weighed on Claudia – I never got to that level at all with her. Claudia, as you know was working both politically and culturally; I was tied into her culturally, the culture of the emergence of our people and so on. And of course it was her own political background that led her to open up on the cultural level and uplift, like Robeson.

Richard Hart In Jamaica we took very much the same view as Pearl about Padmore. We totally ignored the Party advice, because he was giving us tremendous material for the anti-imperialist propaganda that we were putting out. So that was very much our attitude, although we were theoretically inclined.

Trevor Carter Let's not move into the rifts and the schisms that we had. That was the strength of Claudia. Claudia was able to understand what the Communist parties were saying about somebody like George Padmore. As I said this morning, for people like me who learnt my politics here, in the Communist Party, I took orders. It sounds a bit rough but there was a line, and some of us followed that line. But Claudia came, and although the Communist Party of the United States was, in a way, to the right of the British and in a sense was more fundamentalist, Claudia did not feed us the perspective of the American Communist Party, or its attitude to people like C.L.R. James and Padmore. Although she spoke to us about it – I knew her views, Billy knew her views – when she came to the broad movement she was skilful and strong enough to be able to deal with that. That was her strength.

Symposium on Claudia Jones
28 September 1996

Session 4: Carnival

Corinne Skinner-Carter In the 1950s there was a TV programme called 'Six-Five Special', which was something similar to what 'Top of the Pops' is now: it looked as though it was chaos, everybody was jumping here, and it was the first of that kind of programme that people from all walks used to go in there and do their thing. So Claudia decided that that's the way she wanted the carnival to be. The BBC was coming in to film it, so they're going to get the BBC to do this programme like 'Six-Five Special'. I remember Edric saying, 'Claudia, that chaos that you see on that stage is organised chaos, it's not what you think'. But Claudia thought she'd be able to keep all these people in harness. We had all these well-known people, people who the ordinary people in the street could have never had the chance to meet, people thought of as untouchables, people like Paul Robeson. So, we had this act at St Pancras Town Hall, this was in 1958, this was the first one.

And on the night of the occasion, we had all these people, all these cameras and everything, and people were prancing and trying to get up on the stage to touch people that they had never touched before. And I remember Edric standing up and saying, 'My people, my people. Please, please stand back. My people, my people.' But nobody was taking any notice, they were just pushing and making a real carnival out of it. And we had a big chap called Big George, I think he was a bouncer or something like that in the West End, and Big George got on the stage and he was shielding Edric from all these pushing people that were coming up. Anyway, that was the beginning of the carnival.

Claudia proceeded to have this carnival every year, which coincided with the Trinidad Carnival, not at the bank holiday. So the times that we had these carnivals was during the winter time. She had two at Seymour Hall, and one of one of them included Sparrow from Trinidad. She brought Sparrow up from Trinidad! Later on we got a coach and we went up to Manchester, where Kitchener lived at the time. At that time Sparrow was the 'king' in Trinidad, because Kitchener wasn't there of course, so they brought one 'king' to meet the other 'king' in this country.

Then other years we just had carnival and the beauty queens. And we also had costumes, we had costume competitions. It used to be funny because in those days people didn't have cars, so everybody had to get on public transport, and it was very funny in the winter to see people dressed up in costumes, getting on London Transport and coming to places like Seymour Hall or the Lyceum. Needless to say only a few people came in their costumes because a lot of people were embarrassed to travel that way. But we did it.

Alex Pascall I've found that, Terror, the Calypsonian, won the first calypso monarch title here in 1957 at Chelsea Town Hall, so there must have been something, either as a Calypso or some type of competition. So therefore I'm wondering whether there was not some other carnival. We have never mentioned 1957. Trevor, you could correct that?

Trevor Carter From the time I was here in 1954 the only time I think we had any kind of parade or carnival was something we attempted to do at the League of Coloured Peoples, in 1954, I think. And I could remember playing the records then. Terror was here at the time, and Terror was competing with Scott, and not very successfully. I think he sang at Victory Hall once or twice at some of the dances organised there by Scotty, his name was Scotland. I think Pascall, you are right, the Chelsea Town Hall was the first time Terror sang calypsos in that sort of big public place. Not that calypsos weren't sung – they were sung in all the nightclubs – but that was the first time it became a public thing, in Chelsea Town Hall. Although calypso was popular, particularly after the cricket, the victory at Lord's when Beginner sang his calypso. Jamaican music was much more popular, that was the thing that was driving the Black community.

David Roussel-Milner Memory is a difficult thing. Abner Cohen in one sense was right, because within memory it all becomes one big party. It's very difficult sometimes to divide this particular performance from that ... But I particularly remember, I'm sure it was 1962, when Pat Castagne was the producer, and I was appointed to assist him – I'm not sure whether that led to some of the difficulties, but ... I remember Sparrow was having some difficulty with the band behind him, they weren't playing very well, and so he turned on them. And I must say this for them, although he was cussing them in words I wouldn't dare to repeat, they carried on playing all the way through. But it was quite a night. The sad thing about that night was that Claudia had a Parker pen which somebody had given to her, and I let somebody else borrow it, and it was the last it was seen, and she was vexed with me, and it was the only time I ever saw Claudia vexed, really vexed.

But as for the trip which followed, up to Manchester Free Trade Hall in 1962 with Sparrow. On the coach we had Sparrow and Horace James, who made that journey a fantastically memorial thing. I remember there was Stanley Jack and Yolande Fermin sitting in the back of the coach, for obvious reasons. Alex was there, and quite a few others, Corinne. But as I say, memories do get very confused....

Alex Pascall I will fill in a few of the bits. David, let me take up from there ... 1962 was a thrilling year for me, because it's the year at Seymour Hall when I met for the second time, after one year's absence ... how should I put it? The lady I wanted to marry wouldn't talk to me, and we happened to dance that night and she became my wife. That's why 1962 is so important for me. Yes I remember Pat Castagne, I was the drummer with Bing Morriset playing for Allister's dance group. We had Stanley Jack, Patsy Jack was not yet his wife – Patsy Fleming she was, who came as a limbo dancer from Grenada. We had a couple of other dancers, they were Jamaicans, I remember that.

Female Speaker Helen Fleming, not Patsy. She was one of the dancers.

Alex Pascall Ivan Chin and his Combo. When they started to play Sparrow asked them which part of the universe they came from. Really beamed the guys to the high success. I mean Sparrow's arrival was ... It was like the expected coming of Jesus Christ for those of us who were here, because we were starving for what was the real back-home southern Caribbean thing, as everything we were able to get was Jamaican. And if you recall, Sparrow sang that night, 'Throwing Coins'; he changed it from 'three coins in a fountain' to 'throwing coins in a fountain'. And he took the hell out of the Bajans. That was really nice. Sparrow's behaviour has always been, if you don't pay him right or his money is not right, he's gonna give you hell before he performs. Claudia was no exception, and she had to coddle him and everything else, to get Sparrow on stage. And so, it was also the night when Cy

Grant sang, because remember Cy never was close to us as the people down there.

(I want to say this about Cy, in greatness of Cy, the lyrics he sang were never written by Cy Grant. They were written by Bernard Levin who sent the lyrics and Cy took ages to translate them into what he then called calypso in answer to Harry Belafonte. That's unbelievable, I mean, Cy himself would admit that now, because that's history.)

That night Victor wore that famous costume and won the carnival prize, the prize for disguise, and Sir Learie Constantine was also in the hall that night, and Claudia Jones was the person who was able to bind it altogether.

There was Laurel Aitkens. We must bring him in here to see how he brought ska and calypso together, that's very important, how Latin and all that came in. In dealing with the trip from London, Laurel Aitkens, in his dark glasses, stripe suit, and he had a pianist that could not play anything else but plum-de-plum-de-plum-de-plum-de-de-de-plum. The coach trip, I've been longing and wanting to talk about this for donkey's years, because we could churn it up together. Horace James giving Sparrow hell, Sparrow had all this press-and-curl ... Sparrow could not take fatigue. And this was the first time we saw him lose his complete peace. We had to separate them. The coach trip was excellent, I don't think before we have ever had a coach with so many artists of the different parts of the Caribbean. Let's not leave the Africans out from that at all, because Ambrose Campbell the Nigerian who put what you may call high-life into this country was always with us. Jean Martin who was once a beauty queen in the Caribbean, in Grenada, she was also part of the trip.

Alex Pascall This was the period when the tune 'Desafinado' had just come out, because Sparrow was on a guitar, working it out; the same guitar he took when he put Ivan Chin and the boys behind, and he said, 'I will sing the calypso myself', and he strummed his own guitar. But Ivan and the rest didn't take it on. Ivan's gone but Ivan needs an immense amount of credit as we write the history about Hans Crescent and the West Indian Student Centre.

Obviously Claudia expected people to turn out because Sparrow was coming so Claudia had hired this vast hall. We arrived in Manchester, it took ages to find the pianist who was supposed to be playing for Laurel Aitkens, and when he couldn't get him, Girl Satchmo said, 'Well you could use my pianist'. Now that guy was a singer, I've never seen a striped suit so remarkable, the suit was better than what he could play on the piano. And he never ended, though

Satchmo wanted to sing, 'Oh that ship ...' She lives in Leytonstone now and has gone sort of gospel, so you can't talk to her much about those days. And we had hell to get her song over. Very few people turned up, it was very disappointing. But Sparrow was amazing. The people who came, Black, white and the indifferent, all were happy to know that Sparrow has come to this country.

It was Sparrow and Claudia who discussed the return of Lord Kitchener to the Caribbean. I hope in doing all the documentation now we will record that and make Kitchener see that it is Sparrow and two other calypsonians who paid his passage to go back to the Caribbean.

To recall the history of that period in dealing with calypsos. Britain used calypsos [records] at that time to sell to Africa and the Caribbean as part of its economy after the war. Calypso never took off here at all.

Don't leave the blue spot gram out of that period please, because there was nothing else. The Jamaicans had their turntable and the ugly box as people used to refer to it, but what a box it was. And we had the blue spot gram [gramophone], a damn big box that we bought expensively, and it didn't have nothing inside it except it was pretty. They conned us with that damn thing.

There are other stages on the carnival I would like to talk about ... When did it go onto the street? We must go back to the Colhern where people started to meet ... Sonny Black tells me about how active he was.[1] I don't know; Sonny Black needs to come and declare himself whether he was.[2]

... My life has been carnival. You see there is something in it, as you were saying before, if you cannot see us a Caribbean people, then you can't see carnival.

Joe Mogotsi I've been here from 1961. The people mentioned, artists you were talking about, I am wondering what role Stretch Cox played.

Corinne Skinner-Carter Stretch Cox came up when they were doing a film called *Fire Down Below* in 1956. He was around doing a lot of dancing, a lot of limbo dancing. But Claudia was here in 1958; Stretch Cox left this country in 1959.

Joe Mogotsi Well I dispute that, because I came here in 1961. We actually worked with Stretch Cox and Stanley Jack, I worked with them in this country.

Colin Prescod Is it possible, Corinne, that he returned from Trinidad?

Corinne Skinner-Carter He might have done, and I know that ... Well Stanley was here for a long time after that, yes.

Donald Hinds I just want to fill in some names which have been mentioned. I wonder if somebody would help me out here. I think the first carnival was in January 1959, not 1958, January of 1959 I think it was. We find that the second carnival was announced for the 6 February 1960. That's in the paper so I suppose it must be true. And then, there's mention of one of our winners, Beryl Cunningham is mentioned here. Of course part of my job was to interview the carnival queens; I always looked forward to it. Also Stanley Jack – his name was mentioned, and here we have 'Stanley Jack, Pat Fleming, *November Wedding*'. And that was 1962.

I also have, which of course I haven't got here, photographs, Claudia and Fay Sparks, and Mario Grimaldi of the Grimaldi-Siosa Lines, which was sponsoring the trip to the Caribbean, and also Claudia with Marlene Walker. You mention a black girl, she was again another black girl, a beauty queen. Also another photograph with again Marlene Walker, Beryl Cunningham, and the High Commissioner. We got everybody in, the High Commissioner was there to meet them. And in that particular photograph I've mentioned there are Della, Della McKenzie, and another one you probably don't know a lot of, Brenda Tye. Nowadays I don't know how it would be handled, but here we have Claudia and Miss Jamaica, Carol Joan Crawford. So we have it documented somewhere: check the *West Indian Gazette*.

Corinne Skinner-Carter Claudia thought about bringing people together in that way would be a way of letting the British people see how our behaviour is not one of riotous behaviour. But that if we let them see what our culture was like, that we are easy-going, soft, pleasant type people, they might want to join us, they would be inclined to join us. The best way to join people is through their culture and through, she felt, and I think I feel too, music and dance.

Jenny Mckenzie This is a statement and a question. I first went to carnival in 1975 and before that I didn't know the history of it, and I've been playing mas for the last five years and have really got into the spirit of it. Now this year was the only year I didn't go, and just a few weeks ago somebody told me that somebody else had started carnival. I was told that it was started in the Notting Hill area by a particular woman, not Claudia Jones, and I wasn't told the name. This person said it was a white woman who started the carnival, OK? And I remember my mother referring to the 1958 Notting Hill race riots, 1958 was the year I was born. So, what I'd like to ask is, how it is that somebody else could have been credited with starting carnival?

Trevor Carter Let me deal with it. Rhaune Laslett has her rights as far as that thing is concerned. She was a social worker who was involved in community activities. Anywhere you go in Britain, whether it's Plymouth or Cornwall, there is a British carnival, and there was going to be a kind of carnival in Notting Hill Gate, what in Brooklyn they will call a 'blockarama'. And she invited a steel band. She invited a steel band and that's all it was. But the media in its way attempted – I don't know if it's conscious or not – to take it away from us, give it to somebody else. But it is right that she did invite Sterling, Ralph, and Russell to play.[3] And if I am right, I think Corinne you and a few people were behind the truck, just a few people, and that's how it happened. But the spirit of carnival wasn't introduced by this woman, that was the important thing.

Corinne Skinner-Carter That event is something like we used to have in every area in London, we used to have a Chelsea Carnival, a Hornsey Carnival, this carnival or that carnival. At these carnivals there used to be floats that paraded around some streets in that area and ended up at the town hall of that particular area. I have done a lot of those carnivals. I used to be on a float that represented the electric board, the LEB. You get on the float, in a costume designed to match whatever it is you are advertising. When you get to the town hall there are big speeches and lots of things. I did the Lord Mayor's Shows; the Lord Mayor's Show was something like that as well. Well ... at the carnival in Notting Hill, Russell and the others were asked to go on a float, and on that float they were playing their music. And because they said that they were going to be on the float, a lot of people who they knew came ... And we decided to dress up in our sailor costume and decided to follow the float all over Notting Hill. That might be 1965 ... I'm not quite sure but it might be ... it might be 1964 or 1965.

David Roussel-Milner I recall discussions, particularly at my mother's flat in Hampstead, about going out onto the streets, but there was a fear that if one broke the link with Mardi Gras one would destroy carnival, and obviously you can't go on the streets in February. The ideal time would be August Bank Holiday, which I think was the first Monday of August at the time.

But as to why it happens, in my introduction I quite deliberately went into the distortion of Black history, of hiding Black achievement throughout history. And Abner Cohen, a man of his standing, has done a great disservice as his book, *Masquerade Politics*, is being looked upon as the bible of Notting Hill Carnival history. In it he does say that it was started by Rhaune Laslett who talked about some dream she had of reviving the Notting Hill Fair, which had died out at the beginning of the century. But he makes mockery of Claudia Jones, he makes mockery of us, because he talks about one big party, and we know there weren't just the six carnivals, there were other events that went on that had some association with carnival ... We definitely have to put the lie to somebody like this, the Emeritus Professor of Anthropology at SOAS across the road, and stop this nonsense, and stop it dead. Let people like Claire Holder and all of them know that the carnival was started by the mother of carnivals, the only mother of carnival, and that's Claudia Jones, and not Rhaune Laslett.

Geraldine Connor I wrote a masters degree at SOAS, and in fact I did it on culture and identity in the music of Notting Hill Carnival, and disagreed with Cohen. It's written, but nobody knows me there. But I think that we do have to lodge this in the right place, formally. I think the other thing we have to do is to call our Notting Hill Carnival the Claudia Jones Carnival, and I think the sooner we start to move on those kinds of lines the better for all of us.

Alex Pascall I continue to research the BBC's libraries in whatever way I can ... There is lots of material, especially audio material that cannot even be identified. What I have found in doing the series on the influence of Black persons and Black music and musicians on musicians here, is that I cannot identify a lot of the voices. In those days they would just say, 'Here comes another calypsonian, and he's coming up the road now', and you don't know who the hell he is. There are a lot of recordings there whose voices I do know, and I've tried to get some accreditation to it to help them put it together. I was pushed off completely.

On films, I would have to try to get somebody who is inside there to continue to research it, because they are privatising all of those areas now. It is something we have to move on swiftly before the year 1998, because the privatisation within the BBC will remove and erase everything that hasn't been erased before.

About Mrs Laslett. Why I can talk about that is not that I was in the Notting Hill Carnival from the start, let me make it quite clear. But in 1968 I knew that Fitzroy Coleman was the first man who amplified a guitar and had a little box pulling down the street. Let history be written, Fitzroy Coleman carried the first mobile amplified guitar ever on the streets of Britain here, nobody did it before then, and he needs his credit on this. That was 1968. In my little book I have credited all these people in the poem that I have written.[4] Johnno with his cuatro; Johnno was a calypsonian himself but nobody regarded Johnno in what he did.[5] I mean all that goes to Claudia's credits.

Let's come down to Mrs Laslett. Andre Shevington, whom I have interviewed – most of the people who you are talking about today I have interviewed through 'Black Londoners' – Andre said to me that he was close to Mrs Laslett and she said to him, the Sunday carnival, the children's street thing is missing something; and she heard about the guy with the tin pan ... And Andre went to Sterling and Russell, and it was through Andre Shevington that they came in to the carnival.

Russell Henderson has described the entire routing of the first carnival they made which was longer and it's still longer than the route we are following at this moment. As a matter of fact it went all down there to Hyde Park Corner so that is the route we should map as we write the history of carnival.

Nineteen sixty-two ... that period needs to be analysed likewise, because of the movement of the steel band, although we had TASPO coming here before.[6] You need to take the songs that were made by the calypsonians here that became the road marches in Trinidad, so that we remember road marches were taken from England by Caribbeans back to Trinidad. Vivian Comma who came to write the music for the film *Fire Down Below*, all his music has been stolen, no credit given to him for writing the songs in *Fire Down Below*. It's a serious history, and it's all to do with carnival. Look at poor Vivian, eighty years-old now, still bending on the streets, belief in his mas and his calypso. I am bringing these names because we're going to come to a roll of honour when we look at what we are asking for in tracing Notting Hill's carnival as Claudia Jones's Carnival, and not as Carnival Limited.

Pearl Connor Actually the problem that we're talking about is the general robbery and rape of our people in the music and the entertainment world. So you are talking about something happening here in the centre where we should be able to have aid to get these things sorted out, and lucky we have done it, and it needs to be done. This is what this is the beginning of, isn't it? Right?

Colin Prescod I am about to call for this proposal ... Claudia Jones initiated something, and this particular cultural intervention in this country is what we have been talking about. What she did was to harness the energies of the Caribbeans.

You wanted to have rolls of honour, let's make this happen. So getting it right is absolutely important. I think that Alex began a while ago doing it, and other people have been joining in. Alex began it by mentioning Black arts monuments ... The first amongst these Black arts monuments might be the naming of the Notting Hill Carnival as the Claudia Jones Carnival. It seems to me that some people here may be wanting to recruit themselves to that purpose ... It seems to me that here there may be something which is brewing, which would constitute a perfectly feasible approach to getting some substantial monies to do something of the sort that Alex is talking about ...

Gertrude Elias I feel that we ought to get Camden Council to put a plaque at the house where Claudia had been living because she was at her time the leading Afro-American artist and writer and political leader in this country. She lived at 58 Lisburne Road, NW3, quite near where I lived you see, this is why we became very intimate. But I think that the organisation ought to see to it to get some sort of an initial memorial.

Alex Pascall Thank you. I'm glad you've brought that here, because I had noted Collingham Gardens and Hans Crescent: there are a number of places where her spirit has walked through in our development, such as the town halls. And if we hit the boroughs by finding specifics in every one of the boroughs, to thread some of the other people who are attached to Claudia, like Lambeth where the paper developed, your mother's flat at Eton Place and so on, then we are really hitting the local government areas.

I have made a proposal that has gone to Greenwich via the other boroughs to set up a monument for the Caribbean people's presence in Britain. This is going to be headed by Sir Shridath Ramphal; that is on the way, and is going to be.

So I am stating that we should look at the planning; and construct a roll of honour of the people's names that helped in the development of Carnival. Mrs Laslett of course could be there, we are not throwing out Mrs Laslett. But what I don't want, which the Metropolitan Police wanted, let me tell you openly here and now, they offered Mrs Laslett the chair of the Notting Hill Carnival. Yes they did, they did – ask Andre Shevington. In the whole turmoil of what we were going through, Mrs Laslett was called by the police and the borough to return to take over the carnival; they will pass the monies and everything through her. And she felt in her honest opinion that she could not go down that road. I am agreeing that it is not her saying this, because in my the first interview with Mrs Laslett before anybody spoke to her, she told me that on the tape, 'Alex, you are the first person who has come in to talk to me'. Andre Shevington brought me to her home, she was lying on the bed when I interviewed her in her crippled state, and she said, 'Nobody else has taken notice of the contributions that I have made for Notting Hill Carnival'.

I've written back to Professor Cohen telling him of all the mistakes in the book. Probably not as David has done. I welcome what you all have done, because people see it as their bible and so on.

Fay Llewellyn I'm a librarian at the Institute of Education, and I stumbled across Claudia Jones and felt very angry that there wasn't anything much about her in print. I came here and found some information, and I'm quite willing to spearhead anything or to do anything that anybody needs to do. I've been doing some research for a book for children. I feel very angry about it. I think that we should at least get the carnival to have a float, because I can't believe that there wasn't anything about her. My generation has no idea of Claudia Jones, and I think that we need to get them to give us something free. It's very commercial now and people are making money from it. I think that is the first way to go, give out flyers to all the young people and get everybody on the streets knowing what's going on, and then from there things will grow.

Colin Prescod I want to thank you all for having answered the call Marika and I made. Some of you are here who said that you couldn't possibly be here, and that's really impressive. I came in off the plane, I was late, and I was struck by the wonderful energy in the room and the warmth, and now I am moved to tears, because I think it's been an absolutely wonderful day. And, thank you all very much, and we will do our best to transcribe this stuff and to make it strong for Claudia, and indeed for all the causes that she struggled for.

Notes

1. The Colherne was a pub where Black people used to meet. On Sunday nights Caribbean musicians performed there from the early 1960s. According to Sonny Black, Sterling Bettancourt (ex TASPO musician) and Russ Henderson were the initiators of the calypso/jazz Sunday nights at

the Colherne. (Telephone interview with Mr Black, London, 28 May 1998.)

2. Sonny Black came to Britain in 1961 as the manager of the Dixieland Steel Band which had won the Music Festival in Trinidad. Though he claims that Claudia was to some extent distrusted by many Caribbeans who were anti-communist, Mr Black readily acknowledges thast she 'had set up – started Caribbean culture in Britain'. After Claudia's death, but inspired by her, he briefly published a newspaper – the original *Caribbean Times*. At the time of our telephone conversation, Mr Black was the artistic director of the Commonwealth Arts and Cultural Foundation.

3. Sterling Bettancourt was a steel percussion player. Ralph Cherrie was also a musician. They both played with Russell Henderson. Mr Sonny Black recalls that Mrs Laslett had asked Russ Henderson to play at a street party that she was organising. Afterwards Henderson suggested that a carnival committee should be set up. Despite Mrs Laslett's doubts that this would work, the committee was formed. Selwyn Baptiste was the first chairperson and Henderson was the treasurer. Among the members was Horace James. Telephone interview, London, 28 May 1998.

4. Alex Pascall, *'We Ting': Notting Hill Carnival*, London 1991.

5. Johnno and his cuatro (a stringed Venezuelan instrument): 'Johnno' Thomas from Trinidad, was involved in Carnival from its early street days.

6. The Trinidad All Steel Percussion Orchestra was formed in 1950, of Trinidad's most accomplished performers. It toured Britain for the Festival of Britain in 1951, and then Europe.

Index

Africa Freedom Day concerts 105

Africa Unity House 100, 105, 108, 117 n29, 120 n62

African Arrow 183

African National Congress 100, 105

African Women's Day 106

Afro-Asian Caribbean Conference 99

Afro-Caribbean Organisation 170, 172, 176 n14

Aitkens, Laurel 207

Alfrey, Phillys 132

Anti-Apartheid Movement 105, 122 n77

Armah, Kwesi 168

Armour, Ronald 119, 55

Ash, Ranjana 11, 48, 51, 95, 101, 163, 182-3, 189, 193

Ash, William 11, 48, 182

Association for the Advancement of Coloured People 92, 95

Atwell, Winifred 189

Awolowo, Chief 134, 197

Bailey, Frank 78

Bain, Allister 161, 206

Bard, Phil 27

Bashorun, Aloa 94, 118 n31

Beginner, 205

Black Liberator 172, 177 n22

Black peoples in Britain 89

Black Sash Movement 180

Black, Sonny 60 n67, 208, 215 n2

Blackman, Peter 68, 167, 176 n10

Bogle l'Ouverture bookshop 189

Bolsover, Phil 65

Bowles, Vince 148 n5, 149, n6

Bowrin, George 50, 63, 70, 83 n4, 85 n34, 99, 148 n5, 200

Branson, Noreen 64, 67

Britain: anti-black riots, 92, 142, 180, 190, 192; racial discrimination 90, (bill against) 104; immigration 91, 180, 141, 143

British Caribbean Association 104, 121 n71, 192

British Road to Socialism 67, 74, 75, 83 n7

Brockway, Fenner 74, 93, 97, 98, 99, 100, 132, 167, 168

Brothers in the Fight for a Better Life (CPGB) 66

Buckle, Desmond 67

Burns, Emile 68, 75

Butler, R.A. 96

Byfield, Clem 120 n55

Cambridge, Ricky 50, 51, 73, 87 n65, 121 n66, 148, 164

Camden Black Sisters 173

Cameron, Earl 151, 167, 176 n10

Campbell, Ambrose 207
Campbell, Theo 125, 133, 138, 147, 193, 196, 199
Carew, Jan 50, 51, 101, 121 n65, 122 n79, 132, 193
Caribbean Labour Congress 69, 78
Caribbean News 69, 85 n31, 126, 190, 200-1
Caribbean Workers' Party 106
Carnival 150-162, 202-214; beauty contest 158, 209; venues 159, 205; Manchester 159, 161, 206-7
Carter, Trevor 11, 49, 71, 72, 80, 84 n19, 98, 114, 157, 184, 187-191, 203, 205, 210
Castagne, Pat 150, 205, 206
Cattouse, Nadia 49, 51, 101, 105, 140, 158, 164, 165, 181, 199
Chandrisingh, Ranji 63, 67, 70, 83 n4
Charter for the Rights of Coloured Workers (CPGB) 64
Chen, Olive 134
Chin, Ivan 161, 206, 207
China Peace Committee 112, 113,
Cochrane, Kelso 94-7, 134, 142, 156, 180, 182, 199
Cohen, Abner 178-9, 205, 211, 214
Coleman, Fitzroy 161, 212
Colonial Defence Association (Cardiff) 71
Coloured Peoples Progressive Association 93, 95, 96, 117 n26
Coloured Peoples Publishing Co 132, 135
Comma, Vivian 212

Committee of African Organisations 94, 95, 105
Committee for Afro-Asian Caribbean Organisations 100, 105, 111, 117 n29, 164, 182
Committee for Democratic Rights in the USA (CPGB) 78
Committee of Inter-Racial Unity 104
Commonwealth Prime Ministers' Conference (memoranda to) 103
Communist Party of Great Britain: policy on colonies 62; on racial discrimination 64; and black members 68
Communist Party of the USA: policy on race 27; policy on gender 29; National Women's Commission 30, 31
Connor, Edric 105, 122 n79, 140, 151, 156, 158, 181, 191, 199, 204
Connor, Geraldine 211
Connor, Pearl 11, 47, 51, 94, 106, 119 n55, 140, 158, 179, 185, 189, 199, 202, 212
Constantine, Learie 81, 88 n82, 140, 149 n14, 179, 207
Cowl, Margaret 30
Cox, Idris 68, 70, 78, 84 n19, 184-5
Cox, Stretch 208
Crevelle, Clive 85 n34, 127, 149 n6
Cunningham, Beryl 209

Dankworth, John 140
Davis, Ben 27, 31, 35, 38, 43, 56 n1, n2, 73, 75, 76, 78

Davis, Ossie 48
Dee, Ruby 48, 167
Delmar, Elaine 161
Dixieland Quartet 161
Doyle, Mikki 39, 52, 58 n21, 87 n62, 152, 163, 164
Doyle, Charlie 39, 52, 58 n21
Du Bois, W.E.B. 26, 33 n30, 76, 190
Dutt, R. Palme 62, 67, 78, 185

Eber, John 94, 95, 118 n31
Edwards, Jackie 161
Elias, Gertrude 12, 80, 191, 213
End Racialism in Britain (CPGB) 79
England, Carmen 157, 189
Ettlinger, Eleanor 95
Evers, Medgar 101, 120 n64
Ezzrecco, Frances 93, 94, 96, 97, 117 n28, 167

Fairman, Bill 170, 172
Fairweather, Jimmy 126, 141, 198
Faulds, Andrew 105, 122 n79
Fermin, Yolande 206
Fleming, Helen 206
Fleming, Pat 209
Florent, Josephine 50, 61 n68
Flynn, Elizabeth Gurley 23, 26, 31
For a Lasting Peace and People's Democracy (CPGB) 68
Foster, Bill 27, 31, 36
Fox-Pitt, Cmdr 97
Freedomways 27, 33 n35, 137

Gaitskell, Hugh 99
Gannett, Betty 23, 36, 38, 57 n7
Garvey, Amy Ashwood 44, 92, 94, 123 n83, 153, 180, 193, 197
Garvey, Marcus 45

Gollan, John 78, 79
Gordon, Garnet 95, 97
Grant, Cy 151, 158, 191, 207
Grant-Somers, Diana 134
Gunter, Henry 71

Hall, Gus 78, 167
Hart, Richard 12, 62, 69, 70, 71, 203
Healey, Denis 99
Heart of the Race 175
Henderson, Russell 212
Hinds, Donald 9, 133-9, 142, 146-8, 164, 196-200, 209
Hobsbawm, Eric 108
Holder, Boscoe 150, 161
Holder, Ram John 181
Hornsey & Islington Inter-Racial Group 95
Hunton, Alphaeus 167, 176 n11
Hussein, Yusuf 67, 84 n19, n23
Hutt, Avis 73

Immigration 180; demand for control 91; Immigration from India 91; Immigration from the West Indies 90; Immigration Act (1962) 79, 98-9
Indian Workers' association 51, 61 n74, 100, 105
International Affairs Committee 78
Inter-Racial Friendship Co-ordinating Council 94-7
I Think of My Mother: Notes on the Life and Times of Claudia Jones 173

Jack, Stanley 206, 208, 209
Jackson, Esther 57 n8, 80, 81, 88 n76

Jackson, James 57 n8, 80, 81, 88 n76
Jagan, Cheddi 132, 188
James, C.L.R. 140, 188, 194, 203
James, Horace 206
Jeffrey, Pansy 12, 60 n67, 118 n37, 192
Jenkins, Clive 100, 105, 108, 181
Johnson, Bari 105, 167, 176 n10
Johnson, Buzz 173
Johnson, Revd. Hewlett 40
Johnson, Howard 'Stretch' 37, 39, 57 n12
Jones, Claudia, *in the USA*: early life 20; joins Communist Party 21, 195; arrests, imprisonment 22; illness 23; deportation 25; *in Britain*: contact with Ben Davis 35; financial help from the USA 36, 37, 40, 41, 72; relations with family 38; ill health 36, 39, 40, 53, 54, 72, 147; places of abode 40, 53, 163; relations with CPGB 41, 64, 71-82; poverty 42, 52, 191; passport problems 42; holidays in France 40, 43, 52; friends 44, 179; relations with A. Manchanda 50; *West Indian Gazette* 52, 53, 92, 126-7, 180-1, 196-7, 200-1; Gazette's financial problems 134-5, 148 n1, 198; in the USSR 52, 108-110; in Japan 54, 110-2; in China 54, 112-4; as community organiser 92-103, 181, 185, 190; speaks on Civil Liberties in USA 101; work with anti-racist and anti-imperialist organisations 103; calls herself Trinidadian

110, 113, 175; organises Carnival 150, 156, 191, 199; organises talent quests 139; attitude to culture/art 156-7, 182, 191, 202; death 163; missing autobiography 164, 198; cremation 165; memorial meeting London 167; memorial meeting Peking 169-170; dispute over headstone 170-2; international perspective 109, 182, 192, 193, 194, 203
Jones, Claudia, Lectures 174
Jones, Claudia, Memorial Committee 165, 170, 172
Jones, Claudia, Organisation 172
Jones, Claudia, Symposium 16, 178-215
Jones, Lyn 49, 51, 59 n42, 123 n83
Jordan, Colin 153
Jouhl, Avtar 51, 52, 71, 81, 106
Journey to an Illusion 147

Kaye, Solly 79
Kelly, Ken 133, 146, 149 n17, 200
Khelifa, L. 167
King, Dr Martin Luther 144-6, 181
King, S.G. 127, 132, 148 n5
Ku Klux Klan 91, 92, 116 n14, 129
Kunene, Raymond 100, 119 n55, 121 n65, n66, 165, 167, 168
Kuti, Mrs Ransome 110
Kuya, Dorothy 49, 60 n57, 71, 79

Labour Monthly 77, 87 n59
La Corbiniere, Dr Carl 93, 95, 96, 97, 132, 200
Laine, Cleo 140, 151

Lamming, George 105, 132, 140, 164, 167, 168, 181
Lang, Robert 105
Langford, Diane 18
La Rose, John 50, 60 n67, 132, 187
Laslett, Rhaune 162, 179, 210, 211, 212, 213
Lawman, Cherry 147
Le Maitre, Cris 64, 67, 68, 70, 83 n9, 84 n19, n23, n26, 187
Levi, Eric 163
Ling, Madame Soong Ching 113
Littlewood, Joan 157
Llewellyn, Fay 214
London Labour and Colonial Freedom (CPGB) 66
London Majlis 121 n65
Lord Ambassador 161
Lord Kitchener 161, 205, 208
Lucas, Isabel 167, 176 n10
Lynch, Cliff 183

McBurnie, Beryl 188
McColl, Ewan 158
McKenzie, Della 134, 147, 209
McKenzie, Jenny 209
McNish, Althea 151
Magil, Harriet 27
Manchanda, Abhimanyu 50, 80, 94, 97, 104, 105, 134, 135, 137, 163, 164, 167, 172
Manley, Norman 97, 99, 132, 200
March on Washington, support for 100, 153, 181
Marshall, William 132
Matthews, George 67, 81, 191
Matthews, Robert 183
Metropolitan Police 93, 118 n31
Middleton, Peggy 167
Mighty Sparrow 140, 150, 161, 207-8

Mighty Terror 161, 205
Mitchell, Yvonne 151
Mogotsi, Joe 13, 194, 208
Monroe, Carmen 181
Montagu, Ivor 95
Moore, Richard B. 29
Moses, McDonald 95, 118 n36
Mosley, Oswald 92, 98, 153
Movement for Colonial Freedom 94, 95, 99, 100, 103-5, 118 n32

Naipaul, V.S. 190
National Negro Congress 30, 32 n8
National Paul Robeson Committee 77
New Beacon Books 181
New China News Agency 41
New International Society (Manchester) 71
Nigerian Resume Independence Conference 134, 197
Nigerians in Britain 68, 91
No Colour Bar for Britain (CPGB) 65
Nurse, Rupert 161
Nyasaland African Congress 95
Nyerere, Julius 104

Osborne, John 151

Padmore, George 44, 64, 202, 203
Pan-African Congress (1900) 90
Pan-African Congress (1945) 44
Pascall, Alex 13, 49, 173, 205, 206, 211, 213
Patterson, William 25, 33 n23
People's National Movement 99
Petit, Antoine 111
Phillips, James 167
Picasso, Pablo 42
Pierre, Curtis 150, 161

Pinnock, Winsome 173
Pinder, Winston 79, 170, 172, 176
n14, n17
Pitt, Dr David 84 n26, 93, 94, 95,
96, 98, 100, 132, 140, 164,
165, 172, 179, 181
Pollitt, Harry 42, 63, 71, 85 n39
Prescod, Colin 9, 122 n79, 208,
212-3, 214
Prescod, Pearl 101, 123 n83, 140,
153, 156, 158, 165, 181, 189
Pritt, D.N. 43, 95

Reid, Betty 72, 80, 82, 109
Robeson, Essie 44, 45, 59 n50,
n52, 96, 100, 105, 106, 132,
152, 165
Robeson, Paul 25, 32 n20, 35, 44,
45, 48, 103, 105, 132, 138-9,
152, 165, 181, 187-9, 199;
Robeson Papers 59 n49; *see
also* National Paul Robeson
Committee
Robinson, Helois 36, 57 n8
Rogers, George 97, 119 n44
Roussel-Milner, David 14, 48,
138, 149 n10, 157, 178, 185,
194, 205, 210
Roy, Namba 132
Russell, Sam 80, 109

Sahota, Taja 51, 55, 78, 81, 105-6
Salkey, Andrew 50, 122 n79, 132,
140, 151, 169, 181
Salkey, Pat 50
Satchmo, Girl 207-8
Sawh, Roy 49, 60 n59
Scargill, Arthur 174
Scottsboro Boys 188
Seeger, Peggy 158
Selvon, Sam 132, 140
Sesay, Mrs L.J. 106

Shankar, Ravi 182
Shevington, Andre 162, 212, 214
Sivanandan, A. 100
Skinner-Carter, Corinne 14, 140,
152, 153, 158, 199, 204-5,
208, 209, 210
Soper, Lord 101, 140
South Africa Day Reception 108
South African Coloured Peoples
Congress 105, 168
South African Freedom
Association 95
Southlanders 161
Soviet Woman 108
Soviet Women's Committee 169
Sparks, Faye 209
Spencer, Carmen 134, 147
Star's Campaign for Inter-Racial
Friendship 108
Stennett, Enrico 183-4
Stonehouse, John 99
Strachan, Billy 14, 63, 64, 66, 67,
69, 70, 71, 79, 188, 200-1

Talent quests 139
TASPO 212
Tigh, Brenda 134, 209
Thomas, Ade 63, 83 n4
Trinidad Steel Band 150

Walker, Marlene 209
West African Students' Union
100, 179
West Indian Circle (LSE) 67
West Indian Federal Labour
Party 95
West Indian Gazette 45, 52, 53,
108, 110, 126-148, 171, 193
West Indian Newsletter 68
West Indian Students and
Workers Association 78, 95,
126, 127, 129, 131, 148

West Indian United Association 95

West Indians in Britain (CPGB) 73

West Indies Committee (CPGB) 68, 77

Williams, Eric 43

Williams, Jenny 73

Williamson, John 39, 57 n11, 77, 165

Williamson, Mae 37, 39

Winston, Henry 32 n6, n7, 80, 88 n78, 108, 110, 123 n89, 167

World War II 90

World Congress of Women 110

World Conference Against Hydrogen and Atom Bombs 110

Wright, Richard 187